Supporting Transgender
& Gender Creative Youth

Gender ᴀɴᴅSexualities ɪɴ Education

Dennis Carlson and Elizabeth Meyer
General Editors

Vol. 4

The Gender and Sexualities in Education series
is part of the Peter Lang Education list.
Every volume is peer reviewed and meets
the highest quality standards for content and production.

PETER LANG
New York • Washington, D.C./Baltimore • Bern
Frankfurt • Berlin • Brussels • Vienna • Oxford

Supporting Transgender & Gender Creative Youth

Schools, Families, and Communities in Action

ELIZABETH J. MEYER & ANNIE PULLEN SANSFAÇON,

Editors

PETER LANG
New York • Washington, D.C./Baltimore • Bern
Frankfurt • Berlin • Brussels • Vienna • Oxford

Library of Congress Cataloging-in-Publication Data

Supporting transgender and gender creative youth:
schools, families, and communities in action /
edited by Elizabeth J. Meyer, Annie Pullen Sansfaçon.
pages cm. — (Gender and sexualities in education; v. 4)
Includes bibliographical references.
1. Transgender youth. 2. Gender identity.
I. Meyer, Elizabeth J., editor of compilation.
HQ77.9.S86   305.3—dc23   2013031493
ISBN 978-1-4331-2210-1 (hardcover)
ISBN 978-1-4331-2209-5 (paperback)
ISBN 978-1-4539-1210-2 (e-book)
ISSN 2166-8507

Bibliographic information published by **Die Deutsche Nationalbibliothek**.
Die Deutsche Nationalbibliothek lists this publication in the "Deutsche
Nationalbibliografie"; detailed bibliographic data is available
on the Internet at http://dnb.d-nb.de/.

The paper in this book meets the guidelines for permanence and durability
of the Committee on Production Guidelines for Book Longevity
of the Council of Library Resources.

© 2014 Peter Lang Publishing, Inc., New York
29 Broadway, 18th floor, New York, NY 10006
www.peterlang.com

Printed in the United States of America

Table of Contents

Dedication

To all the courageous gender-creative and transgender youth in the world: through your courage, strength, and clear sense of self, you are educating all of us and helping make this world more open and better for all who follow.

Acknowledgments

We would first like to thank the driving force behind this project and the lead investigator on our research team, Kimberly Manning. She had the vision and the drive to bring this project together and led the grant writing and conference organizing that produced this volume. This book simply would not exist without her. We are grateful for her dedication to the topic, her ability to juggle and multitask, and her leadership on this project. She is an amazing colleague and friend, and we consider ourselves quite fortunate to be able to work with her on such a meaningful project.

Another key player in organizing the conference that led to this volume is Jake Pyne. He was an amazing resource who helped make the first National Workshop on Gender Creative Kids (GCK Workshop) such a success. He brought his considerable expertise on the subject of transgender and gender-independent youth as well as his networks that strengthened the diversity of participants who attended and presented at this workshop. In addition to his knowledge and networks he put significant time and effort into all the nuts and bolts of coordinating and planning the conference. We could not have done it without him.

In addition to Jake's contributions, there were several other Research Assistants (RAs) who contributed to the work that was presented at the conference and included here in this volume. Andrea Clegg worked on the education project and the GCK workshop, and provided valuable legal and policy research for Elizabeth

Meyer's chapter. She was also active in supporting work related to the parents' project described in Annie Pullen-Sansfaçon's chapter. Audrey-Anne Dumais Michaud and Marie-Joëlle Robichaud were also essential contributors to the parents' project and Audrey-Anne provided support during the GCK workshop as well. Anika Stafford joined the project as a Research Assistant in 2013 and provided valuable research support for the Introduction and Conclusion. We are grateful for the time, energy, and ideas that all these graduate student assistants brought to the project.

We also would like to thank and recognize all 70+ participants who traveled from across Canada and the United States to be a part of the first National Workshop on Gender Creative Kids. We were so grateful to work with and learn alongside the diverse range of professionals and family members who were able to attend. The chapters included here represent about a quarter of the ideas presented at the conference. We wish we had more room and more time to include more, but hope that this is just the beginning of future opportunities to build on and share what we have learned. The Social Sciences and Humanities Research Council of Canada funded this workshop, and we would like to acknowledge their financial support of the project.

Finally, we must give great thanks to our managing editor, Lee Airton. Lee provided ongoing support to the logistics of putting this book together. In addition to supporting the writing and research of some first-time authors, Lee helped keep us on track for deadlines, compiling author information and contracts, and ensured this book was fully complete and ready for delivery to the publisher. This is no small feat to accomplish while still trying to complete one's own doctoral dissertation. Thank you, Lee, for all of your efforts.

Introduction

KIMBERLEY ENS MANNING, ANNIE PULLEN SANSFAÇON,
AND ELIZABETH J. MEYER

Although transgender people have long attested to having been conscious of their gender identities from early childhood, the idea of the "transgender child" has only recently entered the consciousness of the North American public. Since 2007, when mainstream media began to air and publish stories about gender-creative children, Americans and Canadians have gradually become aware of childhood gender-nonconformity, including transgender kids.[1] It would seem that anywhere from 2.3% to 8.3% of children engage in varying degrees of cross-gender dress and behavior (Moller, Schreier, Li, & Romer, 2009, pp. 118–119), many of whom will later self-identify somewhere along the LGBTQ (Lesbian, Gay, Bisexual, Trans, Queer) spectrum (see, for example, Green 1987; Knafo, Iervolino, & Plomin, 2005; Wallien & Cohen-Kettenis, 2008). Tragically these same young people are also among the most vulnerable to "gendered harassment" (Meyer, 2006, 2008b) and suicide (Cole, O'Boyle, Emory, & Meyer, 1997; Klomek, Marrocco, Kleinman, Schonfeld, & Gould, 2008; Savin-Williams, 2001).

This edited book, and the conference that gave rise to it, was born out of a desire to begin a national conversation in Canada about childhood gender-creativity. Unlike the United States, which has seen the rise of a number of new nongovernmental organizations actively working to address the needs of gender-creative children and their families, Canada currently lacks a national forum for discussing and realizing social transformation on behalf of children and families. Indeed, as we began to research the social lives of gender-nonconforming children in late 2010, we were dismayed to learn that Canada lacked an organization similar to Transkids Purple Rainbow Foundation (TKPR), Trans Youth Family Allies (TYFA), Gender Odyssey Family, and Gender Spectrum (just four of the newly emergent American organizations working on behalf of gender-independent children and their families). We also found few sustained research agendas focused on the social and political dimensions of childhood gender-nonconformity—in the Canadian academy or elsewhere. As scholars variously concerned with questions of gender equity, ethics, social action, and educational practices, this organizational and research deficit was alarming. As advocates (two of us belong to families that also include a gender-creative child), we were left hungry for resources.

Faced with the need for research and social action we decided to undertake a project that could contribute to the development of both simultaneously. Our first step was to procure a Social Sciences and Humanities Research Council (SSHRC) Insight Development Grant to run three interlinked, multidisciplinary pilot studies and host a national workshop on childhood gender-creativity. A subsequent grant from SSHRC enabled us to expand the scope of the workshop and to disseminate findings in the form of this edited book and through a national website, gendercreativekids.ca, which went live in the summer of 2013.

At the heart of our project is the concept of Social Action Research methodology, which involves a research process not only aimed at discovering, interpreting, and revising human knowledge on different aspects of the world (Centre for Social Action, 2012), but that also aims to address a problem and take action for change. In Social Action Research, stakeholders are viewed as "knowers" (Fleming & Ward, 2004). Many acknowledge this research methodology as a highly empowering approach (Preston-Shoot, 1992; Rimmer, 2005). Central to the approach is a deep concern for the understanding of "the relationship between oppression, power, and change" (Mullender & Ward, 1991, p. 13). At the core of this approach also lie practice principles, which we have embedded throughout the work undertaken in the context of the project. Those principles can be summarized as a belief that people have the right to be heard, to define the issues facing them, to choose to participate or not, to set the agenda for action, and most important, to take action on their own behalf (Fleming & Ward, 2004; Mullender & Ward, 1991; Mullender, Ward, & Fleming, 2013; Pullen Sansfaçon, 2012).

We have taken this concept and underlying principles seriously not only in terms of how we have designed our pilot studies (see Pullen Sansfaçon, Dumais-Michaud, and Robichaud, in this volume) but also in terms of how we have approached the very question of "research dissemination." We are keen to contribute to an emergent academic literature about childhood gender-creativity and, indeed, see this edited book as part of that endeavor. However, we are equally interested in creating dialogue with parents, youth, teachers, activists, and providers otherwise working in isolation from one another. This book and the website are thus also envisioned as invitations for connection, solidarity, and community action.

THE ERASURE OF CHILDHOOD GENDER-CREATIVITY

Until recently, the issue of gender-nonconformity among children was largely relegated to the realm of psychology, psychiatry, and pediatrics: a "health" issue diagnosed as "Gender Identity Disorder" in accordance with the *Diagnostic Statistical Manual*, 4th edition, text revision (DSM-IV-TR). According to the DSM–IV-TR, Gender Identity Disorder is marked by a preoccupation with cross-sex activities and appearance, a strong preference for cross-sex roles, and a strong desire to live or be treated as the other sex (American Psychiatric Association [APA], 2000a). However, and as many clinicians from these health fields increasingly recognize, it is not childhood gender-nonconformity that is in itself "the problem", but rather the lack of acceptance by society at large (Isay, 1997). And, indeed, in late 2012 it was announced that the DSM-5 would be removing the term Gender Identity Disorder and replacing it with Gender Dysphoria. The implications of this change are enormous in so far as being 'gender-nonconforming' (or gender incongruent as described in the DSM-5) is no longer considered to be, in and of itself, a lifetime disorder. Indeed, the new focus of the diagnosis is on the presence of distress regarding one's body; thus, those transsexuals who transition and no longer have such distress, as well as those gender-nonconforming people who have never experienced this distress, are no longer pathologized. While the diagnosis of a key feature of transsexual experience (bodily discomfort) remains problematic, the achievement of the shift to Gender Dysphoria is that it lessens the stigma attached to gender variance, while still providing a diagnostic route to transition treatment for those who require it. As the hard-won result of much strategic activism, this change is an important step forward toward the demedicalization of gender-creativity.

That said, the implication of this shift in diagnosis for children largely went unnoticed. Unlike the decision to modify the definitions of Autism Spectrum Disorder and Asperger's Syndrome in the DSM-5 (which garnered much public discussion), the removal of "Gender Identity Disorder" from the DSM-5 did not garner any mainstream media attention in Canada—especially as this decision pertains to children and youth. Given that as many children may be gender-independent as inhabit the Asperger's/Autism spectrum, this lack of discussion is a grave omission.[2]

A lack of connection is also evident at the political level. To date, there has been almost no media attention focused on another recent initiative that holds serious consequences for gender-nonconforming children in Canada: a private member's bill to protect "gender identity" within the Canadian Human Rights Act. Although Bill 279 marks the second attempt to provide protections to transgender individuals in Canada, there has been almost no discussion of the bill (and its previous iteration) in the mainstream media. Moreover, the limited debate surrounding the bill has largely been confined to the gay press and the Christian right, with the latter often focusing on the erroneous threat that the "Bathroom Bill" might impose on young children. According to the Campaign Life Coalition, if the bill were to become law young girls could face leering male pedophiles dressed up as women in the bathroom stall.[3] Yet, as was acknowledged during discussion at the Canadian Senate Committee on Human Rights, it is transgendered individuals who face danger in sex-segregated bathrooms (Buechner 2012). What is left unsaid are the ways in which this bill, if passed, may increase explicit human rights protections for gender-nonconforming children in the context of their public lives, including but not limited to safe and appropriate access to sex-segregated facilities such as bathrooms.[4]

Why is dominant Canadian culture so ignorant as to the possibility of childhood gender-nonconformity? Why is it that health-care providers and teachers so often say, "But how can the statistics be that high? I have never met a transgender child." At issue here, we suggest, is a complex erasure of the lived realities of gender-nonconforming children. Just as the lives of transsexual and transgendered people have largely been rendered invisible in this country (Namaste, 2000, 2005), the gender-creative child can not exist in a world that does not recognize the possibility of a childhood inhabited outside of the gender binary. Yet as Bauer et al. (2009) note, invisibility on the social agenda can give rise to hyper visibility in daily life, with each individual instance treated as a "social emergency." In a sense the gender-creative child is unintelligible—unintelligible in speech, dress, comportment, social relations, and even in humanity. Indeed, transphobia remains so deep in North American society that to even put the words "transgender" and "child" together can be seen as an aberration. As Andrew Solomon (2012) notes, "Being trans is taken to be a depravity, and depravities in children are anomalous and disturbing"[5] (p. 600).

At work here, we suggest, is the most intense form of gender regulation our society is capable of producing. Butler (1990, p. 17) describes gender regulation as a kind of "matrix of intelligibility" through which the "heterosexualization of desire requires and institutes the production of discrete and asymmetrical oppositions between 'feminine' and 'masculine,' where these are understood as expressive attributes of 'male' and 'female.'"[6] Building on this notion, we argue that gender regulation governs gender expression in the home, gender clinic, school, and community, constantly working to "privatize" childhood gender-nonconformity and thus keep it out of the public eye. Whereas over forty years of activism has produced profound legal and social changes with respect to the recognition of lesbian and gay rights in Canada and the United States (Smith, 1999; Warner, 2002), many social mores regarding gender and sexual identity remain intact. Indeed, some scholars argue that gay and lesbian rights are seen as legitimate not because they ultimately disrupt heteronormativity, but because they offer a kind of "homonormativity" in which same-sex couples are just like "us" after all (Bryant, 2008; Duggan, 2003; Stryker, 2008). Expressions of gender-nonconformity, whether by a child, teen, or adult, however, challenge a society that is organized largely on the basis of a binary understanding of identity. Gender-creative self-expression, to a large extent, remains taboo. One of the main reasons there has been so little public discussion about gender-variant children and youth in Canada, therefore, is because well-meaning parents do not allow their children to be gender-creative outside of the house.

The vast majority of gender-variant children are what Hellen (2009) describes as "non-apparent," and that is children who suppress their gender-nonconformity as a consequence of parental and/or societal pressure (see also Kennedy & Hellen, 2010). This is especially the case for gender-nonconforming boys who tend to generate greater cultural anxiety than do girls (Feder, 1999; Sedgwick, 1991). In many cases, parents and other concerned family members will thus actively discourage, if not outright forbid, their "little man" from participating in what they deem to be "girl" activities. And while many of them, no doubt, are deeply concerned about keeping their child safe from the ignorance of others, few caregivers are able to get beyond their own sense of loss and shame to allow their "son" or "daughter" to appear publicly (or even privately) in accordance with the gender expression with which the child is most comfortable (Ajeto, 2009).

In Canada the parental desire to "cure" the gender-variant child has been compounded by the work of Dr. Kenneth Zucker, a highly influential psychologist who has been treating and publishing about gender-variant children for more than twenty-five years. At the Centre for Addiction and Mental Health in Toronto, Zucker is Psychologist-in-Chief and Head of the Gender Identity Service in the Child, Youth, and Family Program. He and his colleagues have developed a controversial form of gender reparative therapy to encourage gender-nonconforming children to identify with their sex assigned at birth, and thus avoid what they see as an undesirable future of the child growing into a transgender adult (see Tosh, this volume). Working from the assumption that gender identity is malleable in early childhood, and that interventions are necessary to shield the child from the discrimination of society as well as to resolve disturbed attachment issues with the mother (a form of "psychopathology"), they advocate gender-variant children play with same-sex peers and that parents set limits on cross-gender presentation and play (Zucker, 2008; Zucker & Bradley, 1995). Not surprisingly, reparative therapy has been strongly criticized for being homophobic, transphobic, and misogynistic (Bryant, 2008, Feder, 1999; Isay, 1997) and has recently been rendered illegal in some states (Eckholm, 2012).

If gender-nonconforming behaviors are not suppressed at the site of the family and/or gender clinic, however, they will most likely be from the moment the child enters primary school. Elementary school is a particularly formative period for young children as it is a time when they are internalizing how to "do" gender according to heterosexual norms (Blaise, 2005). Queer and feminist education scholars have therefore been concerned with deconstructing gender discourses in the classroom (Arnot, 2002; Blaise, 2005; DePalma & Atkinson, 2008; Letts & Sears, 1999; Meyer, 2009, 2010). For gender-creative children, however, cis-normativity in the school is not just a problem of reproducing oppressive norms, values, and behaviors; it is also often a question of mental health and safety.[7] According to a recently completed survey by Egale Canada, a national organization that advocates for human rights, 75% of LGBTQ students and 95% of transgender students feel unsafe at school—compared to 20% of straight and cisgender (non-trans) students (Taylor et al., 2008).

The threat of violence is real—both inside and outside of the high school and the elementary school. In some locales, if children dare to reveal themselves publicly they and their families may be subject to the wrath of neighbors, friends, and community leaders. Andrew Solomon (2012) documents in horrifying detail the incredible vulnerability of many American families with gender-creative children—especially families that are racialized, impoverished, and/or whose parents are in same-sex relationships. One military family stationed in Okinawa, for example, was reassigned to a base in Arizona because the army claimed it could not protect their transgender daughter from enraged parents after she had started to dress as a girl (she was five). Another family found itself almost totally dependent on the aid of social assistance when driven out of town by an angry mob that included members of the local Ku Klux Klan. The father, who had stayed behind for work, came home several days later to find the family dog murdered, disemboweled, and nailed to the front fence. Their trans daughter, "the tiniest kid in the class," was eight (p. 657). And still in another family, two impoverished women in a lesbian relationship faced another form of violence: the state's apprehension of their children. The primary rationale? That they were lesbians who had permitted their son to wear dresses.

Some of the worst violence (threatened and realized), it should be noted, has taken shape in the context of conservative religious communities. In a biblically based world in which God has created only "man" and "woman," the gender-creative child serves as a living rupture to the perceived natural order of things. But while the majority of fundamentalist religious adherents would forswear physical violence as an acceptable response to transgender children and their families, many see reparative therapy as appropriate. And, indeed, this is the official position of Focus on the Family, to name just one Christian organization to have engaged the issue[8] For a child to be subject to gender correction because they are viewed as psychologically ill (as is purported by some researchers, such as Zucker and his colleagues) is one form of violence. For a child to be subject to gender correction because they are otherwise not acceptable in the eyes of God is quite another. Indeed, for the many gender-creative children growing up in deeply religious families and communities, spiritual violence may be one of the greatest threats of all.

The "invisibility" of childhood gender-creativity, thus, is a direct symptom of the systemic violence brought to bear on children who dare to deviate from gender-normative expression. But this invisibility comes at a grave cost. When repeatedly isolated and attacked, many end up internalizing the violence. The fact that close to half of trans youth seriously consider or attempt suicide, we argue, is nothing less than a social crisis of acute proportions (Clements-Nolle, Marx, & Katz, 2006; Durso & Gates, 2012; Grossman & D'Augelli, 2007; Scanlon et al., 2010).[9]

Dream Big, Dream Open—*Voir grand, rêver librement*

The family is not only the site of where gender repression can begin, however, but also where it can end. Indeed, just as the family can be a site of trauma and injury, it can also be a site of growth and transformation.[10] The fact that there are increasing numbers of parents choosing to affirm their gender-independent children is a sign of an important cultural shift currently under way in North America (Menvielle, 2012). Why some parents are open to affirmation is currently subject to speculation and is likely the result of a combination of factors including increasing acceptance of homosexuality and gender difference (queer theory being an important interlocutor disrupting "heteronormativity"), the rise of the internet (through which otherwise isolated parents can support one another and exchange resources), and the popularity of parenting styles which seek to honor and cultivate the child's basic sense of self (for example see Ehrensaft; Daemyir; and Walks, this volume). Many of these same families, moreover, are not content to battle for new resources and safe spaces for their children alone, but rather are joining forces to struggle for what our colleague, Ann Travers, has termed, "gender justice for all children" (this volume).

The Transgender Child by Stephanie Brill and Rachel Pepper, published in 2008, was the first book to give voice to children and parents living with childhood gender-nonconformity. This resource guide tackles a variety of issues faced by families including how to advocate on behalf of a gender-creative child and negotiate emerging medical options. *Gender Born, Gender Made*, by clinical psychologist Diane Ehrensaft, published three years later, gave added weight to the idea that gender-nonconformity was perfectly healthy—indeed, to be celebrated as an expression of the diversity of what it means to be human. Brill, Pepper, and Ehrensaft are all founding members of the San Francisco-based organization Gender Spectrum, which holds a large annual family conference on gender-independent children.[11]

In the meantime, scholars, parents, community activists, and health practitioners were beginning to hold localized conversations in Canada. It was not until the fall of 2013, when the first National Workshop on Gender Creative Kids (hereafter GCK Workshop) was convened at Concordia University, however, that Canadians (and colleagues from the United States and Great Britain) gathered to discuss how we might bring research and advocacy together to create change in the Canadian context. The following chapters, including the concluding chapter, which analyzes the final workshop session, offers some of the latest research and thinking on how the affirmation of childhood gender-creativity calls us to revision our understanding of the family, the primary school, and community-based belonging.

OVERVIEW OF THIS BOOK

This book is organized into three sections that reflect general areas of intense contact for gender creative kids and transgender youth. The first section presents clinical and theoretical perspectives. The chapters here provide the reader with an overview of some of the historical trends in research and practice when working with gender-creative and transgender youth as well as offering critiques of some negative practices and new frameworks for more healthy and affirmative approaches. Diane Ehrensaft was the keynote speaker at the GCK Workshop, and her chapter presents much of what she shared at that event. Her 2011 book, *Gender Born, Gender Made*, introduces the term "gender-creative" that we have embraced and applied to the work associated with this research. This new lens can provide families and practitioners with an affirming and nonjudgmental approach to working with gender-creative and transgender youth.

The second chapter by Jake Pyne is essential reading as it provides a comprehensive overview of key terms, themes found in research, and a critical analysis of these themes. Pyne's discussion of the research provides an important foundation to contextualize much of the writing in the chapters that follow. In chapter three, Tosh offers a critical analysis of the DSM-5 and the ways in which activists have worked to voice their critiques and reshape the way diagnoses and pathologies are being used to justify certain forms of 'treatment' for transgender and gender-variant people. This section concludes with Ann Travers's chapter in which she presents a strong argument for a new framework for understanding work around gender: the theme of 'gender justice' is one she introduced in her presentation at the conference and resonated strongly with many participants, as you will see throughout this book.

The second section of this volume focuses on issues in the educational system. Chapter five by Elizabeth J. Meyer presents a professional and developmental framework for educators who are working with gender-creative and trans* youth in their schools. Part of the professional standards include understanding one's legal obligations and this chapter provides an overview of protections that currently exist and are under debate that can impact gender-creative and trans* youth in educational settings. This chapter is followed by Karleen Pendleton Jiménez's work that describes a project in schools in rural Ontario. Her writing offers educators some tangible texts, activities, and ideas for ways to discuss gender that will create spaces for broader understandings of gender identity and expression with a diverse range of ages. Finally, this section concludes with Jennifer C. Ingrey's chapter on teaching transgender topics in preservice teacher education programs. Her work at the University of Western Ontario also provides detailed examples and ideas for other teacher development programs to ensure that they are providing their graduates with the language, knowledge and the skills they need to create safer, more inclusive classroom environments.

The final section of this book presents six chapters that address issues important to parents and community workers. Chapter eight begins with a presentation of the experiences of parents of gender-nonconforming boys. Based on interviews with a small group of parents, Françoise Susset presents three main themes: how parents explain their child's gender expression, how this makes them feel, and what behaviors they adopt in response to their child's gender expression. The next two chapters offer new frameworks for thinking about parenting and gender diversity. Chapter nine by Arwyn Daemyir presents her theory of Gender Diverse Parenting (GDP), which offers parents of all children ideas and ways of being that allow for a more flexible and fluid understanding and expression of gender. This is followed by Michelle Walks's chapter based on her research with queer parents who intentionally 'fail' to conform to dominant norms of parenting and explicitly work to raise 'queerlings.'

The last three chapters in this section profile community-based efforts to provide support and agency to parents and youth and emphasize the 'action' portion of this volume. Chapter eleven presents the outcomes of a Social Action Research project with a group of parents based in Montreal. Annie Pullen-Sansfaçon, Audrey-Anne Dumais-Michaud, and Marie-Joëlle Robichaud describe the research methods as well as some of the outcomes of their work with parents so that readers can appreciate how research can support community-based action and sharing of knowledge. This chapter is followed by a case study presented by Lyndsey Hampton, who writes about creating a support group for sexual minority and genderqueer youth in rural Alberta. In this case study, Hampton offers a detailed overview of the successes and challenges of doing this work in rural areas for others to apply in their own regions. Finally, the last chapter, authored by Lorraine Gale and Haley Syrja-McNally, presents a framework developed by the Children's Aid Society of Toronto. They present the *Out and Proud Affirmation Guidelines: Practice Guidelines for Equity in Gender and Sexual Diversity*, which encourages listening, affirmation, a person-centered approach, and a focus on equity in all of the agency's work. In the book's Conclusion, the team behind the original research project offers a formal summation that highlights key themes from the book and the GCK Workshop and offer suggestions in terms of future research, community work, and activism.

We hope you will use this book as a resource, support, and guide for whatever role you play in the lives of the youth whom you come in contact with. It is designed to be read straight through, or in sections, based on the reader's time and interest. We hope that readers will be intrigued and informed by the careful writing and scholarship shared here. We also invite you to visit our new website, (gendercreativekids.ca) which contains a growing list of resources for families and professionals working to make their homes and communities spaces that will embrace and appreciate their gender creative kids. The dialogue and the work are ongoing and we hope that you will join us in becoming advocates, allies, and activists who work to transform hostile and exclusive environments into inclusive and welcoming ones.

NOTES

1. The terminology used in reference to gender-creative children also includes gender-variant, gender nonconforming, gender-independent, and in the context of aboriginal communities, two-spirited. The term trans* is an umbrella term that encompasses a cross section of identities including transgender, transsexual, and transvestite.
2. As many as 1 in 88 children are diagnosed with autism (Schreibman, 2005). It is important to note that some studies show a greater incidence of autism spectrum disorders among children being referred to gender clinics (de Vries Noens, Cohen-Kettenis, van Berckalacr-Onnes, & Doreleijers, 2010; Edwards-Leeper & Spack, 2012).
3. "Campaign Life Coalition," 2010. See also the website for the Campaign Life Coalition for recent changes in its approach to defeating the bill: http://www.campaignlifecoalition.com/index.php?p=Gender_identity_laws (accessed May 23, 2013).
4. See Currah, Juang, and Minter (2006) for a more comprehensive discussion of the possibilities inherent in legal change.
5. For discussions of how constructions of both queerness and childhood render queer childhoods "unthinkable", see Bruhm and Hurley (2004); Halberstam (2004); and Stockton (2009).
6. Butler (2004, pp. 78–79) discusses this process with explicit reference to children in her later work. Although Butler and others have been rightfully criticized for losing sight of the lives of transsexual women through their focus on the "transgender question" as a theoretical rubric (Namaste, 2009), we nonetheless feel that some of Butler's insights can help identify and unmoor the gendered normative frameworks that limit the lives of gender-creative children and youth.
7. The term "cis" refers to individuals whose gender identity is congruent with their anatomical sex. Cis-normativity refers to the way in which our social world is governed by the norm that sex and gender are synonymous, and divided on the basis of "woman" and "man."
8. See, for example, Focus on the Family's website: http://family.custhelp.com/app/answers/detail/a_id/25950 (accessed May 23, 2013).
9. One representative study of trans* people in Ontario finds that 47% of trans* people age 16–24 considered suicide recently and 19% had attempted suicide in the past year (Scanlon et al., 2010).
10. See Meadow's (2011, p. 742) account of how parents make use of biomedicine, psychology, and secular spirituality to expand gender ideologies and pave the way for social change.

11. Three other recently published books include Pepper's (2012) Transitions of the Heart: Stories of Love, Struggle and Acceptance by Mothers of Transgender and Gender Variant Children; Green and Friedman's (2013) Chasing Rainbows: Exploring Gender Fluid Parenting Practices; Angello's (2013) On the Couch with Dr. Angello: A Guide to Raising and Supporting Transgender Youth. Gender Odyssey, a Seattle-based organization, also organizes a large conference for families and children each summer.

CHAPTER ONE

From Gender Identity Disorder to Gender Identity Creativity

The Liberation of Gender-Nonconforming Children and Youth

DIANE EHRENSAFT

In September 2012 the governor of California signed the following bill: "No mental health provider shall provide minors with therapy intended to change their sexual orientation, including efforts to change behaviors or gender expressions" (CA Bill SB-1772, 2012). This statute matches the Standards of Care set forth by the World Professional Organization for Transgender Health in 2011: "Treatment aimed at trying to change a person's gender identity and expression to become more congruent with sex assigned at birth has been attempted in the past without success (Gelder & Marks, 1969; Greenson, 1964), particularly in the long term (Cohen-Kettenis & Kuiper, 1984; Pauly, 1965). Such treatment is no longer considered ethical" (The World Professional Association for Transgender Health, 2011, p. 16).

Not unexpectedly, as I write this chapter, court cases have already been filed challenging this legislation as a violation of individuals' constitutional rights. Whether the legislation remains on the books or not, its existence flags a sea change in the twenty-first century world we live in, where the rights and opportunities for gender-nonconforming and transgender children and youth are being asserted at home, in the schools, in the mental health community, in the halls of justice, and in our law-making institutions.

In 1972, when I was a new faculty member at Sir George Williams University, in Montreal, Quebec,[1] I received a paper from a student. We were studying gender at that time. In the paper, the student wrote, "Howdy Doody is a genderless male. You can tell his sex by his name." I had no idea what the student meant, and I still do not. But the sentence has stayed with me over these 40 years, and kept me asking, "So what is gender anyway and how do we tell someone's gender?" Just for curiosity, I recently did an Internet search for "Howdy Doody" and first realized that Howdy Doody, one of my favorite TV characters from the late 1940s, was quite a gender bender, with his tight plaid shirt and jaunty kerchief. If Howdy Doody had been a real boy, rather than a puppet, someone might have wanted to send him to a psychotherapist to change his gender expressions to make him more masculine. Over these many years I have learned that we see what we want to see about a person's gender, through the historical lens available to us, and there is a simple answer to the question, "How do you tell someone's gender?" Ask them. It is theirs to say, not ours to tell. This simple answer is the main organizer of my thoughts in this chapter exploring gender-creativity and the ingredients for building a gender-creative world.

In 2011 I published the book *Gender Born, Gender Made* (Ehrensaft, 2011b). I wrote about the True Gender Self, the False Gender Self, and Gender-Creativity, three terms that I coined, adapted from the work of D. W. Winnicott on the development of the personality through the true self, false self, and individual creativity (Winnicott, 1965a, 1965b, 1970). I define the true gender self as one's authentic internal gender identity, a sense of self as male, female, or other. The false gender self is one's gender presentation—actions, expressions, and comportment developed to protect the true gender self from harm or to comply with the social environment's expectations, rules, or guidelines. Gender-creativity is the weaving together of a unique and authentic gender self based on core feelings and chosen gender expressions. These terms then generated the portrait of the gender-creative child: the child who does not abide by the binary gender norms, prescriptions, or proscriptions that might exist in the child's culture, but transcends and transgresses those norms to independently, uniquely, and with artistry evolve into the gender that is "me."

Before landing on a final title for *Gender Born, Gender Made*, the publishing house staff was very much inclined toward the title *The Gender-Creative Child*. I floated this title to a group of experts in the field of transgender health. To a person, I received a "thumbs down." They were concerned that a potential reader, upon seeing the book jacket before knowing its contents, would assume that I was promoting gender as something we choose and create with intentionality, implying that we could choose to create it otherwise. This posed a danger, potentially reinforcing the sentiments of the transphobic world that gender-nonconforming and transgender people are just making bad choices and could be taught to make better choices, aka gender-normative choices, thereby supporting the very mental health practices of "reparative" therapy that the state of California had just banned for minors. The group of experts also thought the title might offend many people in the transgender community, who want to be recognized for just being rather than creating themselves. The group suggested that I not use "the gender-creative child" in the title, as much as they liked the term, but instead let the reader embrace the term after reading about it in the contents of the book when they could come to understand its true meaning. I thought this very wise counsel and, to my publisher's disappointment, stayed with the title *Gender Born, Gender Made*.

The book is now launched, no longer in its infancy. With hindsight, I sometimes regret having let go of the title *The Gender-Creative Child*, as not a single person I have encountered has ever had the predicted negative reaction to the term. Still, the concerns of the experts who thoughtfully counseled against the title got me to clarify what I was referring to when I coined the term "the gender-creative child." It is not the child who creates a gender. It is the child who uniquely and expansively discovers and expresses an authentic gender self, pulling together a gender from the inside and the outside, a gender that is not static but can change and grow over a lifetime, a gender that is not governed by external dictates but internal desires and knowledge. The gender-creative child freely weaves together a core sense of gender identity with the expressions chosen to represent that self. It is the boy with golden curls, jeans, and a tutu that graces the cover of *Gender Born, Gender Made*.

THE NEW GENDER-CREATIVE WORLD

In 2012, Chuck Bennett was 80 years old. He knew he was gay from a young age but kept it under wraps. As he described it, he was born 50 years too soon. He was excited to see the changes that were happening in the world around him, as he awaited legislation allowing gay marriage to go before the electorate in his U.S. home state, Maine (which did pass). Looking back at his hidden life as a gay man in a homophobic culture, he explained, "I'm inclined to look back not in anger …, but with some degree of sadness. Everyone could have been more fulfilled if they hadn't been burdened with this prejudice" (as quoted in Bruni, 2012, p. A23).

I was struck by the bridge between an 80-year-old gay man's pensive words about homophobia and the situation of gender-creative children today. Mental health professionals have taken note of a "gender swell." More and more families have been coming to talk about their children who are defying binary gender norms. Twenty-five years ago, this seemed a rarity. Now it seems a growing trend

(Meyer, 2012; Spack et al., 2012). Yet a recent large-scale study of transgender and gender-nonconforming adults by Beemyn and Rankin indicates that such children have been around for a long time: the majority of subjects interviewed knew from an early age that they did not fit the gender assigned to them at birth and/or the social expectations for that gender (Beemyn & Rankin, 2011). The biggest difference between those adults and increasing numbers of children today is that, throughout their childhoods, these adults, just like Chuck Bennett, hid their experience, deep in their closets or deep in their psyches. Sadly, they were seldom afforded the opportunity in childhood to let the world know who they were, and if they did, it was rarely received with a warm welcome. Take Andre, a transgender man: "Andre—who, as a young child, went to bed each night hoping to wake up a boy—remembers having a nightmare in which his siblings rolled a boulder on him and buried him alive. Being forced to bury his gender identity underneath a 'little girl shell' was like that nightmare to him, and he had 'waves of feeling suicidal' during his childhood" (Beemyn & Rankin, 2011, p. 44).

Andre and his cohort rarely had a chance to be their affirmed authentic gender selves in childhood, and that is truly unfortunate, for their own well-being and for the gender health of our society. We must also remember that many gay men like Chuck Bennett began their childhood as gender-nonconforming little children on the way to discovering their gay identity (Ehrensaft, 2007, 2011b, 2012). So they, too, suffered childhood transphobic gender affronts like Andre did.

The gender-creative child has been able to "come out" rather than hide with the help of an emergent accepting and supportive subculture. At the same time, the gender-creative child is often at least one step ahead of the larger mainstream culture, which means that the child has to step into a milieu that is still not ready and may even feel antipathy toward that child's gender-creativity. A new model of childhood gender affirmation is coalescing, operating from the premise that young children are very aware of their evolving gender identities and desired gender expressions and the role of the family, community, and society is to allow those children's authentic genders to unfold (Brill & Pepper, 2008; Ehrensaft, 2011a, 2011b). Our collective responsibility is to make sure that model gets implemented, not just in our own homes, backyards, or communities, but worldwide, to ensure the human rights of people of all genders across the globe.

Evidence of the emergence of a gender-creative world is all around us. Although not a child, Jenna Talackova, a transgender young woman, recently won the right to compete in the Miss Universe Canada contest. In April 2012, it was announced that Jenna Talackova could compete in the pageant, after first being expelled when officials discovered she was transgender—only women born female need apply. With pressure, the Miss Universe organization switched its position—Jenna, and all future Miss Universe contestants, were eligible if they met the legal requirements for being female (Johnson, 2012).

Other evidence of the growing emergence of the gender-creative world comes most poignantly from the children themselves. As part of my responsibilities as psychologist at the Child Gender Clinic at the University of California–San Francisco, I recently interviewed a 9-year-old transgender girl, Karie,[2] who had recently transitioned full-time from her assigned male gender to her affirmed female gender, to assess whether she was a good candidate for puberty blockers. I asked her, "So, Karie, if someone said to you, 'You know, you're going to have to go back to living as a boy for now,' what would you do?" Without a moment's hesitation, Karie's response: "I'd tell 'em I'll take 'em to court." Then, after a slight pause, "Or they can take me to court." Contrast this to Andre, the transgender man who was forced to bury his gender identity underneath a "little girl shell," a waking nightmare that led to thoughts of suicide. For Karie's generation, with support from family and community, that shell has been cracked open, replaced by a sense of confidence and entitlement to the true gender self that is rightfully theirs, a right open to litigation if anyone tries to deny it.

Andy appeared in the pages of *Gender Born, Gender Made* as the 3-year-old-boy who got furious when his parents corrected people in the street who mistook him for a girl. At the time, the parents, strong believers in honesty and forthrightness, asked Andy, "Well, then what do want us to tell them?" Like Karie, Andy shot back: "Oh, just tell them I'm a chipmunk." By the end of preschool, Andy made it clear to everyone that Andy was a girl, not a boy, a persistent, consistent, and insistent expression of self spanning many months. So, with parent and professional support, Andy became Andi and, as is often the case, the tantrums and despair that preceded the gender transition all but disappeared, replaced by a sunny, happy child. Andi has lived the past six years in her affirmed female gender. When it came time to enter middle school, she applied to an all-girls, academically rigorous, private middle school that advocated equality, diversity, and tolerance. Despite meeting all the academic requirements and being evaluated as an outstanding candidate by all who interviewed her, her application was rejected. The school explained to the parents that it was "not ready" to provide the supports that this transgender child would need to function at the school. The father's response: "My child doesn't need any supports. She's doing just fine. It's *you* who need the supports." To the school's credit, it recognized this need and organized a conference to discuss the role of same-sex schools in supporting transgender children, so that maybe the next transgender girl who applies will discover a gender-creative rather than gender constrictive environment. Andi had also applied to other schools, and was enthusiastically accepted by another school nationally recognized as a leader in gender diversity. In the first week of school, Andi bounded in the house and announced to her father, "Dad, I'm the hottest transgender girl in my class." Andi was demonstrating her resilience and gender-creativity in the context of a gender-creative academic world that was only too happy to embrace rather than reject her as the hottest transgender girl in class.

Building a gender-creative world to shepherd our gender-creative children toward adulthood is a critical task, and it will take a village to get there. For those of us working in the mental health field, we are faced every day with clear evidence that if we catch people early with supportive interventions, we can lower the risks of depression, suicidality, anxiety, drug abuse, sexual acting out, self-harm, learning difficulties that appear in significantly higher numbers among transgender and gender-nonconforming youth than in the youth population at large (Ryan, Huebner, Diaz, & Sanchez, 2009; Ryan, Russell, Huebner, Diaz, & Sanchez, 2010). It will take an integrated effort by families, professionals, and the community at large to ensure that there will be no more sad Chuck Bennetts or Andres and instead a blooming garden of every variety of gender identity and expression that our youth will come up with.

I would like to share the moving story of one man who stands as a model in moving us closer to that gender-creative world. Nils Pickert lives in Germany. His 5-year-old boy likes to wear dresses. The family relocated from Berlin to a small town, one that might not take kindly to a boy in a dress. Nils had to make a decision about how to send his son to school: "I didn't want to talk my son into not wearing dresses and skirts. … He didn't make friends doing that in Berlin; … so after a lot of contemplation I had only one option left: To broaden my shoulders for my little buddy and dress in a skirt myself" (Weiss, 2012, p. 1). For his gender-creative actions, Nils Pickert has been hailed as "Father of the Year" by Gawker Media, and praised in parenting blogs around the world. Nils's son is now feeling confident, because Dad has got his back. When he is teased about his skirts and dresses now, he tells his classmates: "You don't dare to wear skirts and dresses because your dads don't dare to either" (Weiss, 2012, p. 1). If our children are to be given the freedom to step out of constricting binary gender boxes, their footsteps will be so much lighter if we adults step out of those boxes right alongside them.

RE-LEARNING GENDER

To change the choreography of our own gender footwork, our first task is to unlearn everything we ever learned or internalized about gender. In my own training as a psychologist, we were taught a narrative about gender that went something like this. At birth, all children were assigned a sex, male or female, based on what the doctor

saw between their legs. A few babies had the misfortune of being born with ambiguous genitalia, and these children would need to be surgically "fixed" and assigned a
singular gender, male or female, as soon as possible, because after the first two years of
life, it would be near impossible to change a child's "core gender identity," defined as
the sense of self being either male or female, based on sex assignment at birth, which
in turn is based on genitalia and X and Y chromosomes. This identity—"I am boy"
or "I am girl"—is firmly established and immutable by the time a child was eighteen
to twenty-four months, aided by the child's being treated as male or female by those
caring for the child. Then come the preschool years, the era of gender socialization:
children will be taught by their elders what it means to be male and female and how to
act accordingly. For those of us psychoanalytically trained, this same period coincides
with the turbulent Oedipal stage, in which girls fall in love with their fathers, boys
with their mothers, but discover that their parents are already taken and they will have
to find a partner of their own later, and can do so by devoting themselves to identifying with the parent of their same gender who will teach them the ropes of malehood
or femalehood. By the time boys and girls enter grade school, it will be clear that all
children are either male or female and that there is no backsies on that; they will know
how to behave as that male or female; and they will accept that someday they will find
a wife or husband and have their own babies, with the assumption that all healthy families will have a mother and father. If all goes well, the child will be firmly established
as permanently male or female, and staunchly heterosexual. Either of these accom-
plishments not in place means pathology and a need for mental health intervention.

Regretfully, this teaching is not an anachronism of my 1960s training, but is
still alive and well, despite empirical evidence that the theory does not hold up in
practice, the final test of any good theory. Sexuality does not equal gender; they are
two separate developmental tracks. Our core gender identity lies not between our
legs but between our ears, in the messages from our brain. Elders can make every
effort to socialize the children as they see fit regarding gender behavior, and children will still transgress and follow their own path, if given the chance. Gender is
not set in stone at age six—many individuals transition from one gender to another
over the course of their lifetime with no aspersion on their psychological well-being,

Yet predicated on this theory that does not hold up in practice comes a harmful
mode of treating gender-nonconforming children that is profoundly antithetical to
building a gender-creative world. The misguided actions, known as reparative treatment, assert that children who do not accept their assigned gender will need help
from professionals and parents to get them to do so, to avoid gender confusion and
aspersion from an unaccepting public. That help will take the form of evaluating
first for the presence of Gender Identity Disorder and then promoting interventions that will reinforce "same sex" behaviors and expressions, discourage or even

punish "cross-sex" behaviors and expressions, secure strong bonds with the same-sex parent and ask the opposite-sex parent to step back (assuming a heterosexual household), facilitate same-sex friendships and discourage cross-sex friendships, engage in psychodynamic psychotherapy for both parent and child to work through the conflicts and traumas that have led the children to deviate from normative gender development, as defined by the theory stated above that I once learned and has proved to be both wrong and harmful (cf. Zucker & Bradley, 1995).

This is the thinking that we all have to unlearn. The next step is to replace such binary thinking with an affirmative roadmap of gender. I have taken efforts to craft one that I hope will prove helpful. The concepts of true gender self, false gender self, and gender-creativity are the signposts of this new roadmap. Like many of my cohort of gender affirmative practitioners (cf. Brill and Pepper, 2008), I replace the concepts of core gender identity and gender socialization with the partnership of *gender identity*, who you know yourself as, male, female, or other, and *gender expressions*, how you put your gender together and show it to the world. In this partnership of identity and expression, it has been my observation that gender identity is much less malleable to outside forces—it is not very bendable, only hideable, whereas gender expressions are much more susceptible to manipulation by the culture.

The concept of a gender spectrum, in which gender can present in an ever-evolving combination of shades and hues, has replaced the constrictive binary gender boxes. It is a fine and useful model, but I have still chosen to go one step further to develop the concept of the *gender web*, in which nature, nurture, and culture come together to create a three-dimensional intricate weaving of each individual's unique gender self. If we look more microscopically at the three major threads, nature, nurture, and culture, we find several microfibers: within nature: chromosomes, hormones, hormone receptors, gonads, primary sex characteristics, secondary sex characteristics, brain, mind; within nurture: family, school, community; within culture: values, ethics, laws, policies, theories, and practices. Like fingerprints, no two gender webs are alike. Unlike fingerprints, the gender web can change over the course of one's lifetime. It is up to the children to hold the needle that weaves together their gender web. If someone else grabs it from them, they are robbed of their own identity and expression. The gender web is each child's reach for gender authenticity, fortifying the true gender self, managing the false gender self, and calling on gender-creativity to do the job.

CHILDREN'S COLORFUL DISPLAY OF GENDER-CREATIVITY

As children are given increased freedom to spin their own gender webs, we see an ever-evolving presentation of gender identities and expressions among the gender-creative children who are increasingly making themselves be known. This panoply reflects the exciting sea change toward greater gender acceptance, albeit juxtaposed by persistent transphobic and genderist prejudies in Western culture. As superbly stated in the final lines of *The Lives of Transgender People*:

> By identifying themselves in multigendered ways, trangender and other gender non-conforming youth are radically changing the definition of gender and how gender identity will be viewed in the future. ... We live in a world where gender is more complex and more fluid. It is not eough to dispense with the notion of a gender binary; we must embrace and celebrate the idea that gender is bound only by the limits of people's spirits. (Beemyn & Rankin, 2011, p. 166)

In presenting the colorful array of children who are indeed showing up, we take the risk of creating new boxes and categories of gender, but in the spirit of simply sampling the existent varieties of gender webs that our gender-creative children are spinning, I would like to share some of the descriptions that either we as a community or the children themselves have generated:

- Gender-nonconforming/variant/independent/creative children: All children who live outside the gender binary
- Transgender children: Children who affirm their gender identity as opposite the one on their birth certificate
- Gender-fluid children: Children who weave together many possibilities of gender, either at one point in time or over time
- Gender hybrids: Children who experience themselves as some combination of male and female, including:

  1. Gender Prius: Half girl/half boy
  2. Gender Taurus: Girl (Boy) on Top; Boy (Girl) on Bottom
  3. Gender by Season: One for school, other for summer vacation
  4. Gender by Location: One for accepting locations, one for less accepting locations

- Gender Smoothies: Take everything about gender, put in blender, press button, that's me
- Gender Queer Youth: Beyond gender categories at all
- Protogay Youth: Explore gender on way to discovering sexual identities
- Prototransgender Youth: Explore gay identity on way to discovering transgender identities
- Gender Tootsie Roll Pops: One gender self on the outside, one gender on the inside

These descriptors will change, fade, or multiply over time, allowing us to bear witness to our children's ever-expanding creativity in challenging the gender binary.

Playing with the gender-web/gender-creative model, I was struck by a *New York Times* article that made note of the shift in some U.S. colleges' application forms as more applicants are of multiracial identities. Now applicants can choose from a larger menu of ethnic and racial categories. As stated by one bi-racial applicant: "You can put both. You can put one. You can put whatever you feel" (as quoted in Saulny & Steinberg, 2011, p. A1). Imagine offering the same to our gender-creative applicants. No longer would they have to check Male or Female. They could choose from Male, Female, Other, Transgender, Bi-gender, Gender Queer, Two-Spirit, Third Gender, Fourth Gender, Gender Hybrid, Gender Smoothie, Boi, Shemale, Neutrois, Androgyn, Other. How far away this would bring us from a world where boys must be boys and girls must be girls.

PLAYERS IN A GENDER-CREATIVE WORLD: PARENTS AND SCHOOLS

Children and youth spend the vast majority of their time either at home or in school. Whereas adults will have very little control over children's gender identities, they will have tremendous influence over the children's gender health, defined as the opportunity to express their true gender selves with pride and acceptance. This equation for gender health puts a great deal of responsibility in the adults' hands, so we should be ever mindful of the tasks at hand.

Because so many of us have been socialized in our own childhoods to believe that gender is bedrock and binary gender is normative and healthy, we have work to do attending to our own gender ghosts, defined as internalized thoughts, attitudes, feelings, beliefs, experiences that draw us toward culturally arbitrated binary gender boxes and make us anxious when we or anyone else strays from those boxes. As we unlearn gender, our collective task is to substitute those gender ghosts with gender angels, defined as internalized thoughts, attitudes, feelings, beliefs, experiences that allow us to be gender-creative and live or accept others living outside of the culturally defined binary gender boxes.

The first place to let our gender angels wrestle with our gender ghosts is at home, and the key players will be the parents. Any parent of a transgender or gender-nonconforming child may come to the realization that their gender-nonconforming child simply came to them; they did not shape them that way. Any parent may be faced with agonizing cognitive dissonance: I love my child / I think trans people are strange. Now I have one. To allow gender angels to prevail, parents will have to resolve that dissonance, it is hoped with love trumping transphobia, and then develop the resilience to stand up to people who blame the parents for making their children into gender freaks—as in, "How could you let him go out dressed like that? It's creepy." Any parent of a transgender or gender-nonconforming child will have to balance safety against authenticity of expression. It is hoped that there will be room for their child to come out, but parents may also have to shelter their child from harm by asking the child to save that child's authentic gender self for safe places. None of these tasks are easy, and are best accomplished with strong gender angels in place.

The first lesson in strengthening our gender angels is a simple one. When it comes to our children's gender identity and expressions, it is up to the parents to listen, and for the children to tell. Lesson number two: We need to learn to live with gender ambiguity and not pressure our children with our own need for gender bedrock. When we try to pin down our children's evolving gender—they're trans, they're gender-fluid, they're a half-and-half—we may end up imprisoning them in a new bubble of surety and expectation that may actually prevent their true gender selves from coming out. At any one time, all we can know is the cross section of the child we have then; all we can do is meet that child at that crossroads in all the child's explorations and gender-creativity. A third lesson is more complicated. It involves learning how to help our children build a psychological tool kit to meet up with situations that may come their way—language to use when others might ask about their gender presentations; resources to turn to if they are not feeling safe; supports to keep them healthy and thriving, including contact, if possible, with other gender-creative children. A fourth lesson is a corollary of the third: assessing when protective shields might be in order and then communicating to the child that in no way are the parents trying to change the child's gender, but instead sheltering it from an unfair world until that world is safer. The last lesson is to go forth to make that world safer. Children need to know their parents are taking direct action, be it advocating for the child at school, gender-flexing right along with their child, joining with other families and community members to promote gender rights and fair practices in both public and private venues, in the spirit of "If you're not part of the solution, you're part of the problem" (Speake, 2009).

The second key player in wrestling with gender ghosts is the school, where children have their most intensive interactions with non-familial peers. Organizations like Gender Spectrum[3] now offer curricula and student and staff support to build accepting and gender-expansive academic environments for children of all genders. Some schools are welcoming of these programs. Others are caught in a web of transphobic attitudes and misconceptions. The work is to move these schools forward, by evoking gender angels and putting gender ghosts to rest. In early 2012 I learned of a school district in Virginia that had proposed legislation to ban cross-dressing, among a larger list of inappropriate school attire (Garrow, 2012b). A national legal advocacy group asked if I would write a letter to the board challenging the policy. Here are excerpts of that letter, my own personal attempt to call on schools' gender angels:

> I am writing you in regards to your proposed student dress policies. … Whereas I fully support your intent of ensuring that the education of students … is conducted in an environment where safety risks, disruptions, and distractions are minimized through means of an enforceable dress code policy, it is my professional opinion that you are achieving the absolute opposite goal in including [cross-gender clothing] in this policy: "The following clothing is expressly prohibited … : Any clothing worn by a student that is not in keeping with a student's gender and causes a disruption and/or distracts others from the educational process or poses a health or safety concern." This policy related to gender and dress codes as stated is unwittingly mixing apples and oranges in likening clothing worn by individuals to express their authentic gender identity to clothing that is sexually provocative, advertises drugs or alcohol, or is sleepwear rather than school wear. There are increasing numbers of youth who do not identify with the gender listed on their birth certificate or with the socially prescribed behaviors that accompany that gender. There is also a growing body of scientific research that indicates that when these youth are prohibited from expressing their authentic gender selves, which may not be in accordance with their assigned gender as listed in their school records, they are at risk for depresssion, anxiety, sexual acting out, learning and attentional problems, drug and alcohol abuse, self-harm, and at its worse, suicide attempts or actual suicides. Conversely, when the youth are supported in the expression of their authentic gender identities, their mental health significantly improves. Therefore, by your own stated objectives, imposing this dress code based on the gender assigned on one's birth certificate rather than one's affirmed gender puts a whole class of students in the position of lack of safety and, through prohibition of their gender expressions, distractions and disruptions that may very well impede their academic performance.
>
> Indeed, it is understood that both students and faculty may not know how to react to youth who express themselves in gender-nonconforming ways, often through their dress, but the remedy is not to force those gender-nonconforming youth to hide who they are but to provide educational programs and supports for the entire student body and staff (and parents as well) with the goal of developing academic environments that are accepting and inclusive of all enrolled students, whether they are gender conforming or gender-nonconforming. I believe that this would be in keeping with federal regulations ensuring the rights of public school students of all races, ethnicities, sexualities, and genders to an equal education free from discriminiation or harassment. If the presence of gender-nonconforming youth in the classroom is distracting or disruptive to other students, then the educational objective should be to make this no longer true, so that there is a place for students of all gender expressions and identities to feel welcome in your schools. I believe this is an attainable goal, but one that will never happen as long as a dress code related to gender is in your policies.

The bad news was that such a policy was ever considered. The good news is that, in response to community pressure and legal threats, the dress policy related to gender was retracted (Garrow, 2012a). When the community rallies, we witness one step away from gender suppression and one step forward toward gender-creativity, and we can hope that the seeds were planted for the growth of gender angels within school board members who originially stood on the side of gender squelching.

CONCLUSION

Gender webs, gender-creativity, gender angels coalesce into the triumvirate that will both enlighten us and push us forward into a twenty-first-century world where genders multiply and flourish, while binary boxes are relegated to the back-waters of history. I would like to finish with the words I wrote to a mother who asked me, tongue in cheek, if I could offer her a crystal ball as to whether her gender-bending little boy was going to end up gay: "We can only know who he is right now and psychologically prepare for the myriad of possibilities as his gender self unfolds—he might end up gay, or transgender, or gender-fluid, or genderqueer, or some definition of gender that his generation will construct that we haven't even thought of yet. The most critical thing is to leave all paths open to him and communicate that whatever his chosen path, it will be met with love and support, even in the context of a community or culture that might feel otherwise. I do hope that is helpful, not quite like a crystal ball, but a signpost to help us with the most challenging task of all regarding our children's gender-creativity—living for awhile with the ambiguity of not knowing how the story's going to end."

NOTES

1. Now Concordia University.
2. All names and identifying features of children or families are changed throughout this chapter to protect the confidentiality of individuals.
3. Gender Spectrum (www.genderspectrum.org) is a national organization in the United States that offers education, training, and support to create a gender-sensitive and-affirmative environment for all children. Gender Odyssey and TYFA (Trans Youth Family Allies) are two other similar organizations in the United States.

CHAPTER TWO

Health and Well-Being among Gender- Independent Children and Their Families

A Review of the Literature

JAKE PYNE

Recent years have seen an increase in public and media interest in gender-independent children—children who do not conform to social gender norms (Park, 2011; Weathers, 2011; Witterick, 2011). Outspoken parents and advocates are increasingly seeking recognition for gender-independent children and demanding their right to be safe and supported in their families, schools and communities (Kilodavis, 2010; "My Son's Christmas Dress," 2012; Trans Youth Family Allies [TYFA], 2013). However, the availability of supportive community-based health and social services for these families has often been lacking due to a history of pathologizing research that has framed gender independence as an illness in need of clinical treatment (for example, see Zucker & Bradley, 1995). In January 2012, Rainbow Health Ontario (RHO) responded to the absence of community-based services for gender-independent children in Ontario, Canada, by launching the *Gender-Independent Children Project.*

Operational since 2008, RHO is a province-wide program that works to improve the health and well-being of lesbian, gay, bisexual and transgender (LGBT) people in Ontario through education, research, outreach and public policy advocacy. RHO is a program of the Sherbourne Health Center in downtown Toronto, a centre that has been providing comprehensive primary health programs and services to LGBT communities since 2003. Although RHO's mandate is focused on adult populations, the organization's expertise in LGBT health issues has led to requests for consultation regarding gender-independent children. The purpose of the project is to build capacity among health and social service providers to provide community-based support for gender-independent children and their families in Ontario. Guided by a provincial advisory committee comprising educators, physicians, social workers, community activists and parents, this project conducted an extensive literature review and an environmental scan,[1] and developed training and resource materials for service providers and parents. All of these resources can be found on the RHO website: www.RainbowHealthOntario.ca.

This chapter shares the results of a literature review with the intention of bringing evidence-based best practices in this area to a health and social service provider audience. Topics covered include: gender independence and mental health; social stressors; family support; adult outcomes; social and medical transition options; gaps in research; and implications for health and social service providers. The information relevant to the health and well-being of gender-independent children spans the fields of health sciences, education, social work and social services; thus, an extensive review of research in these areas provides an important base from which to build the capacity of providers to effectively serve these families.

UNDERSTANDING GENDER INDEPENDENCE IN CHILDREN

Gender-independent children are those whose gender identity and/or gender expression differs from what others expect of their assigned sex at birth. Other terms used include "gender-nonconforming" (Menvielle & Tuerk, 2002), "gender-variant" (Menvielle, Tuerk, & Perrin, 2005), "gender-creative" (Ehrensaft, 2011), "transgender (or trans)" (Brill & Pepper, 2008) and in the case of Aboriginal children "two-spirited."[2] Gender-independent children are a diverse group. Some may strongly and consistently identify with a gender role that differs from their assigned sex. Others may express a gender identity that blends aspects of multiple genders and is fluid or changing. Still others may be comfortable with their assigned sex, but behave in ways that differ from social norms, for example preferring clothing and activities typically associated with another gender (Brill & Pepper, 2008; Ehrensaft, 2011). Being gender-independent is not intended as defiant behavior on the part of a child nor is it caused by parenting style or experiences of abuse (Children's National Medical Centre, 2003). Only in very rare circumstances will a child alter their gender expression due to a traumatic event (Ehrensaft, 2012). In the overwhelming majority of situations, gender independence is simply an expression of the diversity of human experience (Children's National Medical Centre, 2003; Ehrensaft, 2012; Menvielle, 2012; Menvielle et al., 2005).

The meaning attached to gender-nonconformity varies across cultural contexts. Among Aboriginal peoples in North America, culturally-distinct traditional spiritual roles have existed for those who live between male and female social roles, often as seers, healers and medicine people (Anguksuar, 1997; Balsam et al., 2004). Diverse expressions of gender have been highly valued in some cultural contexts, including but not limited to Indigenous people in the South Pacific region (Besnier, 1994; Roen, 2006), Indonesia (Blackwood, 2005) and other areas of Southeast Asia (Peletz, 2006). In all contexts, social expectations shape the interpretation of, and response to, gender-independent children. For example, in North America, the range of pre-pubertal behavior considered socially acceptable for girls tends to be broad, while feminine behavior among boys tends to elicit severe concern. In fact, one Ontario gender identity clinic reported a referral rate 6 times higher for feminine boys than masculine girls, even though what was deemed 'cross-gender behavior' was more common among girls (Zucker, Bradley, & Sanikhani, 1997).

Of the research that has sought to establish the prevalence of gender-nonconformity among children, results vary widely, since what is considered to be masculine or feminine is generally not objective, nor is it quantifiable. One study found that 2%–4% of boys and 5%–10% of girls behaved as the "opposite sex" from time to time (Achenbach, 1991). Another study found that 22.8% of boys and 38.6% of girls exhibited 10 or more different "gender atypical behaviors" (Sandberg, Meyer-Bahlburg, Ehrhart, & Yager, 1993). The societal stigma that accompanies gender independence may lead some families to require additional support. For adolescents who are considering gender transition, there may also be unique medical care considerations. Clinicians have reported that families often seek support when the child is first entering school or first entering adolescence (Menvielle, 2012).

GENDER INDEPENDENCE IN CHILDREN AND MENTAL HEALTH

The World Professional Association for Transgender Health (WPATH) (2011) states that gender-nonconformity is a "matter of diversity, not pathology" (p. 4). Beginning in the 1960s, however, a subfield of North American researchers and clinicians began to identify childhood gender-nonconformity as a pathology in need of treatment (Bryant, 2006). Avoidance of transsexuality and homosexuality was the stated goal of treatment programs designed to bring youth gender expression in line with social norms, most often through psychotherapy (Green & Fuller, 1973; Greenson, 1966; Zucker, 2008) or behavior modification (Rekers, 1972, 1975, 1977, 1979). In 1980, the diagnosis of Gender Identity Disorder in

Children entered the *Diagnostic and Statistical Manual* (DSM), a publication of the American Psychiatric Association used to classify mental disorders (APA, 1980). This diagnosis was highly controversial and was commonly criticized for pathologizing gender diversity (Menvielle et al., 2005), reinforcing sexist stereotypes (Lev, 2005), and casting a broad social problem (societal intolerance) as an individual pathology (Langer & Martin, 2004). This diagnosis recently became "Gender Dysphoria" in the DSM-5 (APA, 2013), generally understood to be a more accurate and less pathologizing diagnosis (for a more detailed discussion see the Introduction to this book).

While some clinicians continue to advocate for treatment to prevent children from growing up to be transgender (Zucker, Wood, Singh, & Bradley, 2012), other clinicians have deemed these treatments harmful (Wingerson, 2009) and proposed that therapists advocating them are to be "avoided" (Menvielle et al., 2005, p. 45). WPATH (2011) states: "Treatment aimed at trying to change a person's gender identity and lived gender expression to become more congruent with sex assigned at birth … is no longer considered ethical" (p. 16). Thus contemporary approaches to childhood gender-nonconformity are moving away from pathologizing treatments and toward affirmative models in which the focus is not on the child's behavior but rather on parents learning to support their child. In the affirmative approach, the goals of intervention with families are to: de-stigmatize gender variance; promote the child's pride and self-worth; strengthen the parent-child bond; create opportunities for peer support among families; and offer parents the skills needed to advocate for their child in daycares, schools and other social environments (Brill & Pepper, 2008; Children's National Medical Centre, 2003; Ehrensaft, 2011b, 2012; Gale, 2012; Lev, 2004; Mallon, 1999c; Malpas, 2011; Menvielle, 2012; Menvielle & Tuerk, 2002; Menvielle et al., 2005; Pleak, 2009).

Evidence to support an affirming approach is beginning to emerge. A recent study compared mental health in comparable gender-nonconforming children across two treatment programs with different approaches: one clinic in which gender-nonconformity was treated as a disorder and another in which parents were encouraged to support and affirm their child. The children in the supportive program had substantially fewer behavioral problems, indicating that the approach that parents seek and receive may impact significantly on childhood mental health (Hill, Menvielle, Sica, & Johnson, 2010). In another study, children who were strongly pressured to conform to gender norms were "prone to anxiety, sadness, social withdrawal, self deprecation, and other signs of internalized distress" (Carver, Yunger, & Perry, 2003).

Though gender-nonconformity is not itself a mental health problem, social ostracism, hostility and even violence all have an impact on gender-independent children's emotional and psychological well-being, often manifesting in the form of depression and anxiety (Brill & Pepper, 2008; Ehrensaft, 2012). Gender-independent children have been found to be more likely to acquire post-traumatic stress disorder by early adulthood (Roberts, Rosario, Corliss, Koenen, & Austin, 2012). Among trans youth, studies have found high rates of suicidality (Grossman & D'Augelli, 2007; Scanlon, Travers, Coleman, Bauer, & Boyce, 2010) which have been strongly linked to experiences of social exclusion (Bauer, Pyne, Francino, & Hammond, in press). In a recent Ontario study, strong parental support for youth gender identity was associated with a 93% reduction in recent trans youth suicide attempts (Travers et al., 2012). In another study with adolescent trans girls (those born male and identifying as female, or MTF), the correlation between experiences of gender abuse and major depression and suicidality was so strong that findings suggested a direct causal relationship between the two (Nuttbrock et al., 2010).

For some gender-independent adolescents, the onset of puberty may bring on emotional distress as their bodies develop in a direction with which they are profoundly uncomfortable. This distress (Gender Dysphoria) can manifest in depression, suicidality and self-harm (Spack et al., 2012). For these young people, gender transition is an important consideration.

SOCIAL STRESSORS ON GENDER-INDEPENDENT
CHILDREN AND THEIR FAMILIES

Gender-independent children can face a high level of social rejection from peers (Cohen-Kettenis, Owen, Kaijser, Bradley, & Zucker, 2003) and this may increase through their years in school (Menvielle et al., 2005). Parents of gender-independent children may also face rejection from friends and family members (Brill & Pepper, 2008; Ehrensaft, 2011). In one U.S. study of elementary school–aged youth, gender-nonconforming students were more likely than others to be called names, made fun of or bullied at school (56% vs. 33%) (GLSEN and Harris Interactive, 2012). In a survey of Canadian LGBTQ high school students, 95% of trans youth reported feeling unsafe at school (Taylor et al., 2008). Many parents cite safety in schools as their biggest concern (Brill & Pepper, 2008).

In some cases, child welfare authorities have attempted to apprehend gender-independent children out of a misguided belief that parental support for gender diversity constitutes child abuse (Cloud, 2000). Further, some parents are themselves intolerant of gender diversity and may contribute to a child's stress with negative attitudes (Menvielle & Tuerk, 2002). For example, a recent study found that gender-nonconforming children were more likely than gender-typical children to be targeted for abuse and violence from their own family members (Roberts et al., 2012). Despite these serious concerns, social rejection and abuse are not inevitable. Parents, providers and educators are increasingly mobilizing on behalf of gender-independent children and developing resources to support children within their families (Children's National Medical Centre, 2003; Ehrensaft, 2012; Lev, 2004; Mallon, 1999; Malpas, 2011; Menvielle & Tuerk, 2002), schools (Brill & Pepper, 2008; Gender Spectrum, 2012a; Meyer, 2010; Wells, Roberts, & Allan, 2012) and social service organizations (Gale, 2012).

SUPPORTING FAMILIES WITH GENDER-INDEPENDENT CHILDREN

Caregivers may have a variety of reactions to a child who expresses gender independence. While some may not struggle, others may experience shame, anger or grief over the loss of an idealized child (Children's National Medical Centre, 2003). A child's gender expression may become a significant source of conflict between parents or between a child and a parent (Menvielle et al., 2005). Given support, however, most parents of gender-independent children can learn to respond positively to their child (Menvielle et al., 2005). Research has found that for lesbian, gay, bisexual and transgender (LGBT) youth, parental rejection predicts negative heath outcomes and parental acceptance predicts positive health outcomes (Ryan, Huebner, Diaz, & Sanchez, 2009; Ryan, Russell, Huebner, Diaz, & Sanchez, 2010). Indeed, in one Ontario study, strong parental support for a youth's gender identity has been associated with increases in a trans youth's: life satisfaction; physical health; mental health; self-esteem; housing stability; and food security, as well as with decreases in a trans youth's risk for depression and suicide (Travers et al., 2012). Health and social service providers can assist families by supporting parents to process difficult emotions and welcome their child.

Some parents may be anxious about their child's future identity and may discourage a child from exploring a cross-gender identity, or conversely, may rush decisions regarding gender transition. Parents should be encouraged to follow a child's lead and avoid imposing their own preferences for a child's development (Menvielle, 2012). It is also very common for parents to have fears about their child's safety (Brill & Pepper, 2008; Hill & Menvielle, 2009). Supporting parents to develop advocacy skills is an important part of safety planning in schools and other settings (Malpas, 2011; Menvielle, 2012; Menvielle & Hill, 2011). Peer support has been identified as a key resource for families with gender-independent children (Malpas, 2011; Menvielle & Hill, 2011) and peer-based support programs for families are developing in some cities in North America (for example, see Children's Hospital of Los Angeles, 2012; Gender Spectrum, 2012b; National Children's Hospital, 2012; Seattle Children's Hospital, 2012).

CONSIDERING ADULT OUTCOMES FOR
GENDER-INDEPENDENT CHILDREN

As with all children, there is no way to know who a gender-independent child will become as an adult. Some gender-independent children come to identify as cisgender (non-trans) people who are lesbian, gay or bisexual. Some continue to identify as gender-fluid into adulthood. Some come to identify as transgender and seek to socially and/or medically transition to a new gender role. Others may never align themselves with any of these identities (Brill & Pepper, 2008; Ehrensaft, 2011). There is research to suggest that many gender-independent children shift to become more gender-typical as they age (Zucker & Bradley, 1995), though there is debate regarding whether this reflects a natural progression or an internalizing of pressure to conform (Children's National Medical Centre, 2003; Gray, Carter, & Levitt, 2012; Menvielle et al., 2005). In one qualitative study, interviews were conducted with young people who were gender-independent as children, finding that for both those who went on to transition and those who grew to be more gender typical, their trajectories became clearer during the ages of 10–13 (Steensma, Biemond, de Boer, & Cohen-Kettenis, 2010).

Though some research has investigated adult outcomes for these children, primarily sexual orientation and gender identity, these studies are subject to substantial limitations. In some studies, researchers were unable to re-connect with 30% of original participants at the time of follow-up (Wallien & Cohen-Kettenis, 2008). In other studies, samples were garnered from adults who as children were given treatment intended to change their gender expression, potentially impacting respondents' perception of the acceptability of gender diversity and thus their responses to follow-up surveys (Drummond, Bradley, Peterson-Badali, & Zucker, 2008; Green, 1987; Zucker & Bradley, 1995). Studies that have assessed sexual orientation outcomes for gender-independent children have reported vastly different results and these findings can be considered inconclusive (Figure 1).

Figure 1. The findings from studies exploring adult sexual orientation outcomes for children diagnosed with "gender identity disorder" are highly inconsistent.

Studies exploring sexual orientation outcomes for children diagnosed with "gender identity disorder"	Percentage reported to be lesbian, gay or bisexual in adulthood
* Drummond, Bradley, Peterson-Badali & Zucker, 2008	24–32%
** Green, 1987	75%
*** Wallien & Cohen-Kettenis, 2008	68%
*** Zucker & Bradley, 1995	19%

* Includes only children assigned female at birth

** Includes only children assigned male at birth

*** Includes both children assigned male and female at birth

The same studies have measured whether participants continue in adulthood to experience discomfort with their assigned sex (Gender Dysphoria) and whether they continue to meet the diagnostic criteria for Gender Identity Disorder (Figure 2). These findings also vary widely and can be considered inconclusive.

Figure 2. The findings regarding adult "gender dysphoria" outcomes for gender-independent children are inconsistent.

Studies exploring "persistence" of gender dysphoria for children diagnosed with "gender identity disorder"	Percentage reported to continue to meet diagnostic criteria for "gender identity disorder" in adulthood
* Drummond, Bradley, Peterson-Badali & Zucker, 2008	12%
** Green, 1987	2%
*** Wallien & Cohen-Kettenis, 2008	27%
*** Zucker & Bradley, 1995	20%

* Includes only children assigned female at birth

** Includes only children assigned male at birth

*** Includes both children assigned male and female at birth

For a number of reasons, it is difficult to obtain accurate information from these studies regarding the number of gender-independent children who come to identify as trans in adulthood. For example, inclusion in these studies has often been based on the criteria for the Gender Identity Disorder in Children diagnosis (DSM-III), which does not distinguish between the distinct phenomena of *behaviors,* also known as gender expression, which are presumed to be gendered (clothing and mannerisms), versus *gender identity* (how one sees oneself) (Drummond et al., 2008; Zucker, 2005). In addition, existing studies have measured whether participants meet the diagnostic criteria for "gender dysphoria" and "gender identity disorder" at follow-up rather than inquiring into how participants identify themselves, for example, as *trans* or *genderqueer* (Drummond et al., 2008; Wallien & Cohen-Kettenis, 2008). Follow-up has often been conducted between the ages of 18 and 23 (Drummond et al., 2008; Wallien & Cohen-Kettenis, 2008), and yet many come to identify as trans after this age. Further, the terminology relating to trans communities is evolving over time. For example, "transsexual" was the only recognized trans identity at the time of some follow-up studies (Green, 1987). Yet the term "transsexual" refers only to individuals who seek medical interventions to bring their body in line with their social gender identity, now understood to be a smaller subset of a much broader and diverse trans community.

While some parents and providers do experience anxiety regarding the future identities of gender-independent children, it is neither necessary nor possible to determine their adult identities in childhood. Providing support to gender-independent children requires validating how they express themselves and see themselves in the present.

TRANSITION: SOCIAL AND MEDICAL OPTIONS

Many gender-independent children will not want or need to transition to a new gender role. If provided the space to explore a range of activities and gender identities, many place themselves comfortably on a spectrum between male and female or find as they grow that they feel comfortable with their assigned gender role and physical body. Yet others strongly identify as a different gender and are healthiest if they can live in that role by taking steps to socially and/or medically transition. It is important for parents and providers to pay close attention to what young people communicate about their needs. If a young person is in distress regarding their gender role, the adults in their life may need to consider, together with the youth, their options for social and/or medical transition (Brill & Pepper, 2008; Ehrensaft, 2011).

Social Transition

Social transition consists of a change in social gender role and may include a change of name, clothing, appearance and gender pronoun. For example, a male-born child wishing to socially transition would likely begin using the pronoun "she," change her name, begin to present herself as a girl, attend school as a girl and live her daily life as a girl. Children in this situation, along with their families, may make a variety of decisions regarding privacy and how open they wish to be about their history (Brill & Pepper, 2008). For pre-pubertal children, social transition is the only transition option as medical intervention is not recommended prior to puberty (Hembree et al., 2009).

The decision for a child to socially transition is not a simple one and should be made jointly among the child, the parents and, if available, supportive professionals. Some clinicians recommend encouraging parents of gender-independent children to follow their child's lead and avoid imposing their own preferences (Menvielle, 2012). Experienced clinicians have reported that in some children, the need for transition presents itself clearly with obvious distress in the original gender role and obvious well-being in the new role. In contrast, other children are clearly comfortable with their assigned sex but desire to express themselves in ways that are considered less common for their gender role. These clinicians state that for children who are in between these two experiences, the path is less clear (Ehrensaft, 2012; Menvielle, 2012).

Social transition in young children is a relatively new practice and long-term research in this area is lacking. Parent and clinician reports indicate that children's comfort and happiness can improve dramatically with this option (Brill & Pepper, 2008; Ehrensaft, 2012). Clinicians have indicated that there may be children who choose to transition back to their original gender role at the onset of puberty (Menvielle, 2012; Steensma, Biemond, de Boer, & Cohen-Kettenis, 2010). In one study, young people in this position found it distressing to explain this to their friends and families (Steensma et al., 2010). Yet another clinic reported that the one youth under their care who did choose to transition back reported not distress, but gratitude for the opportunity to live as the other gender and clarify their identity (Edwards-Leeper & Spack, 2012). It is possible that some young people who transition more than once might view this as a mistake or a return to a prior identity, while others might view this as their own unique gender trajectory. Children pursuing social transition should be reassured that they can continue to express changes in their identities, and parents are best advised that other transitions may be possible (Menvielle, 2012). Social transition is becoming more common for pre-pubertal children and those families beginning this process can greatly benefit from peer support to assist them in facing social stigma and advocating for their rights within schools and other institutions (Menvielle, 2012).

Medical Transition

Medical transition consists of steps taken to bring the physical body in line with the social identity in cases in which an individual feels a strong incongruence between the two (often referred to as *Gender Dysphoria*). Though historically practiced by adults, some transition options have more recently become available at younger ages. For adolescents who experience distress as puberty approaches, gonadotropin-releasing hormone analogues (GnRHa) or "puberty suppressant hormones" can be administered to provide relief by delaying the development of unwanted secondary sex characteristics. Puberty suppressant hormones are frequently used to treat the premature onset of puberty among other young people. According to current studies, the effects are reversible and puberty commences if discontinued; thus, an adolescent who decides not to pursue transition can cease GnRHa and resume puberty ("Pubertal Blockade Safe," 2012).

The U.S. Endocrine Society Clinical Practice Guidelines recommend that adolescents who maintain a strong and consistent cross-gender identification should be considered for medical treatment using GnRHa at the onset of puberty (Tanner Stage II).[3] If, after an exploration of gender identity, complete transition is desired, cross-hormone treatment can begin at age 16[4] with the potential for surgery approval at age 18 (Hembree et al., 2009; Spack et al., 2012; WPATH, 2011). This protocol is supported by the World Professional Association for Transgender Health "Standards of Care" as well as by long-term studies conducted in the Netherlands (Delemarre-van de Waal & Cohen-Kettenis, 2006; WPATH, 2011).

There are divergent opinions regarding when to introduce puberty suppressant treatment; however, leading Dutch and U.S. practitioners offer a number of rationales for introducing puberty suppressant hormones at the onset of puberty, rather than later: 1) Suspending puberty provides emotional and psychological benefit through an immediate reduction in stress. 2) A reduction in stress facilitates the necessary identity exploration and provides additional time to make decisions. 3) Adolescent treatment outcomes can be more satisfactory than adult treatment outcomes, as the unwanted effects of puberty will be prevented—for example, prevention of breast tissue growth in female-to-males which would later need to be surgically removed. 4) The effects of puberty suppressant hormones are fully reversible, whereas many unwanted pubertal changes are permanent—for example, voice change for male-to-females (Delemarre-van de Waal & Cohen-Kettenis, 2006; Hembree et al., 2009; Meyer, 2012; Spack et al., 2012; WPATH, 2011).

While some parents and providers may doubt the need to make long-term medical decisions at a young age, it is important to understand the sense of urgency some gender-independent adolescents may feel regarding puberty. In addition to the noted irreversible bodily changes which commence during puberty (Delemarre-van de Waal & Cohen-Kettenis, 2006), the stress of navigating the social world in an inappropriate gender role is significant and the risk for suicide and self-harm can increase dramatically during this time (Spack et al., 2012;

WPATH, 2011). Indeed, in an Ontario study that included both trans adults and youth, the timing of transition had a direct bearing on suicidality. Past-year serious suicide consideration was highest among those who were planning a medical transition but had not yet begun, significantly higher than among those who had completed a transition, and among those who were not planning a transition (Bauer, Pyne, Francino, & Hammond). Thus a young person's urgency to transition must be considered in context. Both supporting a young person to transition as well as *not* supporting their transition have long-term consequences. A danger is that parents or providers may believe that delaying or refusing to support transition is a neutral position—this is not the case.

Assessments for GnRHa are often conducted by a team that includes pediatric endocrinologists and mental health professionals (Delemarre-van de Waal & Cohen-Kettenis, 2006; de Vries, Cohen-Kettenis, & Delemarre-van de Waal, 2006; Edwards-Leeper & Spack, 2012), though guidelines also provide for family doctors to diagnose and prescribe (WPATH, 2011). The assessment process may include physical and mental health testing, inquiry into the young person's gender identity and assurance that the youth has strong family support. Eligibility criteria may also include a consistent gender identity and the demonstration of certainty by the youth, and there has been some critique of the reliance on these concepts (Roen, 2011). Currently in Canada, there are some institutions beginning to facilitate puberty suppression and early gender transition for adolescents, for example at the Children's Hospital of Eastern Ontario, the BC Children's Hospital, the Montreal Children's Hospital, the Winnipeg Health Sciences Centre and the Sick Kids Hospital in Toronto. The high cost of GnRHa may not be covered by provincial health insurance plans in Canada; however, it is often included in workplace benefit packages and coverage can also be secured through social assistance for low-income families receiving public benefits.

OUTCOMES ASSOCIATED WITH TRANSITIONING AT A YOUNGER AGE

For many, the prospect of transitioning at a young age raises concerns regarding unsatisfactory outcomes, post-transition regret or long-term physical and mental health implications. Studies to date have indicated positive outcomes in each area. Follow-up studies indicate that unsatisfactory outcomes and regret are associated more with a late rather than an early transition (Cohen-Kettenis & Gooren, 1999; Lindemalm, Korlin, & Uddenberg, 1987). Post-transition difficulties have been found to be highest among those who experience strong social stigma when they are unwillingly visible as trans people in their new gender role (i.e., if they are unable to "pass" as their felt gender when they desire to) (Ross & Need, 1989). Early transition tends to facilitate greater "passing," allowing for less visibility in the new gender role and potentially less stigma (Delemarre-van de Waal & Cohen-Kettenis, 2006). With respect to regret, out of 70 adolescents beginning GnRHa in the Netherlands none changed their mind about pursuing cross-sex hormone treatment at 16 (de Vries, Steensma, Doreleijers, & Cohen-Kettenis, 2010). In another Dutch study which included 27 participants, no individual transitioning before age 18 regretted their decision to follow through with surgery (de Vries, 2010). It is notable, however, that the Netherlands clinic where these studies were conducted currently has very strict eligibility criteria and it is unclear whether the use of different criteria would produce different results.

With respect to long-term physical and mental health, the first report from a long-term follow-up case study was recently conducted 22 years after a 13-year-old female-to-male adolescent began puberty suppressant treatment. The study found this individual to be in psychological and physical good health with no regrets regarding transition. Bone density, brain development and metabolic and endocrine parameters were all within the healthy range and no negative side effects were indicated (Cohen-Kettenis, Schagen, Steensma, de Vries, & Delemarre-van de Waal, 2011). Additional Dutch studies among trans adolescents who were found eligible for treatment between 16 and 18 years, showed a significant post-surgery increase in body satisfaction. These individuals were found to be socially and psychologically healthy (Cohen-Kettenis & van Goozen, 1997; Smith, van Goozen, & Cohen-Kettenis, 2001) and appeared to be psychologically healthier than those who transition in adulthood (Kuiper & Cohen-Kettenis, 1988; Smith, Van Goozen, Kuiper, & Cohen-Kettenis, 2005).

Other studies have found that the mental health of trans adolescents improves with access to medical intervention (Spack et al., 2012). Pediatric endocrinologist Norman Spack, co-director of the Gender Management Service Clinic at Boston Children's Hospital, has suggested that to refuse to assist adolescents with medical intervention may be a violation of the Hippocratic oath (the physicians' oath to do no harm) ("Pubertal Blockade Safe," 2012). Both Dutch and U.S. experts have stated that at this time, it appears the benefits of suppressing puberty at its onset outweigh the risks ("Pubertal Blockade Safe," 2012; Kreukels & Cohen-Kettenis, 2011).

Ultimately, many gender-independent children will have no need for transition, while for a smaller number, transition will be crucial for supporting and sustaining their well-being. Listening to and valuing what young people communicate about their identities, paying attention to signs of distress, and supporting close partnerships between youth, their families and competent providers will facilitate young people's health and well-being.

GAPS IN RESEARCH

There are a number of areas in which additional research is needed to better support gender-independent children and their families. For example, information is needed regarding the experiences of families with gender-independent children from diverse economic, ethno-cultural and racialized communities to ensure that existing resources are able to serve all families well. Research is needed on the experience of social transition among pre-pubertal children in order to understand what factors best facilitate their well-being and that of their families. There is also currently a lack of research to guide decisions regarding fertility preservation for adolescents who delay puberty or who transition prior to developing viable sperm or egg samples. Though some information is available (Rainbow Health Ontario, 2012), additional research is needed. Finally, though existing follow-up reports on adolescent transition have been positive (Cohen-Kettenis, Schagen, Steensma, de Vries, & Delemarre-van de Waal, 2011; Cohen-Kettenis & van Goozen, 1997; de Vries, 2010; de Vries, Steensma, Doreleijers, & Cohen-Kettenis, 2010), additional research will assist in clarifying the long-term health needs of gender-independent children who pursue transition as well as those who do not.

IMPLICATIONS FOR HEALTH AND SOCIAL SERVICE PROVIDERS

In closing, Rainbow Health Ontario offers the following recommendations to health and social service providers to improve services and support for gender-independent children and their families:

- Primary health care providers including family doctors and pediatricians must become knowledgeable and competent in providing care for gender-independent children as these are the providers to whom parents often first turn (Spack et al., 2012; WPATH, 2011);
- Children's mental health service providers must become competent in advocating for gender-independent children and better supporting families to affirm children's diverse gender identities and expressions;
- Early childhood educators, elementary school teachers and school administrators require training to effectively provide safe and welcoming learning environments for gender-independent children and adolescents;
- Social workers and child welfare service providers must become familiar with the unique indicators of well-being within families with gender-independent children to ensure that all child protection decisions are free from bias;

- Examples of prior unethical research and treatment conducted on gender-independent children indicate that new approaches to research and service provision are needed which honor gender diversity and respect the rights of children in research and mental health service settings;
- As mentioned, existing clinical programs which assist young people to transition typically offer this only to youth with strong family support (de Vries & Cohen-Kettenis, 2012; Spack et al., 2012; WPATH, 2011). These policies have implications for the health and well-being of youth who do not have parental support. Providers must develop methods of working with families to foster greater acceptance and must consider transition options for youth whose families may never support this decision;
- Health and social service providers within all organizations, institutions and sectors must uphold the value of gender diversity and ensure that practices are affirming of gender-independent children.

ACKNOWLEDGMENTS

The author would like to thank Loralee Gillis at Rainbow Health Ontario, the members of the Gender-Independent Children Project Advisory Committee and the Sherbourne Health Centre Trans Working Group, without whose input this chapter would not have been possible.

NOTES

1. Environmental scans are used by organizations to assess the relevant factors impacting a particular field, including the role of multiple stakeholders and the gaps in available services and resources.
2. The term *gender-independent* was selected for use with this project as it both destigmatizes gender diversity as well as reframes gender variance as a trait which many parents value in their children: independence.
3. The Tanner Scale is a scale of human physical development based on external primary and secondary sex characteristics. Tanner stage I refers to pre-puberty and Tanner stage II refers to the onset of puberty. There are five stages in total.
4. Some Canadian clinicians are beginning cross-hormones at age 14.

CHAPTER THREE

Working Together for an Inclusive and Gender-Creative Future

A Critical Lens on 'Gender Dysphoria'

JEMMA TOSH

Psychiatric diagnoses related to gender expression have been the focus of much change and speculation, while continuing to accumulate. In the infamous nineteenth-century text *Psychopathia Sexualis,* Krafft-Ebing (1892) described two diagnoses related to gender-creativity ('fetishism of female attire' and 'hermaphrodism') whereas the recent DSM-5 (American Psychiatric Association [APA], *Diagnostic and Statistical Manual of Mental Disorders*, 5th edition) describes ten.[1] This changeability has, in part, been influenced by the demedicalization of homosexuality (Conrad & Angell, 2004) due to the perceived interdependence between sexuality and gender identity, but it also illustrates a long history of medical attention and intervention despite a lack of consensus and understanding. Thus, 'gender identity disorder'[2] (or its current descriptor, 'gender dysphoria') defines the boundaries of 'normal' and 'abnormal' gender expression with significant consequences. It is of mutual interest to feminist (e.g., Caplan, 2011), transgender (e.g., Winters, 2011a), and intersex communities (e.g., Morgan, Wilson, & O'Brien, 2012) that, despite their differences, all are concerned with psychiatric diagnoses and gender-creativity. This chapter will reflect on the conflicted history of the diagnosis, as well as describe a collaborative project challenging its implementation. This project addressed the DSM-5 Chair of the Sexual and Gender Identity Disorders Section and involved contributions and support from lesbian, gay, bisexual, trans, intersex, and feminist activists, academics, and clinicians (Tosh, 2011a). The acceptance of diverse differences in relation to philosophical or political issues was nurtured through the commitment to a common goal: the condemnation of psychiatric intervention with young, gender-creative children. This politically engaged academic intervention illustrates the potential for creating awareness and intervening in professional discussions around psychiatric intervention when groups overcome differences and work together to develop extensive and valuable activist networks.

GENDER-CREATIVITY AND PSYCHIATRY

While psychiatry has gone to great lengths to define and redefine gender abnormality, the (increasingly) narrow concept of gender normality is never explicitly defined. This has resulted in a continual accumulation of diagnoses (Rose, 2006). As Caplan (1995) states, 'There is no condition we can absolutely and indisputably call normality' (p. 33). Rose (2006) argues that psychiatric diagnoses have become so pervasive that mental illness could be the new 'norm.' Consequently, the 'norm' constructed by mainstream psychiatry is not based on frequency or majorities (i.e., a statistical norm), but is an elusive rarity for those aspiring for mental or psychological perfectionism. The 'ideal' as defined by the dominant culture is equated with 'normal' (Metcalfe & Caplan, 2004). This is of particular interest to psychiatry's *Diagnostic and Statistical Manual* (DSM), as feminists have long argued that the DSM does in fact have a clear ideal of 'normal': a white (Ali, 2004), heterosexual (Metcalfe & Caplan, 2004) man (Ussher, 1991). However, it is much narrower than this; it is an idealized version of gender-conforming masculinity that excludes many men as well as women (and those who do not identify with either categories). To rephrase Szasz (1960), psychiatry perpetuates the myth of mental health.

This accumulation of diagnosis has included a vast array of psychiatric terminology and diagnoses;[3] however, 'transvestism,' 'transsexualism,' and 'Gender Identity Disorder' have been the most enduring. The DSM's first edition in 1952 included 'transvestism' under the deviations of sexuality section. This developed from Krafft-Ebing's (1892) work on fetishism that distinguished a fixation of women's clothing as a specific perversion. Originally, the perversion was not the object of the fetish but its limited focus. The fetish of female clothing was not 'abnormal,' but not being aroused by the rest of the woman was considered 'abnormal.' Krafft-Ebing (1892) theorized that 'this limited sexual interest, within its narrower limits, is usually expressed with a correspondingly greater and abnormal intensity' (p. 153). Its association to eroticism and psychopathology has been repeatedly emphasized within psychiatric texts, such as its name change to 'transvestic fetishism' in 1980 (APA, 1980) and subsequently 'transvestic disorder' with 'fetishism' (APA, 2013). This is, in part, influenced by Blanchard's (1985, 1989a, 1989b, 2005) work that has unsurprisingly attracted much criticism from cross-dressing and transgender communities. For example, Blanchard (2005) has additionally proposed 'autogynephilia' (meaning 'love of oneself as a woman') for 'males [who are] erotically aroused by the thought or image of themselves as women' (p. 439). This association of cross-dressing with sexual pleasure is vehemently contested by many (e.g., Conway, 2008; Winters, 2008, 2009) and continues the construction of cross-dressing as a 'paraphilia' which places it in the same section of the DSM as 'pedophilia' and 'sexual sadism,' two diagnoses that are framed as 'monstrous' (Douard, 2009; Jewkes & Wykes 2012). Nevertheless, Blanchard was the APA Paraphilias Chair for the DSM-5 revisions and consequently 'autogynephilia' made its way into the 'transvestic disorder' diagnostic criteria (APA, 2013).

The term 'transsexualism' was first used by Caudwell (1949) in his work entitled *Psychopathic Transexualis* (Drescher, 2010). Harry Benjamin advanced the popularity of the term in his presentation in 1953 (Ekins & King, 2001) and his subsequent publication *The Transsexual Phenomenon* (Benjamin, 1966), although the term didn't appear in the DSM until 1980. In 1980, the third edition of the DSM transformed the construction of gender-creativity by dividing 'transvestism' into three distinct subcategories. 'Tranvestism' became renamed 'transvestic fetishism' and two new terms emerged: 'transsexualism' and 'childhood gender identity disorder.' The difference between 'transsexualism' and 'transvestic fetishism' was stated to be the lack of sexual pleasure, as well as the desire to become or live as the opposite sex that was described as an essential feature of 'transsexualism' (APA, 1980). 'Childhood gender identity disorder' was described as gender-nonconforming behaviors that could develop into adulthood 'transsexualism.' The primary aim of therapeutic intervention with children at this time was to prevent 'transsexualism' in adulthood. This approach drew on the work of John Money (1975) and others (e.g., Rekers & Lovaas, 1974) who reported the successful change in gender identity in children, which has since been the topic of much controversy and criticism (Colapinto, 2000; Diamond & Sigmundson, 1997). However, this aim is still promoted by current members of the APA (e.g., Bradley & Zucker, 2004; Zucker, 2006b). As Zucker, Wood, Singh, and Bradley (2012) state, 'If the parents are clear in their desire to have their child feel more comfortable in their own skin, that is, they would like to reduce their child's desire to be of the other gender, the therapeutic approach is organized around this goal' (p. 383).

In 1994 the APA combined two diagnoses ('transsexualism' and 'Gender Identity Disorder nontranssexual type') into 'gender identity disorder in adolescents or adults.'[4] This symmetrized the diagnosis with the childhood version[5] that had existed since the DSM-III (APA, 1980), due to increasing research into 'gender-variant' or 'feminine' boys in the 1960s (Bryant, 2006). This new diagnosis altered the psychiatric construction from a disordered desire to be the opposite sex, to an internal 'incongruence between anatomic sex and gender identity' (APA, 1980, p. 261). This moved the diagnosis even further from the eroticized construction of 'transvestism.' However, these changes to the diagnoses were very controversial (Bryant, 2006; Hird, 2003), with subsequent requests for its removal (e.g., Isay, 1997) similar to the (eventually successful) campaigns for the declassification of homosexuality as a 'paraphilia' after gay rights protests and an APA vote (APA, 1973). This move also altered the focus of intervention, from coping with a gender identity issue through changing sex (Money, 1986) to what Lawrence (2008, p. 425) describes as addressing 'the gender problem itself.' Ultimately, it enabled interventions aimed at correcting gender-creative behavior.

The diagnosis also attracted criticism for its oversimplification of gender as a straightforward binary of male and female and its dependence on stereotypical Western constructions of femininity and masculinity (e.g., Langer & Martin, 2004). Although the DSM attempted to counter these accusations, it failed to adequately resolve the problem. For example, the DSM-III (APA, 1980) stated, 'Children whose behavior merely does not fit the cultural stereotype of masculinity or femininity should not be given this diagnosis' (p. 265). This was re-emphasized in the revised edition where the text read, 'This disorder is not merely a child's nonconformity to stereotypic sex-role behavior as, for example, in "tomboyishness" in girls or "sissyish" behavior in boys, but rather a profound disturbance of the normal sense of maleness or femaleness' (APA, 1987, p. 71). However, it did not explicitly define 'tomboyishness' or 'sissyish' despite Richard Green originally drafting the diagnosis (Bryant, 2006) and the clear influences from his 'sissy boy syndrome' (Green, 1987). There was also no clarification of what a 'normal sense of maleness or femaleness' would mean. This was despite clinicians challenging the use of a rigid gender binary (Ehrensaft, 2009; GID Reform Advocates, n.d.; Lev, 2005), querying the validity of this approach to gender identity in general (Hegarty, 2009), and highlighting how the diagnostic criteria represented a particularly western perspective (Langer & Martin, 2004). As Lev (2005) states,

> The basis for the diagnostic criteria in children rests in stereotypical definitions of normal male and female behavior. ... The DSM does not appear to recognize the impact of forty years of feminism, and the full range of behaviors and experiences engaged in by normal males and females in contemporary society. (p. 51)

Also lacking are explanations as to why femininity is seen as more problematic than masculinity in gender-creative youth (Hegarty, 2009). Langer and Martin (2004) highlight the uneven ratio of diagnosis, with referrals for feminine, gender-creative children equaling more than six times the number for other gender-nonconforming children. Zucker (2006a) has argued that this is related to the more social acceptability of women expressing masculinity, but this also illustrates the role of social construction in the diagnosis of 'Gender Identity Disorder' (Langer & Martin, 2004). The overemphasis of feminine gender expression by gender-creative children fits with previous feminist critiques of psychiatry as pathologizing and devaluing femininity (Bryant, 2006; Sedgwick, 1991).

The overinclusive and ambiguous criteria have also been criticized as they outline 'normal' gender development in such narrow terms that they pathologize almost all individuals who do not rigidly adhere to cultural expectations of femininity or masculinity. As Spade (2003) argues, the diagnosis of 'Gender Identity Disorder' implicitly creates a dichotomy between abnormal and normal gender development that promotes a 'fiction of natural gender' (p. 25). In doing so, it assumes that all forms of gender expression that fall outside this definition are fundamentally deviant (Lev, 2005).

Paradoxically, while the 'Gender Identity Disorder' criteria risk encapsulating many gender-creative individuals beyond the scope of 'transsexualism' (making it impossible to be 'transsexual' and mentally 'healthy'), they simultaneously exclude many they are designed to support (Lev, 2005). For example, there is a diverse range of individuals who wish to pursue body modification surgery or receive hormonal treatment to ease the distress of gender dysphoria. However, as the diagnosis acts as what Lev (2005) describes as an 'admission ticket,' those who do not fulfill the criteria often find that treatment is not available. For instance, as 'transvestism' is separated from 'transsexualism' based on the criterion of wanting to change sex, a previous diagnosis of 'transvestism' can result in a refusal for medical treatment (Lev, 2005).

Another frequent criticism of 'Gender Identity Disorder' (GID) is the declaration that mental disorders have subsequent distress for the individual. Several have queried the cause of childhood distress as an internal mental pathology that leads to deteriorated social relationships, arguing for the possibility that the distress is a result of social stigmatization from the diagnostic label. Lev (2005) states, 'If gender-variant behavior was not stigmatized by labeling these expressions as psychiatric diagnoses, then transgender and transsexual people might experience significantly less emotional, legal, or social distress' (p. 48). Nevertheless, Zucker (2006a) maintains that '[w]hen children with GID are socially ostracized by their peers, it is their overt behavior that elicits negative reactions, not an abstract label' (p. 548), but he does not consider how abstract concepts are attributed to those behaviors.

Several others (e.g. Bartlett, Vasey, & Bukowski, 2000; Hegarty, 2009) have argued that due to the DSM-IV (APA, 1994) definition of mental disorder being based on inherent distress that does not result from '… conflicts that are primarily between the individual and society' (p. xxii) that 'Gender Identity Disorder' does not fit the psychiatric definition of mental disorder. Bartlett et al. (2000) cite parental descriptions to illustrate that anxiety lies with those around the child in response to their gender-creativity and that the child's distress is often in response to restrictions on their gender expression. For example, a mother states that her child 'gets very mad at me when I won't let him dress in my dresses' and that they 'seemed content and happy' when dressed as a girl (Meyer & Dupkin, 1985, as cited in Bartlett et al., 2000, p. 761).

Nevertheless, as Lev (2005) highlights, the diagnoses of 'transsexualism' and 'Gender Identity Disorder' have legitimized gender dysphoric distress as well as creating previously nonexistent avenues for treatment. However, the diagnosis continues to pathologize a wide variety of individuals and often fails to enable access to support and treatment to many who need it. This leaves gender-creative individuals in a very conflicted space, as within current medical systems they need the diagnosis yet it disadvantages them also (Lev, 2005). Moreover, the renaming of the diagnosis as 'Gender Dysphoria' (first put forward by Fisk, 1973, 1974) resulted in premature celebrations of a symbolic success on par with the demedicalization of homosexuality (Tanner, 2012). While the new name does move toward a pathologization of distress rather than gender-creativity (the term 'dysphoria' means 'abnormal distress'), the criteria have moved in the opposite direction, and it is the criteria that psychiatrists will use to diagnose and implement treatment (Tosh, 2013). As Winters (2011b) observes, 'The workgroup has not reflected these principles in the diagnostic criteria for Gender Dysphoria. They retain much of the flawed language from the DSM-IV' (para. 4). For instance, criteria for 'Gender Dysphoria' in children still include 'a strong preference for the toys, games, or activities stereotypically used or engaged in by the other gender' in addition to 'a strong desire for the primary and/or secondary sex characteristics that match one's experienced gender' (APA, 2013, p. 452), showing the continued pathologization of gender-creativity.

FEMINIST, TRANSGENDER, AND INTERSEX PERSPECTIVES

In addition to criticisms aimed at the diagnosis, its criteria, and psychiatric treatment, there has also been disagreement between feminist, transgender, and intersex communities about gender-creativity more generally. For example, some feminists have sided with the psychiatric perspective arguing that transgenderism is a sickness (e.g., Jeffreys, 1997, 2005; Raymond, 1979), although this is increasingly challenged by third wave feminism (from 1992 onward, see Walker, 1992) and the developing field of transfeminism (Koyama, 2003; Scott-Dixon, 2006). Additionally, there has been tension between intersex and transgender communities as both are under the gaze of medical and psychiatric institutions but have distinct perspectives, communities, and aims for social transformation. For instance, Intersex in Australia (2011a, para. 11) states, 'Intersex is not the same issue as transsexuality, although the current medical approach to gender makes it so for some' and 'we simply don't want the trans agenda to dominate in any discussion on intersex' (Intersex in Australia, 2011b, para. 9). The diversity of these communities and the potential for gender-creativity to redefine 'sex' and 'gender' in ways that trouble previous feminist and queer conceptualizations make disagreement and debate inevitable. However, it is this critical reflexivity and questioning that is the strength of these distinct but conjoined movements. Adopting challenging perspectives into each discipline makes it more inclusive and our understanding of sex and gender is deepened. It is the working together of these different communities and the development of a campaign that incorporated difference and contrasting perspectives at its core that I will now describe.

COLLABORATIVE GENDER-INCLUSIVE ACTIVISM

The Division of Clinical Psychology (DCP) of the British Psychological Society (BPS) invited Professor Ken Zucker as keynote speaker to their annual conference in December 2010 (BPS, 2010). Zucker works at the Toronto Centre for Addiction and Mental Health (CAMH) and is considered an authoritative figure in the controversial diagnosis and treatment of children with 'Gender Identity Disorder' (Hill, Rozanski, Carfagnini, & Willoughby, 2006). He was also Chair of the American Psychiatric Association's (APA) Sexual and Gender Identity Disorders Work Group for the DSM-5 (APA, 2013). His invitation was proposed by the DCP conference committee expert group who research potential speakers for the division (J. Unwin, personal communication, November 15, 2010).

This invitation sparked an angry and concerned response from many. Zucker's work at CAMH has been widely criticized by academics (e.g., Bryant, 2008; Hird, 2003; Langer & Martin, 2004; Lev, 2005; Menvielle & Tuerk, 2002; Wilson, 2000; Wren, 2002), organizations (e.g., Burleton, 2008; Choe, 2008; Queerty, 2009), and individuals concerned with LGBT issues and gender-creativity. Zucker's treatment has been described as 'coercive' (Ehrensaft, 2008, as cited in Spiegel, 2008) and in some instances 'abusive' (Burke, 1996). This approach has also been compared to reparative therapy (Pickstone-Taylor, 2003) that was used in attempts to convert homosexuals to heterosexuality, and was condemned by the American Psychiatric Association in 2000 (APA, 2000b).

Zucker's approach involves emphasizing the potential benefits to the child of acting in ways that are expected of their biological gender and encouraging 'sex-typical' clothing, toys, games, and activities (Zucker & Bradley, 2004). Those involved in the child's life who accept their 'atypical' behavior are considered 'problematic' and either discouraged from supporting the behaviors or are 'removed.' For example, Hird (2003) describes a case study by Zucker wherein the family were advised to fire the child's nanny as she was seen as encouraging cross-dressing behavior. Zucker's justification for this treatment, which he admits lacks empirical support (Zucker, 2006a; Zucker, 2004; K. Zucker, personal communication, December 3, 2010), is to reduce social ostracism. However, he overlooks his own role in this segregation. To identify 'gender dysphoria' as pathological and requiring treatment in addition to enforcing a rigid gender binary only encourages social exclusion to those who challenge hegemonic and normative constructions of gender. For instance, Feder (1997) highlights how this collaborative intervention between school, parents, and psychiatrists legitimizes the gender-creative child as 'deviant' and thus gives (conforming) children 'a particular kind of power' (p. 200) through teasing, name-calling, and harassment. These responses to gender-creativity not only exclude children who do not conform, but also act as deterrents for other children not to play with gender.

While many groups who opposed Zucker's invitation agreed with criticisms in relation to the narrow conceptualisation of gender and the controversial approach to gender-creativity in childhood, there were contrasting views in relation to the diagnosis more generally. While there was relative agreement that the pathologization was problematic and unfair, the diagnosis is a requirement for gender-creative adolescents and adults to access treatment and support. Therefore, there were concerns that criticisms of the disorder could potentially make accessing treatment difficult or potentially impossible. These issues were discussed early on by those involved with the campaign. Consequently, it was agreed that the focus would be on Zucker's approach with children. This would enable the diverse group to communicate a clear message that represented the perspectives of those involved. It was also agreed that 'Gender Dysphoria' reform as part of an ongoing process of challenging gender-creative pathologization would be more effective than a sudden declassification due to these complex issues of institutional barriers (see GID Reform Advocates, n.d.; Winters, 2005).

Several months of organization and mobilization accumulated on Friday December 3, 2010, amidst freezing temperatures in Manchester, UK. This campaign, which began with only a few emails being sent out to enquire if others were aware of this keynote presentation, soon developed into an international and multifaceted response aimed at the DCP. The Psychology of Sexualities Section (POSS) of the BPS was the first to formally contact the DCP, stating its objections and including a statement describing the objections in more detail (Tosh, 2011b). At the same time, activists were organizing and advertising protest meetings in Manchester. The DCP conference organizers quickly became aware of these meetings and were keen to discuss these issues with myself and other protest organizers. However, the meeting with the conference organizers had limited success, as we were informed that the keynote would go forward despite the objections from POSS and the protesters. Nevertheless, the DCP were keen to arrange a panel to enable a discussion at the conference, but it was difficult to find a suitable speaker at such short notice. The DCP arranged for Polly Carmichael to debate these issues with Zucker as she works at the Child GID clinic in London, but as Carmichael cites Zucker in her own work (e.g., Carmichael & Alderson, 2004), it is unlikely that feminist, transgender, and intersex objections would have been voiced at the debate if this panel went ahead.

The Psychology of Women Section (POWS) sent its objections soon after this and the protest meetings increased in frequency and numbers, as activists organized what the messages would be and how best to communicate them at the conference. I initiated an online petition at the request of several individuals who wanted to participate but were unable to attend meetings (iPetitions, 2010). On the day of the conference, this petition had collected over 330 signatures from individuals in the UK, the United States, Canada, and Australia and included comments from a wide range of concerned individuals. For example, Professor Spurlin stated, 'This is just another example of the perpetuation of misogyny and homophobia in culture under the guise of medical authority' and Misha Balch of Gender Alliance of the South Sound stated, 'Zucker's work … is an affront to the dignity of transgendered people everywhere. Transgenderism is a reaction to a society that rejects "whole people" whose personalities do not conform to the patriarchal polarized socio-political constructs of "male" and "female"' (iPetitions, 2010).

The DCP then began to receive criticism from within the division, from the Faculty of Sexual Health and HIV. The Faculty sent its concerns formally to the DCP just after the conference, and the Community Psychology Section of the BPS sent their objections on the first day of the conference. The Community Psychology Section also produced a statement outlining their concerns, particularly emphasizing the human rights legislation that Zucker's treatment potentially breaches (The UK Community Psychology Discussion List, 2010).

In addition to these formal responses within the BPS, the awareness of and support for the protest were increasing outside the organisation. Several media outlets published articles and blogs on these events and encouraged people to support the protest either by attending the meetings or signing the online petition (e.g., Intersex in Australia, 2010; The Lesbian & Gay Foundation, 2010; Lockhart, 2010). There was also a lot of discussion within professional and activist networks via email lists, blogs, and online groups. This accumulation of interest and support demonstrated to DCP conference organizers and delegates on the day of the protest that although there were more than 60 people protesting in the snow, the views they represented were supported by many more. It also enabled us to achieve more than previous protests had been able to do, particularly in terms of having our perspective heard at the conference (N. Kennedy, personal communication, December 3, 2010). The DCP conference organizers invited two protesters into the keynote presentation to ask Zucker questions and meet with him face to face. Natacha Kennedy, who organized the protest against Zucker in London in 2008, and I attended Zucker's keynote presentation and voiced our concerns.

Once inside the conference Kennedy and I were escorted to the room where Zucker would present his keynote. The polite and professional atmosphere of the academic conference was in striking contrast to the overt and passionate chants originating from outside. The Chair of the DCP delivered a critical introduction to Zucker's keynote, which was responded to by another DCP member who emphasized Zucker as 'inspiring' and 'one of the world's leading experts' on 'gender identity disorder' before describing her professional relationship with him. This very brief introduction was awkwardly positioned between the Chair's critical introduction and Zucker's presentation, but illustrated the tense and polarized positions in relation to his work.

Zucker's presentation summarized research that conformed to his previous presentations and publications apart from a brief summary of the proposed revisions for the DSM-5. The questions following the keynote included critical reflections that examined the underlying validity of the approach, often replicating criticisms already discussed in published literature. For instance, Kennedy summarized her own PhD research on transgendered children and highlighted the contradictions between her findings and Zucker's work. Kennedy's research with transgendered adults found that the vast majority were very secretive during their childhood and adolescence and were unlikely to be referred to a service during this time (Kennedy & Hellen, 2010). Therefore, Zucker's work generalizes from a specific sample of the trans community, and one that Kennedy and Hellen (2010) argue is in the minority. The persistent query (e.g., Langer & Martin, 2004) of whether these children were distressed by their Gender Dysphoria or other people's responses to their 'atypical' behavior was also raised. This was in addition to concerns regarding the lack of supporting evidence for the successful treatment of 'gender dysphoria,' which Zucker has previously acknowledged (e.g., Zucker, 2006a).

REFLECTIONS

Those who attended the keynote presentation heard Zucker's perspective but only after an introduction that highlighted the controversy and complex ethical issues of psychiatric intervention with gender-creative children. The audience also listened to probing questions once Zucker's presentation had ended. Several delegates had also come out to speak to protesters and many took pictures of the banners and signs. If this group had not mobilized and responded to Zucker's invitation the DCP keynote would have been a very different experience. The commitment by those who were determined to intervene as well as the emails and phone calls of support and encouragement helped develop this ongoing campaign.

Connections between different sections, organizations, and networks enabled us to approach the DCP from a variety of positions, as clinicians, academics, and activists as well as gay, lesbian, bisexual, heterosexual, transgender, gender-creative, intersex, and feminist individuals. This was key in bringing together a diverse range of perspectives, and included building bridges between communities such as feminist and transgender activist groups. This collaboration was built on two aspects of the campaign: regular meetings and working with conflict and complexity. By this I mean that rather than attempting to bring together this eclectic group into a consensus and stifling creative responses or promoting a single perspective over others, we encouraged everyone's voice to be heard and even for conflicting strategies to be employed. This atmosphere of acceptance and respect made the protest a positive and inspiring experience. As one protest attendee stated, 'There was a sort of radical organizing and openness to plurality of opinions and tactics I haven't seen much of in other trans activism' (Foibey, 2010, para. 4).

Regular meetings enabled the group to discuss issues at length and decide on ways forward together, even if it meant that several strategies were being mobilized simultaneously. For example, there were comprehensive discussions over the concepts of freedom of speech and censorship, and the group followed both strategies of trying to have Zucker's invitation retracted as well as finding ways of responding to his presentation via a panel discussion. This fluidity of the campaign strategy enabled the group to be reactive to events as they occurred and be inclusive by supporting multiple perspectives and creative activist responses.

Psychiatry's construction of gender has a long and complex history that continues with ongoing critique and activism. This complexity needs to be engaged with at the very center of academic and activist responses to psychiatric gender 'norms.' While those involved in this intervention held different views on sex, gender, and gender-creativity, we were able to move forward together because we all agreed on one thing: that we should have the freedom to play with gender.

CONCLUSIONS

Psychiatric diagnosis related to gender-creativity is an important area for academic and activist intervention. It is an issue for all genders of any variety, as the definition of 'normal' gender expression delineates an idealized form of masculinity that has long been critiqued and problematized by many (e.g., Kimmel & Mahler, 2003; Miedzian, 2005). This collaborative project between feminist, transgender, and intersex communities illustrated the potential for working together on areas of commonality, without the need to lose distinct perspectives or identities. The creativity that we put into our gender expression should be reflected in our academic and activist work; when addressing complex issues, working with multiplicity, contradiction, and conflict is a valuable part of the process of transformation.

ACKNOWLEDGMENTS

Parts of this chapter have been described in previous publications. These include: papers in the *Psychology of Women Section Review*, the *Psychology of Sexualities Review*, and *Clinical Psychology Forum*, as well as a forthcoming book chapter entitled 'Critical Feminist, Queer and Trans Psychology: Deconstructing Gender and Sexuality' (published in German) and my PhD thesis submitted to Manchester Metropolitan University, UK. This content has also been presented at the National Workshop on Gender-Creative Children, Concordia University, Montreal, Canada; Asylum Conference, Manchester, UK; Psychology of Women Section Conference, Windsor, UK; Congress on Working with Childhood Sexual Abuse, Nottingham, UK; Interrogating (In)Equality Conference, the University of British Columbia, Vancouver, Canada. It has also been described in invited talks at the Psychology of Sexualities AGM, London, UK; Disorders of Sex Development Group, Royal Manchester Children's Hospital, Manchester UK; Discourse Unit: Centre for Qualitative and Theoretical Research, Manchester Metropolitan University, UK; Centre for the Study of Gender, Social Inequities and Mental Health (CSGM), Simon Fraser University (SFU), Canada.

NOTES

1. These are: 'transvestic disorder' with or without 'autogynephilia' or 'fetishism,' 'gender dysphoria in children' with or without a 'disorder of sex development,' 'gender dysphoria in adolescents and adults' with or without a 'disorder of sex development,' 'gender dysphoria in adolescents and adults posttransition,' 'other specified gender dysphoria,' and 'unspecified gender dysphoria' (APA, 2013).

2. I use quotation marks when referring to psychiatric diagnoses or categories to differentiate from the behavior, identity, or communities. For example, by placing 'gender dysphoria' in quotation marks, I am not employing scare quotes, but indicating that my discussion relates to the discursive concept, rather than gender dysphoria that is experienced by individuals. Separating the concept from the material reality does not minimize or disregard the embodied experience, but enables critical interrogation of socially constructed concepts (Hacking, 1995).

3. Psychiatric nomenclature reference the following diagnoses in relation to gender-creativity: 'fetishism (female attire)' (Krafft-Ebing, 1892), 'transvestism' (APA, 1952), 'transvestitism' (APA, 1968), 'transvestic fetishism' (APA, 1980, 1987, 1990, 2000a), 'transvestic fetishism with gender dysphoria' (APA, 1990, 2000a), 'transsexualism' (APA, 1980, 1987), 'gender identity disorder in adolescence or adulthood nontranssexual type' (GIDAANT) (APA, 1987), 'gender identity disorder in adolescents or adults' (APA, 1990, 2000a), 'childhood gender identity disorder' (APA, 1980, 1987, 1990, 2000a), 'gender identity disorder not otherwise specified' (APA, 1990, 2000a), 'gender dysphoria' with or without a 'disorder of sex development' (APA, 2013), 'autogynephilia,' 'autoandrophilia' (Blanchard, 2005), 'transvestic disorder with autogynephilia' (APA, 2013). Prior to the demedicalisation of homosexuality, transgenderism was theorized to be an advanced form of homosexuality. The terms related to this era include: 'eviration' and 'defemination,' 'effemination' and 'viraginity,' androgyny and 'gynandry,' and 'metamorphosis sexualis paranoica' (Krafft-Ebing, 1892).

4. While transsexualism was no longer a diagnostic category, the DSM-IV (APA, 1994) defined it as 'severe gender dysphoria' (p. 771) often resulting in the desire for sex reassignment surgery or hormonal treatment.

5. 'Gender identity disorder of adolescence or adulthood nontranssexual type' (GIDAANT) only featured briefly in the DSM-III-R describing a gender-creative individual (particularly related to cross-dressing) who did not wish to change their biological sex. Fundamentally, it was a non-eroticized version of transvestism. GID also experienced a brief episode in the 'Disorders Usually Diagnosed in Childhood' section of the DSM-III-R, but was quickly reinstated as a 'sexual and gender identity' disorder in the DSM-IV with adult and child versions (although transvestism remained under the paraphilias section).

CHAPTER FOUR

Transformative Gender Justice as a Framework for Normalizing Gender Variance among Children and Youth

ANN TRAVERS

PRELUDE

Whenever we are crossing the Canadian–U.S. border, my instructions to my daughter—and her response—are always the same: "I will be calling you 'he.'" She: "Why?" We have had many discussions about this and none of them have been satisfactory for either of us. But before we leave home each time, I insist that she refrain from wearing a skirt or a dress until we are across the border (if we are driving, it is not unusual for us to pull into the nearest shopping mall parking lot to enable her to "change back" into herself). I tell her I don't like it either but not everybody understands that we are who we say we are. Most of the time she and I are in solidarity in the face of the failure of others to understand who she is—or who I am, for that matter—or to realize that the categories they impose upon her are contrived and oppressive, but the erasure of her identity is real and it hurts every time. The last time we flew to the United States, I watched as she came through the sensor gate behind me. I did not even notice that one of her fists was clenched until the guard who was waiting to wand her asked her to open her hand. When she did, she revealed a delicate, iridescent pink hair scrunchy. She was trying to find a way to hang onto herself in the face of such denial. I was stunned by her ingenuity and torn up by the way she was left empty handed.

As she grows up, my beloved one will increasingly engage with gendered and racialized "vectors of security and vulnerability" (Spade, 2011, p. 117) unmediated by our queer multi-racial family structure and antithetical to the values that, at least most of the time, characterize, our family culture. Right now she is only 8 years old and I fear that the truth about the extent of the potential danger lying ahead would harm her development. She is a radiant Black child and dual citizen of the United States and Canada, who, in her own words "was born a boy but likes being a girl." For the time being she rides on my magic carpet of White, middle-class privilege but this will take her only so far. Although I have always been visibly queer, I purposely curtail my own regime of greater trans emergence so as to maintain the privileges I enjoy and that enable me to protect her.

When she was 5, still so small really, she told me that the bathrooms at the Unitarian church we attend made her sad. The image I have in my mind of her as she said this is of a small and anguished child, frozen before two doors. She literally did not know where to go—but she knew that loss would be the result of either choice she made. As a gender-nonconforming person myself, I have horrible childhood memories of censure and denial. I don't think I initially cared much about who was a boy and who was a girl until I was told, in no uncertain terms, that I was one and not the other and that the female category assigned to me was a despised and devalued one.

I hate the gender binary and the transphobic, homophobic, racist and sexist ideology of the two-sex system (Fausto-Sterling, 2000, 2012; Hill Collins, 2005; Lemert, 2002): the transformative gender justice–driven social change I long for speaks to that. My perspective is inevitably partial and I hope it does not foreclose options that are important to others; that is certainly not my purpose and, as always, I have much to learn.

INTRODUCTION

I worry a bit about recent media coverage that has brought issues relating to transgender and gender-nonconforming children and youth to public attention. I do find some relief in the potentially positive benefits of greater tolerance but most of the trans people featured in this coverage conform to binary norms.[1] I recall the recent oppressive and 'concerned' media attention given to a Toronto family who chose not to divulge the sex of their new baby—Storm—to anyone (Poisson, 2011). I am concerned that the malidentified 'science of sex difference' (Connell, 2009)[2] that justifies gender inequality may be used to support a medical model that limits our understanding of issues relating to transgender people to a mode of transsexuality likened to a 'birth defect.' I am also concerned that mainstream trans-inclusion policies may be oriented toward waiting until a transgender or gender-variant child, youth or person shows up on the scene for inclusive measures to be undertaken. This means that the multiple and interlocking oppressive structures that shape our lives (Hill Collins, 2005) and impact everyone—not just the visibly marked 'others'—escape scrutiny.

In this chapter I will outline and advocate for a transformative gender justice framework designed to push the envelope of inclusion past tolerance to much needed structural change. This framework is informed by recent critical perspectives and builds on my (2008) queered version of Fraser's (2007) definition of gender justice. The willingness to identify and resist oppressive power relations is a key feature of critical race theorizing, anti-capitalist/globalization scholarship, queer feminism and critical trans politics. These traditions inform the paradigm of transformative gender justice I outline in this chapter as a basis for child and youth advocacy. As such, a transformative gender justice framework takes explicit aim at oppressive social structures and cultural patterns and refutes powerful mainstream ideologies that mask the undemocratic character of actual governance and social policy. I begin the chapter with a brief overview of issues relating to transgender and gender-variant children and youth and then go on to introduce Fraser's (2007) definition of gender justice as a requirement of democracy. I discuss tensions between queer feminist and transgender scholarship in order to link a queered version of Fraser's definition of gender justice to critical race and critical trans theorizing as a basis for a transformative gender justice paradigm. The chapter concludes with a discussion of what this paradigm means for child and youth advocacy, in both the short and the long term.

Invisibility

We know that whatever the statistic is on the prevalence of transgender and gender-variant children, it is likely to be artificially low as a result of the totalizing pressure of much of the gender categorization and socialization children are subjected to (Berkowitz & Ryan, 2011; Hellen, 2009). Understandably, gender-variant children and youth are often invisible due to their tremendous efforts to avoid teasing, persecution and scorn from peers, teachers and family members (Whittle, Turner, & Al Alami, 2007). If, as the limited data currently available to us show, transgender and gender-variant children and youth are disproportionately victims of "gendered harassment" (Meyer, 2010), self-harm and suicide (Cole et al., 1997; Klomek, Marrocco, Kleinman, Schonfeld, & Gould, 2008), we can safely speculate that more children and youth would exhibit gender-nonconformity if greater cultural flexibility concerning sex and gender identities was the norm. As it stands, the intense social policing of gender and sex identity among children makes it appear as if gender-nonconforming children are a rather tiny minority; the gender socializing/censoring environment of most family, peer, school, sports and religious settings reflects the circular reasoning of the *Thomas* Theorem: "Situations that are defined as real become real in their consequences" (Macionis & Gerber, 2011,

p. 332), meaning that the overwhelming practice of sorting children into boy and girl categories and teaching them to adhere to complementary gender roles makes it appear as if these are natural lines of demarcation. This means that most transgender and gender-variant children and youth are "non-apparent" (Hellen, 2009) or stealth. Inclusion strategies, therefore, must focus on shaping environments in general as well as responding to the needs of a particular child or youth.

Still, the erasure of gender variance in North America is no longer as pervasive as it once was, and children and youth with atypical sex identities and gender presentations are becoming increasingly visible in many of our communities and schools (Brill, 2008; Ehrensaft, 2011). Most of the knowledge about this population's lived experience necessarily must come from the minority of transgender and gender-variant children and youth whose parental support and/or anxiety makes them visible (Ajeto, 2009; Ehrensaft, 2011). Given the White, middle-class pedigree of most of the parent activists I have encountered, and I include myself in this category, this knowledge is necessarily shaped by the "invisible knapsack" of White privilege (McIntosh, 1990) and entitlements of class privilege, making it limited in terms of its ability to address the full diversity of experiences. The ways in which racialized vectors of vulnerability and security (Spade, 2011) impact gender-nonconforming children and youth of color, for example, are under-researched.

Violence against transgender youth and adults is not formally tracked in most jurisdictions in North America, but newspaper and anecdotal reports collected by community organizations indicate that transgender people of color in the male-to-female (MTF) spectrum are particularly vulnerable to violence as a result of the triple burden of transphobia, sexism and racism (Currah & Minter, 2000; Spade, 2011). In addition, institutions, social policy and everyday cultural interactions actively maintain a gender binary, resulting in both institutional and informational erasure of transgender people, thereby neglecting their unique needs for health care, social services and public education and other supports (Bauer et al., 2009; Namaste, 2000).

Research in nonclinical settings has highlighted that gender-variant children and youth are particularly vulnerable to coercive pressure to conform to societal gender norms, resulting in bullying and gendered harassment by peers, and often debilitating social stigmatization (Brill & Pepper, 2008; Ehrensaft, 2010; Hellen, 2009; Kennedy, 2008; Meyer, 2008b; Whittle et al., 2007). In a study investigating school climate, Egale Canada (Taylor & Peter, 2011) reported that 95% of transgender students felt unsafe in schools, 90% reported being verbally harassed because of their gender variance and 50% said that their teachers and other adults in positions of authority failed to intervene when homophobic or transphobic comments were made. Other studies have reported that doctors, teachers and classmates often misunderstand gender-nonconforming children and youth (Hellen, 2009; Meyer, 2008a), which can result in their increased feelings of social isolation. Consequently, many are at risk of being diagnosed with learning disabilities and/or psychological problems because of stress, depression and suicidal tendencies (Glavinic, 2010; Grossman & D'Augelli, 2007). One study shows high rates of violence by parents against gender-nonconforming children (Roberts et al., 2012).

Parenting activist Arwyn Daemyir is not alone (see, for example, Roberts et al., 2012) in claiming that "gender-nonconformity is predictive of PTSD" (2012). We know that among children and adolescents, a sense of belonging is crucial for optimal development (Statistics Canada, 2010). The impact of gendered harassment and bullying on intellectual and social development among gender-variant and/or queer adolescents is an important dimension (Meyer, 2010). White Holman and Goldberg (2006) emphasize the particular vulnerability of adolescents to violence because of economic dependence, the prevalence of age-peer violence in schools and power differentials between adults and youths.

TRANSFORMATIVE GENDER JUSTICE

Writing from a radical democratic orientation, Fraser (2007) insists that gender justice for women—which she defines as material and cultural inclusion—is a basic condition of democracy. Fraser defines gender justice in terms of "participatory parity," that is, economic and cultural equality for women. For Fraser, gender justice requires both *recognition* and *redistribution* for authentic democracy to be realized. In an earlier work (Travers, 2008), I applied a queer (anti-essentialist) interpretation of Fraser's measure of gender justice to make the argument that mainstream sport contributes to gender injustice through its role in normalizing and perpetuating gender inequality. The concept of participatory parity proved useful in documenting the cultural and economic power of sport in providing hegemonic or dominant images of heroic (white and heterosexual) masculinity, in normalizing the ideology of the two-sex system that is at the heart of gender injustice for women, queer and transgender people and in the highly gendered occupational structure of sport itself.

Queer Feminism and Transgender Scholarship

Before I continue, it is important to acknowledge the tensions within queer feminist and transgender scholarship relating to child and youth advocacy. Butler (1990, 2004) argues that the Gender Identity Disorder (GID) diagnosis in the *Diagnostic and*

Statistical Manual of Mental Disorders (DSM) is used oppressively against queer, gay and trans youth, as does Burke (1996). According to Butler, normative gender structures are the problem and GID, therefore, is not the solution. Other scholars and transsexual activists have cautioned us against ignoring the positive role played by GID in ending the legal legitimacy of police attacks on queer and gender-nonconforming people and in acting as a "gatekeeper" for access to and affordability of much needed health care for some transsexuals (Richmond, et al., 2010).

The schisms between queer transgender theories that favor gender ambiguity and fluidity, and transsexual rights literature that is not informed by queer theory are difficult to bridge but key to forming anti-oppression alliances. Significant debates in transgender studies include those between queer-identified proponents of transgender identities as modeling an anti-essentialist gender future (Burke, 1996; Butler, 1990, 2004; Halberstam, 1998, 2005, 2011, 2012; Noble, 2006) and transsexual-rights authors and activists (Namaste, 2000, 2005) who may or may not see themselves in the LGBT moniker but are most concerned about ending the mental distress, discrimination and violence that transsexuals in Western culture face (Elliot, 2010).

The need to abolish the institution of compulsory heterosexuality and the limited options for gender and sexuality it encodes and enforces is a central theme in queer theory. As Blaise observes, for queer theorists such as Judith Butler, "the concept of genderedness becomes meaningless in the absence of heterosexuality as an institution" (2005, 22). Butler's (2004) "new gender politics" "places transgender, transsexual, and intersex movements at the center" (Elliot, 2010, p. 68). The concordant privileging of the gender troubling figure is at odds with the assimilation, human rights and survival agendas of many transsexuals (Namaste, 2000, 2005). Key struggles for this latter group relate to health care, identity documentation and sex-segregated facilities (Spade, 2011, pp. 142–143). But Elliot (2010) is quick to point out that there is no hierarchy of victimization/violence between the former and the latter; gender ambiguous people and identifiable transsexual persons experience high rates of discrimination and violence. A transformative gender justice paradigm, therefore, targets the naturalness of the sex binary and its intersectional structuring role in terms of the distribution of life chances. Meyer identifies the "need to unplug from the heterosexual matrix without privileging particular gender identities or sexual behaviors" (2010).

Recent North American media coverage of transgender children and youth[3] has me concerned that transgender children, youth and adults who feel at home in more familiar identities (consistent with the gender binary) may be more visible and/or accepted in mainstream media than those whose gender identity and/or expression is ambiguous or fluid. Gender self-determination is significantly limited by the options available; it is impossible to know whether many trans children and youth would choose binary-normative transformation if ambiguity were normalized and a full gender spectrum was proudly and publicly on display. As this is not the current reality, hormone blockers at puberty followed by cross-sex hormones in adolescence may be a crucial intervention for some youth in order to decrease their visibility as transgender or gender-variant and therefore the likelihood of discrimination and violent assaults; and some youth will undoubtedly choose this path on the basis of a clear identification with a traditional sex category. It is a mistake to deny them this in the hope that the world will change and make it unnecessary.

Intersectionality

The structuring role of gender regimes is unintelligible without understanding the ways in which gender operates within racist, classist and neoliberal nationalist systems. In her 1998 text *Fighting Words: Black Women and the Search for Justice*, Hill Collins describes the intersection of race, gender and social class as constituting a "matrix of domination." According to Spade, this inspired Kimberle Crenshaw's (1998) coining of the term "intersectionality," whereby "people who experience multiple vectors of subjection … face unique harms not captured by racial justice movements that use male experience as the norm or feminist movements that use white women's experiences as the norm" (2011, p. 31). In later work Hill Collins explains that ideas about gender, race and sexuality are imbricated in North American "black gender ideology." She emphasizes that

> the assumption that racism and heterosexism constitute two separate systems of oppression masks how each relies upon the other for meaning. Because neither system of oppression makes sense without the other, racism and heterosexism might be better viewed as sharing one history with similar yet disparate effects on all Americans differentiated by race, gender, sexuality, class, nationality. (2005, p. 88)

This one history is characterized by Lemert in terms of "European diaspora morality" (2002, p. 5). One of modern Europe's biggest exports, European diaspora morality normalizes the hegemony of whiteness, wealth and [non-trans] heterosexual masculinity. This morality justifies an unequal distribution of cultural and material resources—the very components of participatory parity incorporated in my (queered) employment of Fraser's definition of gender justice—among various groups of people in North American society and beyond.

Skidmore observes that "narratives of transsexuality are always already about race, class, and sexuality as well as gender" (2011, p. 294). Richardson and Meyer emphasize that "transgender histories are also shaped by colonial regimes of racialization": such histories therefore "begin from a position that transgender bodies are raced bodies functioning within a socio-historical context and actively creating their own cultural and epistemological frameworks" (2011, p. 252). Trans scholars of color and anti-racist, anti-poverty allies have penned correctives to the white, middle class, often homonormative (Duggan, 2004) reference point for much queer and trans theorizing. According to Duggan, homonormativity refers to "a politics that does not contest dominant heteronormative assumptions and institutions, but upholds and sustains them, while promising the possibility of a demobilized gay constituency, and a gay culture anchored in domesticity and consumption" (Duggan, 2004, p. 50). As Skidmore contends, this notion of homonormativity provides a "rubric for understanding how certain queer subjects can be produced as acceptable while other queer subjects are produced as pathological" (2011, p. 295). According to this logic, visible white and/or 'respectable'[4] transgender subjects who conform to binary sex and gender norms could experience a measure of inclusion without unsettling the structures and systems of gender inequality. Bucar and Enke are even more specific: "Seeking gay rights and civil rights requires policing sex and gender expression and also maintaining dominant race and class exclusions; and indeed, this is what homonormativity does best" (2011, p. 304). This is partly what worries me about the current spate of transgender children and youth making the rounds of talk shows and mainstream news programs. With rare exceptions, such as Kilodavis's (2011) *Princess Boy*, rather than presenting transgender or gender-nonconforming children and youth as gender troubling figures, they instead seem to confirm an essential gender binary by presenting or being packaged as transsexual beings who are born as one sex but identify innately as the other. The transgender young people made known through such media do display some racial diversity but the limitation of transgender issues to transsexuality fails to represent the range of visible and invisible individuals and identities. As Bucar and Enke (2011) observe,

> the vast majority of transsexual-identified individuals in the United States will not have a single surgery related to sex change, due to lack of access and/or lack of desire. Thus, any media coverage that focuses primarily on SRS [Sex Reassignment Surgery] disproportionately excludes from its purview poor people, people of color, all gender variance that is not medically mediated, and the countless ways in which trans masculine and trans feminine people negotiate the sex/gender expectations of the culture around them. (2011, p. 323)

Let me provide a deeply troubling example of an "anti-poster child" for childhood gender variance. In "Minding the Gap: Intersections between Gender, Race, and

Class in Work with Gender-Variant Children," Saketopoulou (2011) writes about a 10-year-old gender-nonconforming child she refers to as "DeShawn," who is hospitalized for severe mental illness. Caught up in the crossfire of racialized and gendered identity clusters, DeShawn's gender variance is harshly policed. He appears to be seen as "beautiful" by the author alone, a compassionate and gender affirming clinical psychologist working in the hospital. As Saketopoulou details, the vectors of gender, race and class interact to create a situation wherein DeShawn is made vulnerable by racism, poverty, childhood trauma and gender variance. In the end, DeShawn is left violated and alone, as Saketopoulou leaves the hospital and him behind. The complexity of his vulnerability is too great to be contained by the talk show format; and his story, if it were to hit the news, would likely cite non-systemic failures, such as biological explanations for mental illness in combination with the failure of his parents to provide adequate care and role-modeling, as an explanation for his tragic circumstances.

A transformative gender justice paradigm locates 'the problem' outside of the individual child, youth or adult and squarely within the socio-cultural realms of wealth inequality, racialized sex-typing and gender categorization. We are not able to dismiss binary-based and stereotypical sex-typing as merely indicative of outdated attitudes. This is because it sits squarely within ongoing and deeply structured relations of gender inequality—structures of gender inequality that stink of the hatred of women and the feminine and that are integrally linked to structured relations of violence, racialization and systems of class privilege. These are the cultural contexts or 'worlds' (Haraway, 1991) that children and young people emerge in and engage with in contemporary North America.

Spade eschews the liberal LGBT rights agenda that has transformed the burgeoning mass social movements of the sixties into non-profit organizational structures that are characterized by internal hierarchy, philanthropist funding and legal reform agendas. Spade argues instead for mass struggles against the neoliberal elimination of social 'safety nets' and against the prison industrial complex, insisting that "we need to shift our focus from the individual rights framing of discrimination and 'hate violence' and think more broadly about how gender categories are enforced on all people in ways that cause particularly dangerous outcomes for trans people" (2011, p. 29). This critical trans politics intersects with critical race theorizing about trans issues to further radicalize my queered definition of gender justice as participatory parity: by demanding not just recognition for trans and gender-variant people but also a thorough redistribution of the vectors of vulnerability and security that disproportionately harm women, queers, trans people, people of color and so-called 'illegal immigrants.' This is a specifically *transformative* understanding of gender justice and hence of the larger project within which to situate our advocacy and activism on behalf of trans and gender-variant children and youth. Meyer (2010) concurs, pointing out that advocacy and activism designed to achieve gender justice for children and youth requires the integration of an antiracist/anti-oppression framework that links the processes of gendering, racialization and economic marginalization.

Situating the gender binary within European diaspora morality's white, masculine, heterosexual and upper-class privilege and replacing it with a gender spectrum grounded in an anti-oppression epistemology is an important conceptual step. A gender spectrum model generates a "gender affirming" in contrast to a "gender coercive" approach to parenting, health care, education, coaching, social services and support (Pyne, 2012). The transformative gender justice paradigm I outline in this chapter pushes for the transformation of a gender binary into that of a gender spectrum (Fausto-Sterling, 2012) within the context of a larger anti-oppression framework (Meyer, 2010). But it importantly recognizes that the worlds most children, youth and adults live in make it incredibly difficult to adopt fluid identities (Elliot, 2010) and that gender fluidity is not an ideal shared in common by all transgender and gender-nonconforming people. A transformative gender justice paradigm focuses on gender self-determination: not within an individualistic, human rights framework but rather in opposition to the existence and structuring role of gender/race/neoliberal/ "national security state" (Mohanty, 2012) regimes.

Once we jettison the ideological foundations of the sex binary we are able to ground our social justice work on behalf of transgender and gender-variant children and youth in an ethos of transformative gender justice for *all* children and youth. One of my concerns is that people and institutions will wait for a transgender or gender-variant child or youth to "show up" before adopting trans-inclusive measures. This misses the point in two ways. First, as I emphasized at the outset of the chapter, the majority of transgender and gender-variant children are non-apparent—therefore waiting for one to show up to adopt inclusive measures misses the point. As parent activist Arwyn Daemyir (2012) emphasizes, "The harm of coercive gender assignment begins before self-assertion of gender." And second, transformative gender justice is needed also for children and youth who "have non-normative interests for their sex" (Meyer, 2010, p. 62). A coercive gender system is limiting for everyone, so efforts to advance the gender spectrum as the norm is a pro-active and structural way of working toward inclusion for transgender and gender-variant children and youth. As Loralee Gillis, Director of Ontario's Rainbow Health, encourages: "Let's put the lens on the structures (as problematic) rather than the kids" (2012).

I emphasize that achieving gender justice for the children who happen to stand outside of gender norms requires the eradication of or at least the lessening of the gender coercion and policing that *all* children are subject to. A transformative gender justice framework requires that we employ a focus on the maldistribution of life chances within Western systems characterized by significant degrees of social inequality. The intersections of race, class, sexuality and nationality create environments that are more hostile to some children and youth than others. Attention to these intersecting dynamics is key to advocacy on behalf of transgender and gender-variant children and youth because their 'transness' or 'gender variance' is integrated within these systems of privilege and vulnerability.

A transformative gender justice perspective views gender variance in a way that is hostile to neoliberal models of freedom through consumption. The sympathy and support media coverage/exploitation of gender-nonconforming children and youth may garner are inadequate on their own for creating the conditions for safeguarding them. The sympathy and support need to be developed to resist oppressive gender structures. To do this, people must come face-to-face with historical and contemporary denigration and violence toward adults of this ilk. These transgender news and talk show darlings of the moment will transform into the "monsters" we are taught to fear (Shildrick, 2002, pp. 80–81 and they will, in many instances, be treated accordingly.

Transformative Gender Justice: Connecting Harm Reduction Strategies to Broader Social Transformation Objectives

A transformative gender justice paradigm translates into advocacy and social change activism for transgender and gender-variant children and youth in powerful ways. While the steps we need to take may be different in terms of immediate and long-term progress, they must be congruent and designed to address the transformative understanding of gender justice I advance in this chapter. A queered, trans-positive and intersectional understanding of Fraser's (2007) criteria of participatory parity as material redistribution and cultural inclusion drives advocacy and social change efforts in particular ways. To illustrate how this might be so I identify a few transformational long-term goals and focus on immediate possibilities for harm reduction that are consistent with these goals.

The Long Haul

Long-term goals for transformational social change include removing gender as a mandatory identity category for government documentation; providing safety nets for all community members to ensure a baseline standard of living above the poverty level; ensuring access to gender affirming health care; and engineering a cultural shift away from a gender binary infused with sexism, racism, homophobia and transphobia and toward an egalitarian and open-ended gender spectrum. The need for immediate harm reduction interventions, consistent with these long-term goals, is urgent. I conclude this chapter with a few examples of recommendations for immediate harm reduction that tie into long-term goals for social transformation. In making suggestions I choose as my targets public sector institutions and suggest both general and sector-based objectives for advocacy and reform.

Harm reduction in key points of contact

Immediate and significant harm reduction for transgender and gender-variant children and youth can be achieved via the following short-term goals/interventions with regard to key points of contact between children and youth and the public sector. In keeping with the ethos of the transformative gender justice paradigm, many of them target children and youth as a whole for benefit; this is appropriate and necessary given what we know about the invisibility of many transgender and gender-variant children and youth, intersectionality and the harm that restrictive and sexist gender categories inflict on the many children and youth who would not categorize themselves as trans or gender-nonconforming.

Key points of contact between transgender and gender-variant children and youth—apparent or non-apparent—and the public sector include education, the health care system, social services for children and families, the criminal justice system and sport and physical recreation. In general we should advocate for the training of public sector service providers to adopt anti-homophobia orientations and gender affirming approaches and to be able to identify and intervene on behalf of children and youth who are experiencing gender coercion, homophobia or transphobia. Another general step for public sector change is for the replacement of sex segregated bathroom and locker room facilities in all publicly funded institutional spaces with sex integrated facilities. For this latter objective it is necessary to incorporate structural changes to ensure privacy and cultural changes to incorporate teaching and learning about bathroom and locker room etiquette. A few sector-specific suggestions are listed below.

Education

- provide nutritious public school breakfast and lunch programs for all students in publicly funded elementary and high school education settings
- reform public school curricula to include content relating to the scientifically superior model of the gender spectrum over the gender binary
- require all school boards to adopt specific anti-homophobia and anti-transphobia policies with corresponding teacher training and community outreach/ education

Health care system

- advocate for accessible and high-quality health care for all
- train doctors, nurses and mental health providers in a gender affirming approach
- provide support for children and youth around issues relating to "minority stress" (Meyer, 2003)
- use the GID diagnosis to enable those in need to access hormone blockers, cross-sex hormones, various sex reassignment surgeries and gender affirming counselling

Social services and the criminal justice system

- increase resources to protect children and youth from abuse, coercion and violence, including the provision of sufficient community-based shelter programs
- provide material and social support rather than criminalization for youth involved in the sex trade or living on the street (safe houses; gender affirming detox programs; medical and counselling services; education programs; no-hassle welfare and unemployment insurance programs)
- respect affirmed gender in all facets of the criminal justice system
- enact criminal amnesty for non-violent youth offenders

Sport and physical recreation

- adopt Griffin and Carroll's (2010) On the team: equal opportunity for transgender student athletes"[5] standards for public school sport and recreational activities (where teams are sex segregated, students are able to play on either team with no hormonal or surgical treatment required) but go further with a 'no gender questions asked' policy and practice
- increase sex-integrated sport and recreational opportunities for children and youth and incorporate egalitarian values in the organization and culture of these activities
- eliminate sex segregated locker room and change room facilities, incorporating provisions for privacy and socialization regarding change room etiquette

It can be expected that there will be more resistance to some short-term changes than others but they are worthy rallying points for transformative gender justice social activism and advocacy. This is the case especially because the visibility of such efforts itself will have a positive impact on visible and invisible transgender and gender-variant children and youth.

EPILOGUE

Two years ago (May 2011) the Burnaby⁶ School Board adopted a specific anti-homophobia policy amid resistance from some of the parents in the district. As the school board was considering this policy, they were opposed by a group composed primarily of parents with a fundamentalist Christian Right religious affiliation (Kaitlin, 2011) and supported by a diverse group of students, educators, parents and members of the LGBT community. While there to make a petition to the school board in support of the policy myself, I spoke with a high school student who had shown up to support the adoption of the policy and who was worried that it would not pass. I felt tears come to my eyes as I said this: "I think it will pass, but even if it doesn't, something great has already happened. There is some kid in your high school who you may never know who will make it because they saw you here, a straight, non-trans student, standing up for them, stating clearly with your presence that homophobia and transphobia are unacceptable in your schools and that they are worthy of respect. Their parents may be standing across the street from us right now, chanting that beliefs about LGBT people should be imparted by parents, not the school system, having no idea that their own child is one of the many who is harmed by homophobic and transphobic attitudes and environments. But this kid sees you, and the rest of us, out here and it may be enough to help them hang on, make it through high school, find the space to live authentically and without self-hatred."

Our visible advocacy for social change on behalf of transgender and gender-non conforming children and youth, while more or less successful at given times and in given environments, may in itself act as a lifeline to the visible and the invisible young folks among us. Resiliency in the face of oppression may be the short-term or even the main result of some of our advocacy and activism on behalf of this population. For this reason a key feature of our work must involve visibility. We need to show transgender and gender-variant children and youth that they have allies, that they have options, and that they are worthy of our protection. I know it helps my daughter, as it would have helped me 46 years ago, to know that she is not alone.

NOTES

1. That is, people who transition from male to female or vice versa, with no ambiguity or challenge to the two-sex system.
2. Connell claims that the field should be more aptly named "sex similarity research" (1987: 170)
3. See, for example, April 7, 2013: http://globalnews.ca/video/459161/ambc-michelle-and-garfield; March 1, 2013: http://healthland.time.com/2013/03/01/do-schools-need-new-rules-for-transgender-students/; February 27, 2013: http://www.dailymail.co.uk/femail/

article-2285357/It-best-day-life-Transgender-teen-voted-Homecoming-Queen-keeping-original-sex-secret.html
4. i.e., middle-class consumers (Bucar and Enke, 2011)
5. *On the Team: Equal Opportunity for Transgender Student Athletes*, by Griffin and Carroll, is a U.S. report commissioned by the Women's Sport Foundation and the National Centre for Lesbian Rights. In this report the authors make recommendations for sport policy at the elementary and high school levels that require no medical intervention for transgender students to participate in activities according to their affirmed gender but recommend that, at the college level, one year of cross-hormone therapy be a requirement for participation in the case of male-to-female transgender students but not for female-to-male transgender students. The recommendations at the college level were adopted by the National Collegiate Athletic Association (NCAA) in 2011. While the the Canadian Interuniversity Sport Association (CIS) (Menz, 2011) has yet to adopt a policy on transgender student athletes the Canadian Collegiate Athletic Association has adopted policy to bring the organization and its member colleges fully in line with "on the team" recommendations and NCAA policy (Corbett, 2012). No general policy has been adopted for the high school level in either the United States or Canada to date.
6. Burnaby is a suburban city in the Greater Vancouver area of British Columbia, Canada.

CHAPTER FIVE

Supporting Gender Diversity in Schools

Developmental and Legal Perspectives

ELIZABETH J. MEYER

INTRODUCTION

When working with gender-creative and transgender youth in the school setting, it is important for professional educators to be aware of the developmental and legal issues involved in order to guide their decision making and efforts at providing support. Since no child's gender journey is the same (Ehrensaft, 2011), and each school community is unique in many ways, the guiding developmental and legal principles offered in this chapter are intended to provide a framework for professionals to work within in order to provide safe and supportive learning environments for all youth. The first part of this chapter addresses key issues framed in a child-centered developmental approach, and the second half focuses on legal concerns in both Canada and the United States. Before we can effectively address these areas, we would like to provide the reader with some background information concerning what is currently known about the experiences of gender-nonconforming and transgender youth in schools.

In 2009, the Gay, Lesbian, and Straight Education Network published the first national study on the experiences of transgender youth in schools. In their report, *Harsh Realities: The Experiences of Transgender Youth in our Nation's Schools* (Greytak, Kosciw, & Diaz, 2009), they found that 89% of transgender youth are verbally harassed (e.g., called names or threatened), 55% are physically harassed (e.g., pushed or shoved), and 28% had been physically assaulted. In 2011, a Canadian study reported

74% of trans* students experience verbal harassment about their gender expression, and 37% of trans* students report physical harassment due to their gender expression. This same study also reported that almost two-thirds (64%) of LGBTQ students and 61% of students with LGBTQ parents feel unsafe at school (Taylor, 2011).

In a more recent study that examined the climate of elementary schools, researchers found that nearly 1 in 10 of elementary students in 3rd to 6th grade (8%) indicate that they do not always conform to traditional gender norms/roles—either they are boys who others sometimes think, act, or look like a girl, or they are girls who others sometimes think, act, or look like a boy. Less than half of teachers believe that a gender-nonconforming student would feel comfortable at their school (male student who acts or looks traditionally feminine: 44%; female student who acts or looks traditionally masculine: 49%) and only 34% of teachers report having personally engaged in efforts to create a safe and supportive classroom environment for gender-nonconforming students (GLSEN & Harris Interactive, 2012). This study also found that gender-nonconforming students are less likely than other students to feel very safe at school (42% vs. 61%), and are more likely than others to indicate that they sometimes do not want to go to school because they feel unsafe or afraid there (35% vs. 15%). Gender-nonconforming students are also more likely than others to be called names, made fun of, or bullied at least sometimes at school (56% vs. 33%) (GLSEN & Harris Interactive, 2012).

In light of these findings, it is important for educators to be aware of the hostile climate that many students face in schools as well as what they can do to address these issues to improve the experience for all children and youth in school settings. In this chapter, our goal is to provide an overview of the relevant developmental, legal, and professional frameworks that impact how issues of gender diversity are addressed in schools. The legal frameworks are essential as they provide the expectations for what schools are required to provide. However, these legal frameworks are often the bare minimum of what students need in order to be successful in schools; therefore, ethical issues are important to consider as well. When we work with educators from a multifaceted approach that is grounded in both best practices informed by professional responsibilities—what can be referred to as the 'carrot'—as well as legal responsibilities—the proverbial 'stick'—then there is greater potential for positive and sustainable change at all levels in school settings.

DEVELOPMENTAL FRAMEWORK

Many schools base their philosophies in a child-centered approach to education. This chapter also emphasizes a child-centered approach to working with transgender and gender-creative children and youth. What this means is that the needs and interests of the child, as determined by the child, are placed at the center of any program or plan of action. In this section we introduce Maslow's classic theory of human development in order to frame the professional responsibilities placed on education professionals. This theory was selected due to its widespread inclusion in educational preparation programs; therefore, the intention is to apply frameworks that educators are already familiar with in order to help them transfer what they already know about working with students and their families in order to guide their practice in unfamiliar situations, specifically supporting gender-creative and transgender youth. We first introduce Maslow's hierarchy of needs, which describes a theory of motivation that was developed to understand why some individuals achieve a higher level of functioning and societal success than others, and then link this theory to some themes found across standards for professional teachers' associations.

Maslow's Hierarchy of Needs

Abraham Maslow was a psychologist who was interested in studying exceptional individuals who achieved high levels of success so that he could better understand human motivation. As a result of his motivational studies, he developed a theoretical model that he called a "hierarchy of needs"(Maslow, 1943). This theory asserts that certain essential needs must be satisfied before an individual can focus on higher levels of inter- and intra-personal development. His hierarchy was organized starting with *physiological* needs that are required for survival of the organism such as breathing, food, water, sex, sleep, homeostasis, and excretion. The second level of needs was *safety*, which includes security of body, financial security, and health and well-being. Once safety needs have been met, Maslow theorized that the individual could then focus on more advanced developmental processes based on relationships in social groups in the tier he called *love/belonging*. This tier is defined by ways in which humans need to feel connected and appreciated by their social circle, including family, friends, colleagues, as well as other social groups, such as teams, religious organizations, and clubs. The fourth tier is called *esteem* and describes the human need for mutually respectful relationships. The need to be appreciated and valued by self and others can be manifested in different ways depending on one's inner strength and sense of self as developed through the lower tiers. The last tier in Maslow's model is called *self-actualization*, and refers to the fulfillment needs as determined by an individual based on their skills, interests, and desires. Some examples can include becoming a strong and loving parent, becoming a skilled and competent athlete, becoming an engaged and productive community member, becoming a creative and productive artist, and so on (see Fig. 1). In a more recent study, researchers noted that younger children had higher *physical* need scores than other groups, the *esteem* need was highest among the adolescent group, and the *love/belonging* need emerged most strongly between childhood and young adulthood (Goebel & Brown, 1981). Although the degrees of need may change over time, the need for *love/belonging* and *esteem* is of great importance for school-age children and youth. This can help frame educators' approaches to working with students by understanding that children will have great difficulty focusing on more advanced developmental tasks until their most basic needs have been met.

Figure 1. Maslow's hierarchy of needs.

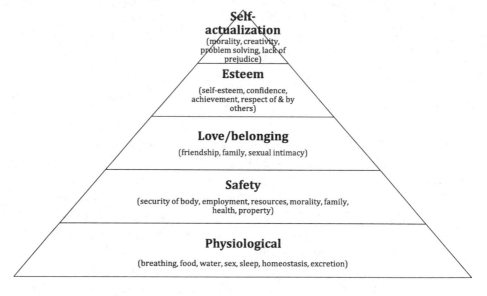

This theoretical model is helpful in understanding how to better support students who may be experiencing issues with safety and belonging in their school or home environments. If these basic needs aren't met, then these individuals will experience extreme difficulties in developing strengths in the areas of esteem and self-actualization. Research indicates that students who are targets for bullying and harassment often avoid school (garnering excessive tardies and absences), disengage from the community, and are at higher risk for dropping out or not continuing on for higher education (American Educational Research Association, 2013; Kosciw, Greytak, Diaz, & Bartkiewicz, 2010).

Teachers' professional associations clearly emphasize the importance of creating safe and respectful environments for all students in their professional and ethical guidelines. For example, the British Columbia Teachers' Federation (BCTF) Code of Ethics states as its first item: "The teacher speaks and acts toward students with respect and dignity, and deals judiciously with them, always mindful of their individual rights and sensibilities" (BCTF, 2006–13). The Ontario College of Teachers presents four main principles for ethical practices: care, respect, trust, and integrity (Ontario College of Teachers, n.d.). In the United States, the California Teacher Credentialing Commission evaluates candidates based on 13 Teaching Performance Expectations (TPEs). TPE 12 addresses professional, ethical, and legal obligations and states, "[Teachers] are aware of their own personal values and biases and recognize ways in which these values and biases affect the teaching and learning of students. They resist racism and acts of intolerance. … Candidates can identify suspected cases of child abuse, neglect, or sexual harassment. They maintain a non-hostile classroom environment" (California Commission on Teacher Credentialing, 2008). This sampling of professional standards provides a guiding framework for understanding how to apply Maslow's hierarchy of needs toward a more developmentally sound and professionally endorsed approach to working with gender-creative and transgender students.

As the Introduction to this chapter points out, many students who are transgender, gender-creative, or otherwise gender-nonconforming experience high levels of bullying and harassment at school. When examined through the lens of Maslow's theories and the standards of professional associations, it is clear that educators and schools are often falling short of their duties to provide a safe and inclusive learning environment. As a result these children and youth may experience many more developmental challenges than their gender-normative peers.

As noted earlier, there has been extensive research that documents the hostile environment in schools for bisexual, gay, lesbian, queer, transgender, (BGLQT), and gender-creative youth (Garafalo, Wolf, Kessel, Palfrey, & DuRant, 1998; GLSEN & Harris Interactive, 2012; Kosciw, Greytak, & Diaz, 2010; Lock, 2002). In order to minimize the psychological and physical harm that these students are exposed to in schools, it is important for school leaders to create safe and inclusive school environments that support students in all of their diversity. When students are denied the space to express themselves and to feel recognized and valued for who they are, they experience isolation, undergo damage to self-esteem, and are vulnerable to bullying and harassment. As a result, these youth are at increased risk for drug and alcohol abuse (Jordan, 2000; Moon, Fornili, & O'Briant, 2007), dropping out of school (Frankfurt, 2000), and suicide (D'Augelli et al., 2005; Hatzenbuehler, 2011). In the face of these potential harms, professional educators should work to find ways to ensure that each school is a safe and supportive place for students of all gender identities and expressions.

LEGAL ISSUES

School leaders have the power and responsibility to enforce and apply the spirit of the law and relevant school policies. Although some administrators may adhere more closely to the letter of the law, interpretations from the courts provide guidance that encourages leaders to apply school policies in a more humane and flexible way that allows for individual expression and recognition of students' asserted gender identities and expressions. The following section is an overview of key laws and case studies that will provide legal guidance for educators working with transgender and gender-creative youth in the school setting.

Canada

The current progressive political climate in Canada was achieved through a long and slow process of legislative reforms that culminated in the *Canadian Charter of Rights and Freedoms* being instituted. This important document was entrenched into the Canadian Constitution by the Constitution Act in 1982 (Watkinson, 1999, p. 22). As part of the supreme law of Canada, this document superseded all existing laws, and for the first time the rights of all persons to be treated equally was given constitutional status. Although public education is governed by provincial statutes, all publicly funded institutions must abide by the spirit and letter of the *Charter* (Watkinson, 1999). This new constitution guaranteed protections for many historically marginalized groups. Gender identity and expression, however, are not included as a protected class for equality rights under section 15 of the *Canadian Charter of Rights and Freedoms*. The original language of this section reads as follows:

> *Every individual is equal before and under the law and has the right to the equal protection and equal benefit of the law without discrimination and, in particular, without discrimination based on race, national or ethnic origin, colour, religion, sex, age or mental or physical disability.* (The Canadian Charter of Rights and Freedoms [s. 15], 1982)

Although the federal government did not explicitly include gender identity and expression in the 1982 text, it also omitted the phrase "sexual orientation." The progressive changes regarding how sexual orientation has been treated in Canada are instructive in understanding where we are today in terms of gender identity and expression. Also, because much transphobic harassment is directed at students who are perceived to be gay, lesbian, or bisexual, there are important overlaps between these two categories of protection. Although equality rights supported by the *Charter* were enforced starting in 1985, sexual minorities were not recognized as a protected class until more than a decade later, following a unanimous decision of the Supreme Court of Canada in the landmark case of *Egan v. Canada* (1995). Although this case was not about discrimination in schools, it addressed the issue of access to public services. The ruling provided that discrimination based on sexual orientation was prohibited by s. 15 of the *Charter* and the justices observed: "Sexual orientation is a deeply personal characteristic that is either unchangeable or changeable only at unacceptable personal costs, and so falls within the ambit of s. 15 protection as being analogous to the enumerated grounds" (Egan v. Canada, 1995, para. 5). This case established the precedent to include sexual orientation as a protected class and had "sexual orientation" read into the *Charter*. Every Canadian was guaranteed equal protection from discrimination based on sexual orientation. Although some provinces were slow to add the term "sexual orientation" to their individual human rights codes, this protection was federally guaranteed as a result of this important ruling.

Since the Supreme Court's 1995 decision in *Egan v. Canada,* various cases have tested the interpretation and application of the equality rights extended in that case. The first test impacting K–12 schools came in May 2001 when the Supreme Court of Canada heard a case from Trinity Western University (TWU), a private religious institution, against the British Columbia College of Teachers (BCCT). In this instance, the B.C. professional teachers' organization had responded to a request from TWU to be fully responsible for its teacher-training program, which it shared with Simon Fraser University. TWU wanted more autonomy in the program in order to reflect its Christian worldview. The BCCT chose not to accredit this institution because it believed the institution was discriminating on the basis of sexual orientation in its demands on its students. TWU required their students to sign a statement that asserted they would "refrain from practices that are biblically condemned," including homosexuality (*Trinity Western University v. British Columbia College of Teachers*, 2001, para. 4)

In its decision, the B.C. Supreme Court found in favor of Trinity Western University, stating that teachers could hold "sexist, racist or homophobic beliefs" (para. 36). However, the Court also made the following distinction:

> Acting on those beliefs, however, is a very different matter. If a teacher in the public school system engages in discriminatory conduct, that teacher can be subject to disciplinary proceedings. Discriminatory conduct by a public school teacher when on duty should always be subject to disciplinary proceedings [and] disciplinary measures can still be taken when discriminatory off-duty conduct poisons the school environment. (*Trinity Western v. British Columbia College of Teachers*, 2001, para. 37)

Although this majority opinion sided with TWU and allowed them to continue mandating anti-gay beliefs in their future teachers, the judges made the important distinction between discriminatory behaviors and beliefs, which is common in cases regarding religious freedom. The decision clearly states that teachers may not discriminate overtly against their students, but does not address the issue of the subtle and persistent homophobic and transphobic behaviors that such attitudes engender and the impact they have on a classroom or school community.

In a second case, Azmi Jubran, a student in Vancouver, was repeatedly called 'gay,' 'faggot,' and 'homo' by his peers during his secondary schooling. In addition to these verbal taunts he was spit upon, shoved in class and the hallways, and even had his shirt burned. After repeated complaints to the school by Jubran and his parents with no satisfactory response, they filed a Human Rights complaint in November 1996. In April 2002, the Human Rights Tribunal of British Columbia found that the school board in Vancouver had contravened the Human Rights Act "by failing to provide a learning environment free of discriminatory harassment" (*School District No. 44 v. Jubran*, 2005, para. 2). This was an important decision because it affirmed the school's responsibility to protect students from discriminatory behavior and to respond effectively and consistently to incidents of harassment. After a series of appeals, the fate of this case was decided on October 20, 2005, when the Supreme Court refused to hear a final appeal and effectively upheld the lower court's decision. This was an important decision as the court acknowledged that the school had made some effort to individually discipline the students targeting Jubran, but that the school had not done enough. The court stated that the school needed to have communicated its code of conduct to students and provided teachers with resources and training on how to deal with homophobia (CLE Staff, 2005; Meyer, 2007). This case sent a clear message to educators that they must mobilize multiple resources and be proactive when addressing issues of school climate and student safety that relate directly to discriminatory harassment in light of human rights protections.

As the above listed cases demonstrate, there are legal precedents that exist to protect students from discriminatory behavior in schools. Although they emphasized issues related to sexual orientation, they are also relevant to issues of gender identity and expression because there have been cases that have successfully argued that discrimination against transgender people is covered under the existing language under the category of 'sex' since 1998 (McGill & Kirkup, 2013; *Montreuil v. Canadian Human Rights Commission and Canadian Forces*, 2009). However, many school boards and educators are ignorant of their legal responsibilities and fail to effectively implement policies, programs, and curricular materials that support full inclusion of sexual diversity in school communities.

Status of protections across Canada: "gender identity and expression"

In contrast to rights protection based on sexual orientation, explicit human rights code protection for transgender persons only began appearing in legislation in provincial, territorial, and federal jurisdictions in Canada in the new millennium. The Northwest Territories was the first jurisdiction to pass such legislation in 2002. It was not until ten years later that three additional jurisdictions followed suit, with Manitoba and Ontario enacting similar legislation in June 2012, followed by Nova Scotia in December 2012. Other jurisdictions have introduced transgender rights legislation that has not, as of this writing, resulted in new laws. Transgender rights legislation introduced in British Columbia in 2011 did not pass first reading. At the federal level, four bills adding gender identity or gender expression to the Human Rights Act, and in three of these cases to the Criminal Code, have been introduced in the House of Commons. The most recent of these bills—Bill C-279—was sent to the Senate in March 2013. For a full summary of provincial and territorial laws, please see Table 1.

Table 1. Provincial protections including gender identity and/or expression as of May 8, 2013.

Province / Territory	Date intro- duced / put into effect	Bill name	Notes
Northwest Territories	February 2002 / July 1, 2004	Bill 1, *Human Rights Act*	
Manitoba	May 2012 / June 14, 2012	Bill 36, *The Human Rights Code Amendment Act*	Introduced by NDP Justice Minister Andrew Swan
Ontario	February 2012 / June 19, 2012	Bill 33, *An Act to amend the Human Rights Code with respect to gender identity and gender expression, "Toby's Act"*	Introduced by MPPs Cheri DiNovo (NDP), Christine Elliott (PC) and Yasir Naqvi (Liberal)
Nova Scotia	November 20, 2012 / December 6, 2012	Bill No. 140, *Transgendered Persons Protection Act: An Act to Amend Chapter 214 of the Revised Statutes, 1989, the Human Rights Act, to Protect the Rights of Trans- gendered Persons*	Introduced by NDP Justice Minister Ross Landry on the *Transgender Day of Remembrance*
British Columbia	May 2011 / did not pass first reading	Bill M 207 – 2011, *Gender Identity and Expression Human Rights Recognition Act*	MLA Spencer Chandra Herbert (NDP)

Four transgender rights bills have been introduced in the Canadian Parliament. In June 2006 NDP MP Bill Siksay (Burnaby-Douglas) tabled a private member's bill, Bill C-326, *An Act to Amend the Canadian Human Rights Act (Gender Identity)*, which did not pass first reading. Three years later, in May 2009, Bill Siksay introduced a second private member's bill in the House of Commons, Bill C-389, *An Act to Amend the Canadian Human Rights Act and the Criminal Code (Gender Identity and Gender Expression)*, which was subsequently re-tabled in February 2010. The bill successfully passed through the lower house in February 2011 by a narrow margin of 143 to 133. Of all the MPs who voted on Bill C-389 at third reading, six Conservatives voted in favor of the bill, including House Leader John Baird; and of the remaining MPs who voted, all but seven Liberals voted in favor of the bill, as did all members of the NDP and the Bloc Québécois. However, the bill died in the Senate when an election was called a month later, although speculation was that the bill was destined to be blocked by the Senate regardless (Ibbitson, 2011). When a new government was elected and Parliament reconvened, two private members' bills were tabled within days of each, the first by Liberal MP Hedy Fry (Vancouver Centre) on September 19, 2011, and the second on September 21, 2011, by NDP MP Randall Garrison (Esquimalt-Juan de Fuca). Procedural considerations allowed for Randall Garrison to proceed with his bill first. Bill C-279, *An Act to Amend the Canadian Human Rights Act and the Criminal Code (Gender Identity and Gender Expression)*, passed second reading on June 6, 2012, with a vote of 150 to 132. Fifteen Conservatives voted in favor of the bill, including Finance Minister Jim Flaherty, and all votes cast against the bill were done so by Conservatives. Support from Conservative members of the House of Commons was secured with the promise that the words "gender expression" would be removed from the bill when it was sent to the Standing Committee on Justice and Human Rights.

Committee meetings on Bill C-279 were held in November and December 2012. After hearing testimony from groups and individuals both for and against the bill, filibustering on the final day of hearings by Conservative MPs resulted in the legislation heading back to the House of Commons unamended and without an official report. Compromise had previously been reached by agreeing to remove the term "gender expression" and by providing a definition for "gender identity," a move which won support from some Conservative MPs while at the same time alienating some members of the transgender community. Sadly, one Conservative Member of Parliament, Rob Anders (Calgary West), took it upon himself to begin circulating a petition against Bill C-279 in which he claimed that the bill—which he and others have dubbed the "Bathroom Bill"—would allow "… transgendered men access to women's public washroom facilities," with the implication being that transgender persons are sexual predators (Wherry, 2012). In response, some people have noted that Rob Anders's discriminatory comments on this issue offer further evidence why such legislation is necessary. On February 27, 2013, House of Commons Speaker Andrew Sheer ruled that the amendments agreed upon in committee could be raised and debated during third reading. Bill C-279 passed the House of Commons by a vote of 149 to 137 on March 20, 2013. Eighteen Conservative MPs voted in favor of the legislation, including Minister of Finance Jim Flaherty (Whitby-Oshawa) and Minister of Foreign Affairs John Baird (Ottawa West-Nepean). Liberal leadership candidate Justin Trudeau (Papineau) was not present for the vote.

Adding both gender identity and gender expression to provincial, territorial, and federal human rights codes would help ensure that the basic democratic rights of transgender persons in Canada are respected and enforced. In this way, members of the transgender community would be able to more easily access and benefit from key sectors of society such as education, employment, housing, and health care—something that most Canadians take for granted. As well, legislation in this area would help ensure that transgender persons are treated with respect and dignity in public places, including washrooms, and while accessing business and government services. Including gender identity and gender expression in the Criminal Code of Canada would also ensure that transphobic crimes are treated as hate crimes, which has implications in the sentencing of offenders. Taken together, enacting legislation that furthers the rights of transgender persons is one step toward building a more just and equitable Canada. The legal context in the United States is quite different, and the next section provides an overview of case law and statewide protections for transgender individuals.

UNITED STATES OF AMERICA

There are currently no federal protections that explicitly protect transgender and gender-creative people from discrimination in the United States. However, all individuals are entitled to the same protection as any other identifiable group. Consequently, a variety of courts from across the country have begun holding school districts accountable for violating the rights of students who are being harassed or treated differently based on their gender identity or expression. The main existing legal protections that are relevant in these cases include: Equal Protection Clause (Fourteenth Amendment), First Amendment, Title IX, and state non-discrimination or human rights laws.

Equal Protection

The Equal Protection Clause of the Fourteenth Amendment guarantees equal application of a law to all people in the United States (Macgillivray, 2007). An equal protection claim requires the student to show that school officials a) did not fairly and consistently apply policies when dealing with the student, b) were deliberately indifferent to the student's complaints, or that the student was treated in a manner that is c) clearly unreasonable.

In 2010, in Mississippi there was a case of a female student, Ceara Sturgis, who didn't want her senior photo taken in the traditional black drape that all females were expected to wear at her school. Instead, and with her mother's support, she tried on a tuxedo and decided that she would feel more confident in her photo dressed in the button-down shirt, jacket, and bow tie historically worn by males at her school. The school officials did not agree with this decision and sent a letter home explaining that only boys could wear tuxedos and her photo would not be included in the yearbook. The American Civil Liberties Union (ACLU) in Mississippi contacted the school district to inform them that they were "violating Sturgis' constitutionally protected freedom of expression"; however, the school's superintendent and principal were unwilling to reverse their decision. The yearbooks were printed and distributed without Ceara's photo or name in them. Consequently, the ACLU filed a complaint against the school for sex discrimination and unlawful sex stereotyping, citing Title IX and the Equal Protection Clause of the Fourteenth Amendment (American Civil Liberties Union, 2010). In November 2011 the school district agreed to settle the case and add Ceara's original photo (in a tuxedo) to the wall of senior photos at the school. The school also consented to modify its policy for senior pictures so that all students would wear gender-nonspecific graduation robes and will update its anti-discrimination policy to include language supporting the Equal Protection Clause of the U.S. Constitution (American Civil Liberties Union, 2011).

First Amendment

The First Amendment of the U.S. Constitution protects students' rights to free speech and expression. In 2001, a student's complaint led to far-reaching changes in his school district and had significant impacts on freedom of expression cases regarding students' gender expression and sexual orientation (*Henkle v. Gregory*, 2001). The federal district court of Nevada allowed the Title IX sexual orientation harassment case of Derek Henkle for punitive damages to proceed; however, the school opted to settle for $451,000 in damages to the student and led to several district policy changes that extend existing protections for free speech and discrimination and harassment to include sexual orientation and gender expression (Lambda Legal, 2002). This case is important because it established students' rights to speak about their sexual orientation in school, and could also be interpreted to include gender expression. This expression is considered protected speech under the First Amendment.

Title IX

Title IX is most commonly known for the impacts it has had on college athletics programs in the United States. However, Title IX of the Education Amendment Acts of 1972 more broadly prohibits discrimination based on sex in education programs and activities receiving federal financial assistance. In 2000, Title IX was applied to a case wherein a student was being bullied because of his feminine characteristics and this was identified as an incident of sex stereotyping (*Montgomery v. Independent School District No. 709*). In this case, the court decided that Title IX damages could be awarded to students on the basis of sexual orientation harassment because it is often based on "failure to meet expected gender stereotypes." A few years later, a Kansas federal district court considered gender stereotyping, and the related anti-gay harassment of a student who did not identify as gay, actionable under Title IX (*Theno v. Tonganoxie Unified School Dist. No. 464*, 2005). The court wrote that "the plaintiff was harassed because he failed to satisfy his peers' stereotyped expectations for his gender because the primary objective of plaintiff's harassers appears to have been to disparage his perceived lack of masculinity." Therefore, they concluded that the harassment of Dylan Theno was so "severe, pervasive, and objectively offensive that it effectively denied (him) an education in the Tonganoxie school district" (*Theno v. Tonganoxie Unified School Dist. No. 464*, 2005). The district settled with Dylan for a total of $440,000 (Trowbridge, 2005).

More recently, the Office for Civil Rights issued guidance in the form of a "Dear Colleague" letter. In this letter there is very explicit wording regarding how Title IX applies in cases of gender identity and expression:

> Title IX prohibits harassment of both male and female students regardless of the sex of the harasser—*i.e.*, even if the harasser and target are members of the same sex. It also prohibits gender-based harassment, which may include acts of verbal, nonverbal, or physical aggression, intimidation, or hostility based on sex or sex-stereotyping. Thus, it *can be sex discrimination if students are harassed either for exhibiting what is perceived as a stereotypical characteristic for their sex, or for failing to conform to stereotypical notions of masculinity and femininity.* Title IX also prohibits sexual harassment and gender-based harassment of all students, regardless of the actual or perceived sexual orientation or gender identity of the harasser or target. (Ali, 2010, pp. 7–8, emphasis mine)

This guidance from the Office for Civil Rights was sent to all school districts in October 2010. In light of the decisions in both *Montgomery* and *Theno*, it is in schools' and school leaders' best interests to ensure the safety and protection of all students in their school—particularly those being targeted by students or staff for their non-normative gender identity or expression. In addition to federal protections that exist, some states have non-discrimination laws that can offer students some relief.

State non-discrimination laws that protect individuals based on sexual orientation and/or gender identity exist in only twenty states and the District of Columbia[1] (National Gay and Lesbian Task Force, 2007). However, according to a study published in 2006, only nine states and the District of Columbia (California, Connecticut, Maine, Massachusetts*, Minnesota, New Jersey, Vermont, Washington, and Wisconsin* [* = sexual orientation only]) have statutes specifically protecting students in schools from discrimination on the basis of sexual orientation and/or gender identity (Kosciw & Diaz, 2006). As of June 2013, Illinois, Iowa, Oregon, and Colorado also added these protections (GLSEN, 2013). Students in these states experienced significantly lower rates of verbal harassment than did their peers in other states. For example, in a case involving a transgender student in Massachusetts, a judge decided that schools should allow students to dress and attend school in the clothing that best reflects their gender identity (*Doe v. Brockton Sch. Comm.*, 2000). In another state decision in 2009, the Maine Human Rights Commission decided in favor of a 5th grade transgender girl being able to use the girls' bathrooms in her elementary school (Curtis, 2009); however, this case was being revisited by the Supreme Court of Maine at this writing (Sharp, 2013). In June 2013, a civil rights panel in Colorado ruled that a school district discriminated against a transgender student when it would not allow her to use the girls' bathroom because she was legally male (Banda, 2013).

RECOMMENDATIONS FOR SCHOOLS

Educational institutions have a responsibility to be safe and inclusive learning environments for all children. Unfortunately, when a transgender or gender-creative child enters the school environment, school officials often see the child as the source of conflict and label them as the problem. We must reframe the problem and not let the child be labeled as such. It is the current structures, policies, and cultures of schools that are the problems to be fixed, and not the individual child. A more developmentally appropriate, and legally defensible, approach would be to examine where the sites of tension and conflict are for the school community and examine why these spaces are not inclusive and affirming for students of all gender identities and expressions. Educators must work to meet each and every child's basic needs (physiological and safety) so that they can enter schools and find sites where they can belong and develop a stronger self-esteem.

Schools should prepare and support students to learn and grow and not be spaces where children and youth must constantly worry about their physical and emotional safety, or feel as if they don't belong. In order to most effectively achieve this goal, the entire school culture should be addressed. Short-term, quick-fix solutions developed because of the presence of a single identified child are inadequate and don't address systemic issues.

Schools that are committed to being safe, supportive, and affirming environments for all children must reevaluate and update policies, professional development, curriculum, library holdings, and community/parent education activities. There is insufficient space in this chapter to investigate in detail each of these areas, but recommendations for schools are provided in other books, including *Gender, Bullying, and Harassment: Strategies to End Sexism and Homophobia in Schools* (Meyer, 2009), *Gender and Sexual Diversity in Schools* (Meyer, 2010), *From the Dress-Up Corner to the Senior Prom: Navigating Gender and Sexuality Diversity in K–12 Schools* (Bryan, 2012*)*, and *Supporting Transgender and Transsexual students in K–12 Schools* (Wells, Roberts, & Allan, 2012). Readers can also find a list of updated resources and references on the website www.gendercreativekids.ca. In addition to whole school reforms, there are additional steps teachers and administrators can take to ensure a more positive experience for a transgender or gender-creative child.

Transforming the culture of a school takes some time and commitment from all members of the school community. In the meantime, the following individual measures can be taken to ensure that students who are potential targets for victimization are protected as much as possible. These recommendations have been compiled from various sources that have provided intentional supports to students who have socially transitioned from one gender to another while at school (Callender, 2008; Luecke, 2011; Wells, 2009; Wells et al., 2012):

a. Stop the **bullying & harassment** targeted at specific students.
b. Offer extra protection **before & after school** (work with local police and school security).
c. Provide in-school **counseling** and/or a safe space for the student.
d. Make **dress code** exceptions for students based on their affirmed gender identity or revise dress codes so that they are gender neutral.
e. Make accommodations for **PE class and bathroom** use in dialogue with the student & family.
f. Use child's **preferred name & pronoun**.
g. Support social transition (from one gender to another) with an integrated **action plan** (see Callender, 2008; Wells et al., 2012).

h. Provide **professional development** for all school staff to be able to understand and respectfully work with this student and their peers.

i. **Consult with experts** to ensure your action plan is comprehensive and affirming of the child/adolescent's own pace and choices.

Each of these steps can provide an essential layer of support and protection to a transgender or gender-creative child in their educational environment. There are additional challenges when that child may not be affirmed in their home and may make collaborating with parents and caregivers particularly challenging. However, as professionals who are entrusted with ensuring the safety and healthy development of children in our care, we believe it is essential for schools to do everything in their power to provide the best education possible for all students.

CONCLUSION

In this chapter, we offered readers two frameworks to consider when working with transgender and gender-creative youth in schools. From a developmental perspective, we advocate strongly for understanding Maslow's hierarchy of needs and ensuring that all students' basic physiological and safety needs are met. We also highlighted the professional and ethical frameworks for several teachers' associations across North America to emphasize the links between developmentally sound and professionally endorsed practices.

The second framework was related to the legal responsibilities of education professionals. We offered an overview of relevant case law in Canada and the United States as well as regional protections that must be considered when developing an action plan in a school community. We brought these two frameworks together to advocate for a holistic approach to affirming and supporting transgender and gender-creative youth in schools. By understanding and applying the legal guidelines and then moving toward a more developmentally supportive and professionally endorsed practice, schools can prepare themselves to be sites that are inclusive and affirming of students from a wide diversity of identities, cultures, backgrounds, and experiences.

NOTE

1. Minnesota (1993); Rhode Island (1995, 2001); New Mexico (2003); California (1992, 2003); District of Columbia (1997, 2005); Illinois (2005); Maine (2005); Hawaii (1991, 2005, 2006); New Jersey (1992, 2006); Washington (2006); Iowa (2007); Oregon (2007); Vermont (1992, 2007); Colorado (2007); Wisconsin (1982); Massachusetts (1989); Connecticut (1991); New Hampshire (1997); Nevada (1999); Maryland (2001); New York (2002).

CHAPTER SIX

"I Will Whip My Hair" and "Hold My Bow"

Gender-Creativity in Rural Ontario

KARLEEN PENDLETON JIMÉNEZ

I have wanted our lives taken seriously and represented fully—with power and honesty and sympathy—to be hated or loved, or to terrify and obsess, but to be real, to have the power of the whole and complex.

(ALLISON, 1994, P. 165)

In every place of research, context is crucial to understanding. Geography influences social relationships and learning. As queer geographer Larry Knopp (2004) articulates, "Space is not just a backdrop for history, and place is not just space with meaning inscribed onto it. Rather, they are both forces in shaping human (and indeed non-human) lives and events" (p. 128). Geography shapes the way gender is expressed. It is a significant part of an intersectional identity. Geographic contexts respond to gender-creativity in specific ways, and perhaps the most common belief is that such transgressions are more acceptable in urban regions, while "the imagining of rural spaces as inhospitable is commonplace" (Gray, 2007, p. 50). Like Gray, who researched queer youth identity in "small town USA," I wish to challenge this easy duality of urban as good for queers, and rural as bad for queers. I do so both because rural spaces deserve more credit, possessing a complexity and vitality too often flattened by stereotypes, and also because the recognition of these nuances will help you in supporting rural gender-creative youth.

In this chapter I wish to offer some of the voices and insights of gender-creative students in rural Ontario, gathered from my research, "Tomboys and Other Gender Heroes." Gender-creative youth live in rural spaces, inhospitable or otherwise. They are experts in the cultural norms of their towns, and in the potential consequences of gender transgressions. I will place their insights in conversation with the popular novel *The Hunger Games* by Suzanne Collins, because as I read the narrative, I found the knowledge closely aligned with the voices of the participants in my study. Brought together, I believe they offer parents, educators, and community members tools for supporting rural gender-creative youth. In particular, I will: 1) provide critical understandings of the complexity of rural gender-creativity, 2) suggest the importance of the use of *The Hunger Games* as a source of recognition and empowerment of rural gender-creativity, and 3) advocate for a curriculum in which youth are encouraged to speak, write, and create; they can't depend on distorted rural representation, they need to put their own lives down on the map.

TOMBOYS AND OTHER GENDER HEROES: THE STUDY

From February to June in 2011 and 2012, I conducted gender equity workshops in eight schools with approximately 600 students. While research invitations were sent to every school in the board/district, all of the schools that ultimately participated were accessed through personal contacts. The students ranged in grade level from 4 to 12. At several of the schools, I returned for multiple days, working with a variety of classes. I was often assisted in the teaching and research by a research assistant.[1] I offered students a collection of activities that served as both equity education, and as media for collecting data. I obtained writing and drawings, and wrote field notes documenting class discussions and theatrical presentations. I audio-recorded the sessions to aid in my memory of the conversations that took place.

I frame the discussion below through the writing responses and drawings I received from participants, through excerpts of *The Hunger Games*, and throughout with attention to geographical context.

EVERYONE SAYS HUNTING IS FOR BOYS

She's a grade 8 student in an inner-city school in a city of less than 80,000. The place is seen as rural to the people of Toronto, and the big smoke to the smaller towns around it. A 10-minute drive from the center of the city to the perimeter will land you in farm fields, but on the way out you'll pass by the only Costco in the region. Her K–8 school features a full spectrum of class divisions, but add them all up and you're still $5,000 below the average annual income of Ontarians.

I provided many of the classes with a writing prompt: choose an object or activity that represents your gender, describe it, say how you feel about it, and tell what you would do if anyone ever tried to take it away from you. I wanted to capture a full spectrum of gendered symbols and practices, and also to offer an opportunity for empathy, a momentary meditation on what it feels like to be asked to repress your gender. The student I am highlighting in this section wrote the following in response:

> Archery is a part of me, because I love to do it, I can hunt with a bow. Everyone says hunting is for boys, but I love it, even though I'm a girl. Country music is an extremely huge part of me. I love country music, all the songs tell a story. All my friends listen to other music, like rap and stuff and think my kind of music is stupid. If somebody ever took my bow, or hunting away from me, I would die. I'm not joking, I've played hockey, I've played baseball, rugby, gone shoppin,' been in million dollar homes. But I like being deep down in the woods, with my bow, my gun, and being able to shoot things. I love being able to crank the country music, and have a good time. I'm a country girl 100% and I don't care if people think I'm weird. I've grown up doing this stuff, and I'll never give it up. Country music, hunting, and archery, are me.
>
> I plan on buying a house, or building a house in the middle of the woods, I have no problem with little bugs around my house, I love to get dirty. I play in the dirt, and honestly I couldn't care less if I drove into town, covered in mud. It does not bug me. (Grade 8 student)

The words are scribbled in pink; they are fierce and proud. She uses her gender as a source of survival, identity, and pleasure. At 13 she is already conscious of her transgressions, claiming the classic masculine activities of hunting and getting dirty, despite opposition, and claiming them even as the stigma of a country identity clashes with her more urban-identified peers. There is a sense of pride in these transgressions, of strength, and of fun. She is aware of gender regulations, but is intent on breaking them. In her words I find gender explained as comfort and history, and a possession to embrace against an urban standard. While I received numerous accounts from rural girls wanting to hunt or fish and being told that these were strictly male activities, for this girl, she seems to be more aware that they are masculine activities in opposition to urban norms. Perhaps this tension arises from her position in a small city, itself conflicted about its identity between rural and urban. In her article "Midwest or Lesbian? Gender, Rurality, and Sexuality," Kazyak (2012) documents that "a range of female gender" is "allowed" in rural spaces as opposed to their urban counterparts (p. 837).

Traditionally masculine clothing like flannel shirts and cowboy boots, as well as work on the farm, driving the equipment, and so on are embraced by a variety of women, whereas such masculine women in an urban context would be viewed as lesbians. This young archer supports queer rural researcher Mary Gray's (2007) assertion that "the everyday lives of rural youth complicate dichotomies of rural and urban ..." (p. 50).

Her words also drew my attention to the literary phenomenon *The Hunger Games* (2010), in their similarity to the character of Katniss Everdeen. Katniss Everdeen is the protagonist of this post-apocalyptic science fiction text, where she lives with her mother, sister, and two love interests, Peeta and Gale. They are citizens of Panem, living at the edge of the nation in District 12 (formerly known as Appalachia). District 12 is known for its coal mining and its poverty, and its citizens often face starvation. There are 12 Districts, each with its own industry and varying levels of prosperity, but all are subjugated by the inhabitants of the Capitol. The Capitol consumes the bulk of the resources, and in order to maintain control over the Districts, they arouse fear by forcing two teenagers (called tributes) from each District, chosen through a lottery, to fight each other until death in an annual event called "The Hunger Games." This text offers a rich narrative for thinking through rural and urban tensions, the devastation of poverty, critical media literacy, and gendered relationships to geography. Compare the words of the grade 8 archer to these scenes describing Katniss's experience of her body and gender expression in *The Hunger Games*:

> I [Katniss] swing my legs off the bed and slide into my hunting boots. Supple leather that has molded to my feet, I pull on trousers, a shirt, tuck my long dark braid up into a cap, and grab my forage bag. (p. 4)

Katniss heads out into the woods, with her bow, and perfect shot, the only place that calms her from the chaos of a world where she cannot protect her family from the violence and exploitation of the Capitol (pp. 4–5). When the Capitol gets their hands on her, the first thing they manipulate and assault is her gendered body (pp. 74–76). The girl hunter needs to be tamed and presentable to urban gender standards.

> Venia and the other members of my prep team have addressed some obvious problems. This has included scrubbing down my body with a gritty foam that has removed not only dirt but at least three layers of skin, turning my nails into uniform shapes, and primarily, ridding my body of hair. My legs, arms, torso, underarms, and parts of my eyebrows have been stripped of the stuff, leaving me like a plucked bird, ready for roasting. I don't like it. My skin feels sore and tingling and intensely vulnerable. ... The three step back and admire their work. "Excellent! You almost look like a human being now!" says Flavius, and they all laugh.

I force my lips into a smile to show how grateful I am. 'Thank you," I say sweetly. "We don't have much cause to look nice in District Twelve." (pp. 75–76)

Looking "nice" is when urban translates into some type of twisted feminine expression. While certain types of femininity are acceptable in District 12, like her mother's and sister's expertise in caring for community members, attention to feminine dress and appearance is a luxury of the Capitol. As Katniss sharply questions, "What do they [citizens of the Captiol] do all day besides decorating their bodies and waiting around for a new shipment of tributes to roll in and die for their entertainment?" (pp. 79–80). The "decorating" of one's body through makeup, stylish clothing, jewelry, and plastic surgery, often considered as hyper-feminine accessories, are embraced by men and women alike in the Capitol. In that sentence, Katniss links hyper-femininity with the slaughter of the poor and rural. Hyper-femininity is portrayed as the repulsive expression of the inhabitants of the Capitol who are "flamboyant " (p. 78), "dyed, stenciled, and surgically altered" (p. 77), "oddly dressed people with bizarre hair and painted faces who have never missed a meal"(p. 72).[2] Hyper-femininity is a central element of urban culture to be despised and resisted by those living outside "the Capitol."

I am reminded of a grade 11 student who exclaimed during one of the gender workshops that he heard that there's a guy in Toronto with purple hair. To be fair, the girl in the row behind him pipes up, "There're a lot of guys in Toronto with purple hair." But either way I note that Toronto and the Capitol have a great deal in common. They are the urban regions of the nations in question, the perceived home of LGBTTQI2S[3] peoples, including those with purple hair. They are also despised by those in District 12 and by those in the rural regions of Ontario as the wealthy, and resource rich, the gluttonous and careless. Therefore, the young archer's masculinity is her love and her comfort, but also a symbol of defiance to the people of Toronto, just as it is for Katniss.

While impossible to generalize rural experience, I believe such findings offer some important points to consider when supporting rural gender transgressive youth. One's gender expression may be intimately tied to one's sense of "country" pride. The policing and condemning of gender expression may be perceived as acts of aggression within a rural community, but also as assimilationist pressures from the urban mainstream. In addition, female masculinity may be seen as gender transgressive for some, eliciting harassment or punishment, but for others it may be perceived as a part of rural life, more accepted than for those living in urban centers.

Consider the writing of another student, a grade 5 girl, who sat at the back of the class during one of my workshops. I perceived her as a tomboy with long hair pulled back, sporting a track outfit, holding her arms stiff across her desk, flexing her biceps. She barely moved the whole session, and kept a steady, serious gaze on me. She may have been only 10, but she seemed tough. I kept an eye on her because I was curious how she would react and what she would write. I was sharing my experiences of being a tomboy with the students, and based on the perceptions I learned where I grew up (the suburbs of Los Angeles), I believed she was one of my kind and might therefore personally understand the discrimination I had faced. I eagerly anticipated her writing, but what I found confirmed that I had little understanding of girl's masculinity in a rural context.

In several of the classes, I passed out index cards in the last 5 minutes of the workshop and asked students to write either one thing they learned from the workshop, or one thing they will change as a result of having participated in the workshop. On her "exit card," she wrote:

> I will change the way of looking at my sister as a girly girl just because she dresses really girly.

From her words, I understand that the gender transgressions were committed by her feminine sister, that femininity, not masculinity, in girls was somehow perceived as the problem. My workshop on gender acceptance offered her the knowledge to accept her sister's femininity, and to stop coercing her to become more masculine. If femininity in girls can sometimes be perceived as an unacceptable gender expression, what is the plight for femininity as expressed by boys?

TOY CARS AND BARBIE DOLLS

In Kazyak's (2012) study of the U.S. Midwest, while female masculinity was often acceptable, rural gay men consistently avoided any identification with male femininity. They understood the stereotype of effeminate gay men, and were relieved to not embody it. Kazyak remarks repeatedly that male femininity did not coincide with rural living. I am not suggesting that masculinity in girls is readily accepted in rural areas, or that femininity in boys is not also despised in cities, but rather that there is a nuance here that shouldn't be missed. There are particular ways of expressing femininity and masculinity in rural areas that differ from the cities, and it can be tied as well to both a resistance to and resentment of perceived gender expression in Toronto.

My findings often supported Kazyak's understanding of the suppression of male femininity. Even with more than 600 writings and images, it is much more difficult to find confessions of male femininity than it is to locate young girls' examples of masculinity. And more often than not, boys recount rigid rules and consequences of the slightest deviations from rural masculine expression. Perhaps the most common expression of resistance against rigid gender rules came from a handful of boys in grades 5 and 6, claiming their appreciation for the colors pink and purple despite what others thought. They did so primarily anonymously on exit cards.

In our classroom discussions, femininity in boys was often linked to being gay. I never had to bring up the issue of homophobia, because my question about gender transgressions in every workshop except one led to a discussion of homophobia. One boy explained that if you hold your hand up and your wrist limp for 10 seconds you'll become gay. Many others asserted that if you liked Justin Bieber and you are a boy, then you're gay. When I asked for them to elaborate, they explained that he had a high-pitched voice. A high-pitched voice is evidence of femininity and is therefore gay sexuality, and any association with this high-pitched voice would therefore also be gay.

The Bieber is a complicated figure who could be a rich source of critical learning on gender transgression. While he has attempted an exaggerated masculine swagger for his audiences, his past appearance as a prepubescent boy with a high voice, pretty face, and relatively long hair has drawn the overwhelming homophobia of the majority of the boys in my study. On the one hand they despise his perceived femininity, on the other they copy en masse his longer hairstyle. On the website Kidzworld ("Everyone Wants Justin," 2013), the phenomenon and contradiction are described:

> Because Justin's not exactly popular among boys (most of his fans are tween and teen girls), many of the guys that go in to get the cut refuse to ask for it by name. Instead, they describe the combed-over 'do with no mention of Justin Bieber. But they want it because the look is so popular with girls right now!

In my study, the most prevalent knowledge that boys reported on personally receiving harassment due to their gender expression was because of wearing this longer hairstyle. However, in at least one instance, a boy embraced the longer hair despite the ramifications being teased.

The boy whips his unconventional longish hair. His longer hair is not quietly contained. It is not explained as the excusable masculinity of a rocker or skateboarder, but rather whipped around like a fashion model. Free flowing hair is traditionally feminine and sexual and he will whip it. When I look at his drawing, I see freedom in his unabashed gender-creativity.

Unfortunately, this is an exception, as I collected very few words or images of boys confident with any form of traditional femininity. I met some very scared and lost boys who, because of their perceived femininity, feared for their futures. I found one such young man in a small grade 11 class in a town of about 6,000 people. The class was part of a rural high school, located approximately 2 hours outside of Toronto, packed with busses in the parking lots. Students can travel more than an hour through the farmland to reach school each day. Because of the quiet during the workshop, I wondered if my descriptions of gender transgression and human rights made any connection with them. It was not until the hour after class as I sipped organic soup at the local café that I was hit with one young man's writing:

> My past is a part of me. This is because of how I acted as a toddler and how it affected me throughout every year of school. As a child, I played with lots of toys. Some mine, some my sister's. I would play with toy cars and Barbie dolls with my little brother and my older sister. Because of this, I had no social identity for if I acted like a boy or acted like a girl. This is what led to my childhood depression that I am continuing to fight.

> During my first year of public school, I was made fun of for the way I acted because I would always talk to the girls and not the guys. I was called rude names and was even labeled gay during my last year at that school. In 2005, I moved to Ontario hoping to get a fresh start but failed at doing so which ultimately led to my past issues coming back even worse.

Because the writing is anonymous, I don't know who he is. But he's the one I'm ultimately doing the research for; he's the one I'm trying to save. He identifies the repeated bullying, the depression, and the inability to locate his gender expression as a natural and legitimate part of the world. There is no evidence of resistance or resilience. I don't know how he'll survive. His words haunt me. Consider his story in comparison to some of the other writings in the class. I offered the following prompt: "In [fill in town name], you know a boy's a boy, if ...", and here were two responses:

> In Roxton[4] you know a boy's a boy if he plays sports, fishes or hunts, works physical labour, plays videogames, loves sex, and is always looking at women.

> In Roxton, I know a man's a man if they drink beer, play hockey and wear old graphic t-shirts. Roxton men don't drink pink lemonade or red wine. That would suggest that they enjoy dinner parties and talking about their feelings. They drink beer, order in

pizza, and watch hockey with some friends. They don't care what they wear—clothes shopping is for girls. If a man was to go to a friend's house wearing a pink tennis shirt, their friends would wonder what horrible thing he had done to receive such a torment from his wife (because, of course, his wife buys his clothes). This, of course, is just the stereotypical male in Roxton.

The grade 11 student described previously, who enjoyed playing with Barbie dolls, is measuring his normalcy against hockey, hunting, and physical labor. The archetypical male of Roxton cannot express feelings or buy clothes, and must continually reaffirm his heterosexuality through his gaze upon women. Even as I offered the workshop to counter such narrow conceptualizations of gender, a one-day intervention is realistically not enough to offer him other enduring representations of maleness. Understanding the more severe treatment of male femininity in rural areas shapes the approach that a parent, educator, or community member would need to take in supporting him. He will likely need access to gender-creative youth representation beyond his immediate community context.

Literature and media can serve as important resources to support rural gender-creativity. As Gray (2007) found, media serves as a crucial tool for rural queer youth in the United States, exploring and affirming their identities. I have already offered Justin Bieber as one such possibility for discussion, and I am impressed with *The Hunger Games* as a potential tool for embracing alternative gender representations. It is not only for the critical insights about regional gender variations that I have incorporated *The Hunger Games* into this analysis, but also because of its popularity. It has become the *Harry Potter* of its time, pulling on board a whole generation of new readers. It is a book that this boy would have access to, that he has probably already read. It is a brilliant book, rich in content for critical pedagogy in the classroom if teachers are willing to lead the way. While young people may not pick up on the many social nuances of the text on their own, an adult's willingness to engage in critical discussions about the narrative might open new possibilities of gender expression. It is a way for adults to value both the diversity of students' gender identities, and their knowledge and interests in popular culture. *The Hunger Games* speaks to a young person's desire to have worth, to have voice, to have an opportunity to express themselves as they are, summed up in the line, "I keep wishing I could think of a way to … to show the Capitol they don't own me. That I'm more than a piece in their games"[5] (Collins, 2010, p. 236). This particular text offers alternative visions of rural male gender expression as well, which could reach the young grade 11 student and affirm his complex gender identity.

For example, in *The Hunger Games* we are offered the character of Peeta, who knew nothing about hunting (p. 359) and was a much better speaker, painter, and cake decorator than a soldier. Katniss and Peeta consciously switch traditional gender roles in order to survive in "The Hunger Games" arena.

> "I won't be much help with that," Peeta says. "I've never hunted before."
> "I'll kill while you cook," I [Katniss] say. "And you can always gather."
> "I wish there was some sort of bread bush out there," says Peeta. (p. 359)

Peeta does not represent the hyper-femininity of the Capitol, but he is assigned the more feminine role of gatherer and cook while Katniss is the expert at hunting. He comes from the same rural District as Katniss, and often expresses his embarrassment at not possessing more traditional masculine traits, such as hunting, fighting, and knowledge of the land. Indeed, he cannot even aid Katniss as a gatherer, knowing more about his family's bakery than the plants of the forest. He was the butt of jokes by other teen soldiers, and often the weak link when the fighting began. But he was loved by Katniss. His very gentleness roused her heart and desire, and ultimately he is offered to us through her eyes. If the readers identify with Katniss, then they probably identify with loving Peeta in spite of, and because of, his alternative gender expression. I would guess that this process occurs unconsciously, but what better opportunity to make gender-creativity explicit than through classroom discussion of a popular young adult text.

"CALL ME LIKE I'M A GIRL"

Out where the fields reach the beaches of Lake Ontario, I found a grade 5 boy clutching his written notes for our workshop. In the workshop, I asked students to write anonymously on Post-its anything they could recall about gender rules, policing, or simple anecdotes they may have overheard about responses to gender expression. Following the writing activity, the students are asked to place their Post-its up on the board in order to get a sense of how gender expression is experienced in their community. He wasn't going to give them to us, but my research assistant eased his fears. He relented and once he was out of the room, we read his pile of Post-its one by one.

> "People leaves me out because I'm new kid and from other country."
> "People don't let me play and don't pass and keep call me like I'm a girl just because I'm from other country."
> "If boys and girls don't need to be called why separate washrooms?"
> "What can you do to get people to stop bullying?"
> "Someone said 'suck it' and then said 'wait you have nothing there,' to me."
> "People keeps bullying me because I'm from other country."
> "What do you do if people leave you out and call you names?"
> "People pushes me and call me names."

It is heart wrenching to read his words. My research assistant and I look up at each other with tears in our eyes. This is the brutality of intersecting oppressions. As an Asian immigrant to Canada he faces anti-immigrant bigotry (Bannerji, 2000) combined with transphobia and homophobia. As an outsider, he is unable to present himself as possessing a "sameness" that is often valued within rural communities (Kazyka, 2012, p. 827). I would guess that, in part, his own cultural gender codes look different, and are therefore subject to attack by his Ontario peers. As well, I think his peers feminize him as a method for attacking him.

Stephen Wei (2004) writes about this phenomenon amongst gay men in Toronto, who often treat Asian men as female. He writes about his own difficulty to see himself as a man under these circumstances, just as this young boy struggles. I choose to finish the chapter with this boy's story because in eight short Post-its, he describes a complexity of gender-creativity that is both devastating and brave, that is messy and articulate, that offers no easy answers. He embodies Dorothy Allison's (1994) call at the beginning of the chapter for "our lives [to be] taken seriously and represented fully" (p. 165). While he endures the harshest types of harassment from his peers, he is unwilling to accept it. He questions their words. He wonders about pedagogical strategies to stop their behavior. Through his example of the segregated bathrooms, he offers a critique and critical questions of the system. He knows something is wrong about the school, and not about himself.

But the story doesn't end there. After offering us his writing, he jumped up to participate in the drama portion of the workshop. He grabbed himself a pink purse as a prop and sashayed across the stage with the girls in his skit. He wasn't going to allow bullying or dehumanizing stereotypes of Asian femininity in men get in the way of an opportunity to put his gender-creativity on stage. The teacher, a smart and loving educator, a friend, and former student, looked over to me in wonder. "Why would he do that?" she asks, given the new and shocking information on his Post-its. I shrug, "It's complicated."

Following the session, the class was dramatically transformed through this boy's words. The teacher challenged them to reveal the racism and homophobia, to acknowledge the harm, to take responsibility, to change the way they saw him and treated him. The class became closer through the sharing of emotions and honesty. The teacher wrote an email to tell me what happened:

> What's right isn't always popular, and what's popular isn't always right, my kids get this now (I think). I have better insights and ideas than some people and maybe am better at sharing them (I thought). I always thought I was in-tune with my kids and our classroom culture, now I know I have to wake up and open my eyes and ears. Yes, over all it's confidence that's attractive, and this has both positive and negative impacts. The idea of the power of the story as transformative proves true. (M. Kofira, personal communication, 2012)

This teacher's account is a testament to the difficult work of supporting gender-creative youth in rural areas. Even those of us with the best of intentions can miss a looming disaster. Coercion and harassment of alternative gender expression are common tactics performed by peers and adults alike. In order to support these young people to survive within their communities, we need to commit to understanding the nuances of regional expressions of gender. We also need to value student knowledge of popular literature and culture, because these are central figures in their lives, and can provide enduring representations of gender-creativity. In addition, these texts alone do not necessarily offer progressive directions for gender expression, but rely on adults willing to follow up with critical discussions and the sharing of students' personal knowledge. Finally, I would advocate for adults to provide opportunities for the young people themselves to write, draw, create, and role-play gender-creative lives (both anonymously and publically). They benefit from the chance to develop the confidence of voice, and to put into the world the rich representations of gender diversity that they might otherwise have difficulty finding in their communities. Ultimately, I believe that the beauty of the stories these young people offered will have the most profound effect on the lives of gender-creative youth and those of us supporting them, the pride and confidence of the archer, the sexiness of the boy's whipped hair, the vulnerability of the grade 11 boy with his toy cars and Barbie dolls, and the defiance of the young Korean boy with his pink purse, unwilling to accept the cruelest of playground taunts.

NOTES

1. With great appreciation to Heather Algie and Star Davey for their brilliance, passion, critical observations and incredible intuitive skills in the classroom.
2. I was first made aware of the connection between the urban corruption and femininity through a conversation with Dana Baitz.
3. This abbreviation refers to lesbian, gay, bisexual, transgender, transsexual, queer, intersex, and two-spirit.
4. Roxton is a pseudonym I have offered to protect the anonymity of the town.
5. An idea first presented to me by Denise Handlarski.

CHAPTER SEVEN

The Limitations and Possibilities for Teaching Transgender Issues in Education to Preservice Teachers

JENNIFER C. INGREY

INTRODUCTION: TEACHING TRANSGENDER ISSUES IN EDUCATION

What does it mean to study a 'fringe' topic? To teach something that is not part of dominant discourses? For the equity educator who is interested in transgender or gender-nonconforming issues (and presents as gender privileged), it means that a lot of negotiation, personal reflection, and rethinking are all necessary work. Teaching for equity and social justice is an un-colonized terrain; teaching for and about transgender issues within an equity framework adds an extra layer of unknowability (Lather, 1991, 2008). In heteronormative understanding, issues of sexuality garner more public attention while gender is subsumed within sexuality or even fades into oblivion. More often than not I deliver introductory sessions on transgender issues. For various ideological and political reasons, transgender is still a new frontier in education. For now, it might be enough to reflect not on the reasons why transgender issues are not integrated in teacher preparation programs in Ontario in particular or in Canada as a whole, but instead on what we can do given the limitations especially within the framework of equity and social justice.

In this chapter, I reflect on three pedagogical approaches in my experience teaching *about* or *for* transgender issues—if not also teaching to be critical of othering and privileging (Kumashiro, 2000)—in the preservice education program

(Bachelor of Education) replete with the limitations of each approach. To reflect on the relevance of these approaches for preservice teachers (teacher candidates), I think through Foucault's (1982) concept of subjectivation, or the becoming of the subject. Sensoy and DiAngelo (2012) argue that teacher candidates must consider their own positionalities (as historically and socially constructed) instead of thinking in terms of individual biases to untangle their subjectivities from their ethical and legal duties to teach for all in inclusive and equitable ways. How teachers think personally is second to the ethical and legal task of teaching all children in an equitable and safe manner. Outlining Ontario policy regarding a teacher's legal responsibilities bolsters this approach and avoids having to convince any resistant learner to 'tolerate' transgender. I also do not apologize for myself as a cisgender individual doing the work of and for a minoritized population. Policy-grounded pedagogy emphasizes basic expectations of equity that all teachers should be competent about as well as confident in implementing in their classrooms.

Throughout the chapter I interlace student voices as authorities on their own experience. These are participants from a larger research project on students' knowledge about gendered subjectivities in school spaces. In terms of my own engaged teaching practice (hooks, 1994), these students direct me to think about the limitations and the next steps in each of these approaches. The talk from which this chapter derives was delivered at the National Workshop on Gender-Creative Kids at Concordia University, Montreal, in the fall of 2012. At the time, I was preoccupied with my non-insider status, concerned about my place as a gender privileged researcher in the field of transgender and gender-nonconforming studies. Initially, the conference only confirmed my fears when the topic of discussion involved the medicalization of gender-nonconformity in youth. People were leaving the session, having "healing conversations" (I was told) because of the painful history that had been conjured. Certain transgender attendees and presenters spoke about feeling pathologized by medicine and research in general, which contested the perspectives of certain cisgender panelists and presenters. In retrospect, I think about how Vivian Namaste (2000) argues sociological research objectifies transgendered people by ignoring the violence and "implications of an enforced sex/gender system for the people who have defied it, who live outside it, or who have been killed because of it" (p. 9). At the time, being subject to the tensions in the room, I felt ill at ease. I feared I would be contributing to this body of harm, this painful history, simply by embodying a normative gender. But then I reconsidered my guilt as counter-productive; freaking out about my gender privilege distracts from the aim of achieving gender justice for all. Indeed, guilt is narcissistic (Butler, 2004); as Boler (1999) argues, it is preoccupied with "individualized self-reflection" instead of a more useful "collective witnessing"

(p. 176). This 'freak out' was an opportunity, a crisis (Kumashiro, 2000), to refine my position and become open to learning from others. Beyond guilt, this chapter is founded in a "pedagogy of discomfort" (Boler, 1999) to thwart the "paralysis [that] is rooted in privilege" (Sensoy & DiAngelo, 2012, p. 142).

THEORETICAL FRAMEWORK

Transgender figures into my theoretical frameworks through Butler's (1990, 1993, 2004) work on gender performativity and the abject. For Butler (1990), gender is a performance, the iteration of repeated acts that make up the fiction that gender is innate or statically aligned with sex. Through transgender, the entire system of gender normativity is exposed, because the very realm of the abject, the illegitimate (i.e., transgender) reveals the boundaries of what is considered livable and therefore, unlivable (1993). Through troubling how gender is normalized, we can work toward a justice to the individuals whose lives do matter (2004). Transgender studies can dismantle and rethink the entire system of gender as Stryker (2006) frames it:

> The field of transgender studies is concerned with anything that disrupts, denaturalizes, rearticulates, and makes visible the normative linkages we generally assume to exist between the biological specificity of the sexually differentiated human body, the social roles and statuses that a particular form of body is expected to occupy, the subjectively experienced relationship between a gendered sense of self and social expectations of gender-role performance, and the cultural mechanisms that work to sustain or thwart specific configurations of gendered personhood. (p. 3)

Transgender is a lived and metaphorical body that allows us to notice the system of gender that we regulate so highly, so closely, and even asks us to seek out who is not represented by the norm. Of course, this theoretical position is much more complex than a mere introduction to 'transgender issues in education' could ever attempt to cover. But it is what informs each pedagogical approach I take.

Furthermore, I consider the work of Foucault (1980) on power/knowledge as part of how students are positioned to regulate their own behaviors and that of others in a panoptic (1975) sense, operating under the mechanism of power to become themselves the effects of power. Students learn through the discursive and material practices in schools that their behaviors, especially those surrounding gender expression and identity, are highly policed and regulated. Therefore, they learn to self-govern as well, or suffer social consequences for what their peers perceive to be gender transgressions, most often stemming from homophobia (Pascoe, 2007) and transphobia (Sykes, 2004). Primarily, students do not understand gender in a vacuum; they are incited to iterate certain gendered discourses and behaviors through the social advantages and privileges afforded them and in tandem, through the fear of social punishments.

From the lived perspective, much work still must be done in learning how transgender and gender-nonconforming individuals experience school in a North American context. Gender is relational; instead of being separated into categories of men and women, or cisgender and transgender, gender conforming *and* nonconforming individuals together can contribute to the body of knowledge that is so lacking. Ultimately, my work is situated in the field of equity and social justice because I see it as a project to rethink the parameters and categorizations of gender for all people, to consider a sort of gender justice, as in Feinberg's (1998) terms:

> And if you do not identify as transgender or transsexual or intersexual, your life is diminished by our oppression as well. Your own choices as a man or a woman are sharply curtailed. Your individual journey to express yourself is shunted into one of two deeply carved ruts, and the social baggage you are handed is already packed. (p. 6)

WHAT IS THE RELEVANT POLICY: FEDERAL, PROVINCIAL, LOCAL?

I am quickly learning the benefits of knowing and using educational policy, guidelines, provincial law, and so forth when teaching at the preservice level. Not all teacher candidates will be convinced of equity frameworks and the re-thinking of gender systems, specifically, unless these issues are pre-empted by policy that outlines legal obligations. Even then, policy may or may not be taken up by individual teachers; but it is a start to legitimizing pedagogies of equity. The policy that I review in this chapter is specific to an Ontario context from the federal level through to the provincial level and then to the ministry and board level of governance.

The Canadian Human Rights Act does not define gender identity explicitly, but it is subsumed under the category of sex (Women's Legal Education and Action Fund, 2010). Of course, this allowance is still problematic for transgender people who typically do not equate their sex with their gender. Indeed, it glosses over the nuances of gender identity, thereby ignoring the realities of many Canadians' lives, as well as denying explicit protection to transgender individuals especially regarding access to health care, employment, housing, and so forth. Although not a direct influence on provincially controlled education, the act protects against harassment in "the provision of ... services ...," which includes education. To represent the specific rights of transgender people, Bill C-279[1] (historically, Bill C-389) was a private member's bill to amend the Canadian Human Rights Act and the Criminal Code with the inclusion of gender identity and gender expression as protected grounds.

The significance of introducing this history to preservice teachers is that they understand that the explicit rights of transgender people have yet to be recognized at the national level, and much work must still be done to ensure their protection.

However, at the provincial level, Ontario one of only four provinces to include gender identity and gender expression in their Human Rights Code through the passing into law of Toby's Act (Bill 33) in June 2012. Named for Toby Dancer, a trans activist and musician, the act responds to specific issues that transgender people face, namely, abnormally high suicide rates due to rampant transphobia, depression and addiction problems, and bullying in schools (DiNovo, 2012). Toby's Act provides explicit protections for transgender people. It is also an important move in light of the passing of Bill 13, the Accepting Schools Act, also in June 2012, that amends the Education Act to address bullying in schools. Bill 13 speaks to the education context, aiming to make "schools and communities more equitable and inclusive for all people, including LGBTTIQ (lesbian, gay, bisexual, transgender, transsexual, two-spirited, intersex, queer and questioning) people" (p. 1). Furthermore, it names gender-based bullying, including "incidents based on homophobia, transphobia, or biphobia" (p. 1). Bill 13 and Bill 33 are paired legislation marking the human rights and education landscape in Ontario as progressive and exemplary.

Beyond these legislative bodies, I turn to the Ontario Ministry of Education level of governance. Three documents work together: The *Policy/Program Memorandum No. 119* (2009c), the *Equity and Inclusive Education Guidelines* (2009a), and the *Equity and Inclusive Education Strategy* (2009b). The latter states "homophobia, and gender-based violence are still evident in our communities and—unfortunately—in our schools" (p. 9) and therefore includes these grounds in its strategies. The memorandum also states these strategies are "designed to promote fundamental human rights as described in the Ontario Human Rights Code and the Canadian Charter of Rights and Freedoms, with which school boards are already required to comply" (p. 3). The *Early School Leavers Report* (Community Health Systems Resource Group, 2005) from the Ontario Ministry of Education also specifies the population of LGBT youth as having experienced "an extremely negative environment" including such statements from youth as the following: "I felt bullied. It was like a death threat. Like a death note. There was a lot of violence. Everything was by fighting" (p. 24). Schools are unsafe for sexual and gender minoritized youth if their rights are not protected at an institutional level. The Egale *First National Climate Survey* (Taylor, et al., 2011) provides some important research on the experiences of LGBT youth in schools. Although I take heed from Meyer's (2006) advice that gender-nonconforming students have distinct experiences from those of homosexual students, at the moment, we do not have the luxury of differentiated policy at the ministry level, and as we have seen, the legal policies that cover gender identity are themselves still in their infancy, focusing on the rights of transgender people instead of gender-nonconforming or genderqueer youth. As a start, the *Safe Schools Report* (Ontario Ministry of Education, 2006) names gender as a discrete category, separate from sexual orientation, that needs protection through the directive that "boards should support and maintain positive school climates that reinforce bullying prevention messages through programs" (p. 7). Exactly how gender should be interpreted is not yet outlined.

At the school board level, the Toronto District School Board (TDSB) is exemplary in their work on gender matters. They have policy and guidelines specifically devoted to gender identity and gender expression, namely, *Policy P071: Gender-Based Violence*, which they name as "any aggressive action that threatens safety, causes physical, social or emotional harm and denigrates a person because *of* his or her gender identity, perceived gender, sexual identity, biological sex or sexual behavior" (p. 1). This policy includes even the *perception* of gender transgression as a recognized example of aggression. Furthermore, transgender accommodation guidelines combine with their Human Rights Policy (P031). The TDSB's work on gender issues is nuanced and grounded in the research on gender-nonconforming youth experiences and can stand as a model for all Canadian educators.

THREE PEDAGOGICAL APPROACHES

The Pedantic Approach: Terminology

One of my first attempts at teaching transgender issues in education to preservice teachers relied on terminology as a set of tools to begin to unpack the mythology surrounding transgender in dominant discourses. To start, transgender itself is an umbrella term that "incorporates a diverse array of male- and female-bodied gender persons" (Valentine, 2007, p. 4). Furthermore, it can be seen as a political or community term denoting kinship among those with gender-variant identities (Namaste, 2000); and more generally, it is about the "myriad specific subcultural expressions of 'gender atypicality'" (Stryker, 2006, p. 3). Because I focus on gender transgressions more broadly in my own research, I also introduce the following terms: gender-nonconforming: "encompassing all transpeople" (Wyss, 2004, p. 714); genderqueer: "anyone who problematizes heteronormative gender regimes" (p. 714); and gender-variant: may include "gender dissonance" (Luecke, 2011); as well as gender fluidity, which is, according to Bornstein (1994), "the ability to freely and knowingly become one or many of a limitless number of genders, for any length of time, at any rate of change. Gender fluidity recognizes no borders or rules of gender" (p. 52). I had previously preferred this term because I liked the idea of 'limitless' genders until I learned some transgender people reject it because it rejects the binary system that some of them wish to live and pass within. It is now just a term I introduce among many, and the list will probably continue to grow.

I framed this approach in a discussion about the practice of labeling, its negative connotations followed by its more productive potential. Conventionally, labeling is associated with name-calling. Labeling is also a technology of power (Foucault, 1988). How bodies are classified, managed, and regulated are processes that are part of the mechanism of disciplinary power (Foucault, 1975). These systems of normalization tell which bodies matter and which do not (Butler, 1993). After showing a YouTube video called *Labels* (picaVpica/pica pica's androgyne videos, 2008), I argued the practice of labeling can be very productive because it offers a starting point. To put language to something is to bring it into existence. And to have a name for someone is to honor *hir*[2] identity. Above all, naming should be about *self*-naming:

> Naming is power. When I tell you who I am I give you the power to name me. When someone else names me, they define who I am and usurp the power that is rightfully mine. The beginning or end of our freedom lies in the power to name ourselves or others. (O'Hartigan, 1994)

As one of my participants during my research indicated, "Labels are important as well because if you don't have anything to like be concrete on. ... I guess it's kind of like the starting point when you kind of get to know someone, you know, like the little facts about them and then you realize that it's much bigger than that ..." (Pliny, age 18). It helps preservice teachers to know that gender terminology is fluid, contextually based, and highly sensitive and should be used as respectfully as possible, giving authority to the child who might be gender-creative, genderqueer, or gender questioning. Self-labeling is a sort of technology of self and power (Foucault, 1988), an intersection of technologies that leads to self-regulation. If not entirely agentic, at least self-naming for transgender and gender-nonconforming people is a way to resist the regulatory norms of gender.

Teacher candidates who do not have academic or life experience with non-normative gender identities often conflate sex/sexuality and gender. A common assumption is that a person exhibiting gender-nonconforming behavior, dress, or other expression is automatically also homosexual. To untangle this conflation, Paechter's (2001) terminology on gender identity, gender expression, and gender role is helpful. Pascoe's (2007) study *Dude, You're a Fag* also teases out the operations of homophobia and transphobia at work here. Pascoe finds, for boys specifically, that the "masculine identity entails the repeated repudiation of the specter of failed masculinity" (p. 5), which includes a homosexual identity. To regulate masculinity, boys tend to throw "homophobic epithets at one another" (p. 5); although distinct entities, sexuality and gender are entwined in this social process of expressing and regulating masculinities.

Another important purpose of defining gender as separate, yet related to other identity categories, is to reject the biological determinism that is prevalent within a dominant culture of positivism. Some preservice teachers presume genitalia is the source of gender; to clarify that gender is a social and personal identity—whereas sex is something borne out of anatomy and genetics—is to help them understand the identities of people who are transgender or gender-nonconforming. Airton's (2009) definition is especially useful because it notes the performativity (Butler, 1990) of gender: "Your *gender* [emphasis in original] is an evolving relationship negotiated among your lived experience, your context and your feelings about your body" (Airton, 2009, p. 224). Whereas Butler's (2004) analysis of the David Reimer[3] case helps us to understand that a penis (or lack thereof) does not a gender make. To talk about transgender in terms of anatomy incites a reparative medical discourse and insults people pained by this violent approach (Namaste, 2000). Reiterations of myths become part of the hidden curriculum (Giroux & Purpel, 1983), and can lead and have led to an assault on people who feel their gender and their bodies do not cohere to society's binary gender norms.

Not only is it necessary to tease out the difference between sex and gender, we must also name heteronormativity and transphobia in misconceptions of transgender experiences. Without acknowledging the hatred, nothing can be done to repair the misconceptions. Sykes (2004) focuses on the "perceived" transgressions of gender performativity, which is the basis for how gender and sex become confused in common understanding. One of my participants, Bert, corrected these misconceptions saying the following: "Even people in the queer community kind of group ... transgendered issues, homosexuality in the same grouping ... and I don't agree. ... Just because I'm homosexual doesn't mean that I'm also transgendered and the same way I have friends who are transgendered but aren't homosexual ...". This simple statement belies the complexities embedded in the matrix (Butler, 1990) of gender, sex, and sexuality; teacher candidates should hear how students make sense of these identity categories from their own experiences.

It is an ongoing process to continue to untangle the complexities of gender identity. I have decided the terminology approach to teaching transgender issues in education is limited, but best served as a precursor to subsequent teaching sessions that acknowledge this complexity. Lived understanding can often exceed our grasp (see Butler, 2004) and move far beyond the hold of terminology. One of my participants defined herself in this way:

… if I had to label myself as something I would say that I'm genderqueer, … more of a gender-fluid thing. I mean, I have male characteristics, I have female characteristics. … I'm okay I guess with being a female obviously, like, I don't want to be a guy, but I don't think I'm fully anything. I don't know how to explain it. It's really hard to explain. (Pliny, age 18)

Pliny does not necessarily articulate a fluidity of expression the way Bornstein (1994) describes it, but perhaps it is her understanding that is fluid. And if a lived under-standing and experience are so difficult to fix, then our work teaching and learning about gender issues through transgender are both certainly something that must follow this organic, evolving path. We are never done because our learning about anti-oppressive education can only ever be partial (Kumashiro, 2000; Lather, 2008).

The Narrative Approach: A Case Study

I developed another approach for an Equity in Education single-day event or-ganized by the Bachelor of Education program office offering such topics as anti-homophobia, anti-transphobia, and anti-racist education, and Aboriginal and First Nations issues in education to all preservice teachers. It was intended to address equity issues in education especially for those students who would not otherwise have access to these topics in their required or elective courses. Only about 35 out of a possible 750 students were enrolled in the one elective course that addressed gender and sexuality issues within a social justice framework. And even that single course does not alone achieve the aims of a true social justice program, according to McDonald and Zeichner (2009), which should infuse social justice throughout.

Moving beyond the terminology approach, I created a case study based on Luecke's (2011) research of the transition of a gender-nonconforming child named Jaden in elementary school. The case described Jaden's gendered expressions and outlined the procedure the school would take in aiding her transition from boy to girl, which included sending an information letter home to parents. The fol-low-up activity prompted the preservice teachers to do the following: a) evaluate the school's response and management of this child's transition; and b) suggest ad-ditional strategies of support. Ultimately, preservice teachers were meant to engage in a critical way with the systemic issue of transgender accommodation in schools; grounding it in a real case meant I was not drawing on popular culture notions of transgender that might reinforce stereotypes. I hoped that the narrative quality of the case, the value of learning through application, and the real-life relevance of the case would contribute to the success of their learning.

After I inevitably had to review terminology (the preservice teachers were asking me where 'queer' fit into transgender issues, and what the differences were between transsexuals, transgender, and transvestites, etc.), I encountered the problem of the washroom. These teacher candidates exhibited concern for other children in the washroom when this transitioning child was present, as if the gender transition itself or the body within which it was happening posed a sexual threat to all other cisgender children. This reiteration of the violent and perverse transgender stereotype indicates something rather alarming, but all too common, according to Davison and Frank (2006):

> Most teachers … are products of the same educational system as contemporary students, and, in the journey from student to educator … they have gainfully navigated schooling in such a way that they, too, have produced discourses of the self that are in line with dominant educational and gender discourses. Without a gender analysis, teachers and administrators, therefore, may be more likely to perpetuate inequities in pedagogy … that seem to them simply naturally embedded in common-sense differences between women and men. (p. 155)

These soon-to-be educators were not troubling their 'common-sense' notions of normative gender. Kumashiro's (2000) framework for anti-oppressive education can help us to understand how repeated discourses of othering must be disrupted, if not altered: "all learning involves an unlearning" (p. 38). To confront the experience of someone outside of normative gender may have been unique for these preservice teachers. Perhaps they felt exposed to knowledge that could either only incite a 'crisis' of unlearning or cause them to reaffirm their own belief system about gender norms. Some of the teacher candidates had positioned the child who was transitioning as a threat to the binary system of gender. Their responses redrew the lines of 'us' and 'them,' between the norm and the other, in a self-protective and policing way. One student even responded, 'What if a student wants to be a super-hero? Do we have to support that identity too?' I reminded them of the relevant policy, namely, the protected grounds of sex and gender identity under the Code as an attempt to sober these ideas.

Personally, I saw these responses as an affront, a re-issuing of violent acts of objectification toward transgender people. As an educator, it is difficult to handle one's own emotional responses and to balance the rage versus the temperance needed to try to teach everyone. I always struggle when I hear othering discourses because my reaction is so immediate; but it is productive to consider that learning is only partial and together we are working toward an "always-shifting end/goal of learning more" (Kumashiro, 2000, p. 34). Equity work is so difficult because everyone is faced with challenges in their personal and academic understandings, and knowledge is never finite. Not only do educators end up in "unknowable places" (p. 39)—those spaces between what we teach and what students actually learn—but we are also simultaneously contributing to "the ongoing, never-completed construction of knowledge" (pp. 43–44). Furthermore, the discourses these teacher candidates reiterate about gender normativity and the intolerance for the other remind equity educators that dominant forms of knowledge are enforced and reproduced through power relations (Foucault, 1980). The gender privileged are rewarded for their expressions of normative gender, as well as their othering of gender transgressions. All of these operations are invisible and go unknown, which is why making them visible creates such resistance in certain privileged individuals. If they have not lived it, they cannot even see the realities of gender-nonconforming people that lead to their denial and/or defensiveness (Sensoy & DiAngelo, 2012).

The case study itself may have been lacking as a pedagogical approach because it presented only one version of gender-nonconformity, the transitioning transgender child, and it did not leave room for more nuanced understandings of other gendered experiences of children. For instance, one participant from my own research told me the following:

> I didn't know I was transsexual until about 19, after I had graduated. So, that when I went to university, that's when you're exposed to vocabulary, queer, trans. You see people who are different that you don't normally see in a small rural high school … we're still a very, very heteronormative environment. And I at the time identified as a heterosexual female so I fit the bill. … I wasn't deviant in any way. (Jack)

In future, I might introduce the concept of becoming gendered (either gender-nonconforming or conforming) (Butler, 1990), or the delicate subjectivation of any youth, especially one not even knowing how to question *hir* own gender identity. For certain, Jack helps us see the ways schooling can limit how one understands the self and perhaps how these teacher candidates have been barred from any knowledge that troubles their 'common-sense' views of gender as binary and unproblematic.

The Diagnostic Approach: Question Cards

The last approach I review is an alternative to and an improvement upon the pedantic and narrative approaches, although not necessarily solving all the limitations of those approaches for teaching transgender issues in education. I developed a diagnostic activity of question cards for the preservice equity class to ascertain the kind of knowledge and interest preservice teachers currently held of transgender issues. This method acknowledges learner subjectivities, and addresses various levels of understanding simultaneously. They wrote their questions on cue cards anonymously and submitted them to me to be categorized and then answered.

Overall, their questions could be grouped into four themes that I scaffold from traditionalist to progressive: biology, sexuality, school support, and naming. Perhaps they felt safer writing these questions without having to speak publicly. Some of the questions derived from stereotypes and myths of transgender, specifically, how anatomy corresponds to an internal gender, or exactly what the body looks like pre- and post-operatively in transsexuals. Otherwise, they were seeking genetic and hormonal sources of transgender, inciting a biologically deterministic framework. Others wanted to know the impact of gender identity disorders on sexuality, or the relationship between transgender and homosexuality. More progressively, some students wanted to know how they could help genderqueer or gender-nonconforming youth in their own classrooms and how schools could support them. Those preservice teachers already using equity lenses simply wanted to know how transgender students should be named because "teachers ... know that naming is a crucial aspect of the relation they maintain with students" (Van Manen, McClelland, & Plihal, 2007, p. 85).

What this approach did not include was, again, the more nuanced understanding of gender identity, especially that it really does impact everyone, even beyond those who are transgender. Similar to Pliny's fluidity of self-understanding, another one of my participants in my research, Bert, told me about his own gender identity in a way that also highlights the fluidity of his understanding and lived expressions:

> I was born a male and I always see myself as male. I've never seen myself as anything else ... I've always seen myself born with male genitalia and you know, I do like hockey, I do like heavy rock music, I do like traditionally male things.

While at another time, Bert told me this:

> I can be pretty feminine at times ... I'm big in the fashion world, I love fashion, I love shopping. ... You can show me somebody's hair and I can tell you why I love it, why I don't and I'm classified as feminine socially sometimes.

What Bert tells us is that his own understanding of his gender identity is itself transitory, becoming clarified, or emphasizing one thing or another at different moments. Although he does not identify as transgender, he also does not identify with the dominant notion that gender or gender expression is static and fixed. He helps to illustrate the linkages between gender and sexuality. This is his lived experience and it must be valued.

Leo J., another participant of mine, did not identify himself as gender-fluid or genderqueer, but told me about how his understanding of gender identity evolved between high school and university:

It just really blew my mind to meet people who … didn't fall into those categories … they don't fit completely that definition … they are still human beings and they're going to be sensitive to whatever you say so you should not really see them as any different.

Bert and Leo offer an alternative view to the stereotype that transgender is only about anatomical transitions or other superficialities that should be dismissed in light of equity education. Preservice teachers need access not only to information about a variety of gendered lives in schools, but also the frameworks upon which to scaffold their understanding of gender as a regulatory system. Furthermore, they need to be educated that the dominant gender system perpetuates norms and conceals the operation of regulation (see Butler, 1990) within which we are all engaged to some degree or another.

CONCLUSION

In *Teaching to Transgress*, hooks (1994) discusses the notion of "engaged pedagogy" to explain that teaching is something that "offers the space for change, invention, spontaneous shifts … [and] calls everyone to become more and more engaged, to become active participants in learning" (p. 11). I consider the National Work-shop on Gender Creative Kids a significant moment in my process of engaged pedagogy; it contributed to my ongoing understanding of gender identities, the lived experiences as well as the theoretical nuances, and the negotiations required to teach transgender issues to preservice teachers. Teacher candidates too engage in their own process, or subjectivation: they are becoming teachers. The teacher who is engaged and asks *hir* learners for the same level of engagement will see teaching as self-work that is continual, partial, and always open to possibilities. As Wood (2009) argues, "Without this type of self exploration preservice teachers will leave their teacher education programs without the necessary understanding of how their racial [and gendered] identity impacts students of culturally and lin-guistically [and otherwise] diverse backgrounds" (p. 172). Not only am I trying to be a reflexive teacher and researcher, but I am also promoting the same for student teachers. Engaged pedagogy allows transgender issues in education to move be-yond tokenism. According to the Ontario Ministry of Education (*Memorandum No. 119*, 2009b), "equity and inclusive education focus is an integral part of every board's operations and permeates everything that happens in its schools" (p. 5). Of course, exactly how gender identity and gender expression are interpreted as pro-tected rights under the Ontario Human Rights Code and then, similarly, through ministry and board policies still requires much more clarification. But the work on transgender equity has begun and it must certainly become a fixture in teacher education programs for it to be most effective. The one-day event that speaks to transgender issues is a beginning, but it is sorely inadequate to counter the twinned dominant discourses of gender normativity and transphobia in schools. Taylor and colleagues (2011) recommend "that Faculties of Education integrate LGBTQ-inclusive teaching and intersectionality into compulsory courses in their Bachelor of Education programmes so that teachers have adequate opportunities to develop competence before entering the field" (p. 140).

For transgender issues in education, teaching to be critical of othering and privileging (Kumashiro, 2000) is a productive anti-oppressive framework to adopt. In the pursuit of gender justice, it is important to know that transgender as a topic is a living thing, one that requires constant attention, alterations, and rethinking. It is a body of knowledge that involves real human beings who have the right to dignity and justice always. Those who choose to learn and study transgender issues in education are also always engaged in an ongoing process of knowledge construction.

NOTES

1. Due to political debates regarding wording and intended meanings, the legislative process is still ongoing as of the publication of this chapter.
2. *Hir* is a gender-neutral pronoun, used in place of *her* or *him*. Often accompanied with *ze*, used in place of *she* or *he*. Used by trans activists, queer theorists, or anybody who rejects or questions the gender-laden language that is available to English speakers.
3. Born as a man, Reimer suffered a faulty circumcision and was raised as a girl. His case was facilitated by Dr. John Money to reconstruct his gender identity which eventually failed because he returned to living as a man as an adult and then committed suicide.

CHAPTER EIGHT

Between a Rock and a Hard Place

The Experience of Parents of Gender-Nonconforming Boys

FRANÇOISE SUSSET

INTRODUCTION

By their varying levels of support or rejection, parents of gender-nonconforming boys[1] have a significant impact on their child's welfare.[2] As a psychologist having worked with many of these families over the years, the author observed that they faced common struggles and challenges. This chapter reports on findings of a study by the author designed to contribute to our understanding of these parents' experiences, more specifically, our understanding of the factors that may influence their responses to their child's gender expression. The author's objective was to explore how three dimensions of the parental experience are related to one another: (1) how they *explain* their child's gender expression, in other words how they answer the question, "Why is my child like this?"; (2) what *feelings* their child's gender expression evokes in them; and (3) what *behaviors* they adopt to limit or support the child's gender expression.

The chapter begins with a brief description of the context from which the research question emerged: the ubiquitous and well-documented stigmatization these children endure and the impact on their mental health and their development. The author then explains the reason parents of boys rather than girls were chosen as the object of the study. This is followed by an overview of what previous research tells us about these parents and their responses to their child's atypical gender expression. This effort to contextualize the research questions serves as an introduction for the principal aim of the chapter: to give parents a chance to be heard. In their own voice, parents describe their concerns and fears for their child; they explain the complex strategies they create and implement to ensure their child's basic safety. Caught between a rock and a hard place, they reveal how the desire to nurture their child's fundamental need for creative self-expression is often in opposition to the necessity to keep their child safe. In conclusion, a number of recommendations are presented to address the issues emerging from the data.

GENDER-NONCONFORMITY IN CHILDREN:
A DANGEROUS PLACE TO BE

Children who express a number of characteristics typically associated with gender roles of the opposite sex are said to be gender-*variant* (e.g., Istar-Lev, 2004), gender *atypical* (e.g., D'Augelli, Pilkington, & Hershberger, 2002), gender-*creative* (e.g., Ehrensaft, 2011) or gender-*nonconforming* (e.g., Meyer, 2008). From their early socialization experiences outside the family context, children who deviate from the strict social norms defining what belongs to the masculine and feminine realm, suffer at the hands of their peers: the sensitive boy who socializes with girls, prefers his piano practice to dodge ball, and is seen as "effeminate"; the girl who doesn't shy away from rough and tumble games with the boys, insists on joining their hockey game, refuses to wear dresses, and is often labeled "tomboy." From such invectives as "fag," "lesbo," "sissy," "butch" to physical assaults, these children are intimidated, harassed and marginalized by their peer group, their teachers (Taylor et al., 2011) and even their parents (Balsam, Rothblum, & Beauchaine, 2005).

However, non-normative gender expression of femininity in a girl and of masculinity in a boy is not an absolute indication of an emerging homosexual or bisexual sexual orientation and even less so of a transgender identity (Cohen-Kettenis & Pfäfflin, 2003); heterosexual, cisgender (i.e., non-transgender) children are therefore also the targets of violence. In a study conducted by Chamberland, Émond, Julien, Otis and Ryan (2010), more than 4,000 Quebec high school and CEGEP (junior college) students were surveyed and asked if they had been the target of homophobic violence in school. Although an alarming 69% of students from sexual minority groups responded that they had been targeted at least once, 35% of students identifying as heterosexual and cisgender also reported having been targeted.

Impact of Stigmatization on Children's Mental Health

In recent years, researchers have attempted to identify the factors involved in the social adjustment difficulties these gender-variant children experience. A recent study by Roberts, Rosario, Corliss, Koenen and Bryn Austin (2012) looked at the risk factors associated with childhood gender-nonconformity in children under age 11. They found that this population is at greater risk for physical, sexual and psychological victimization in childhood and increased risk of Post-Traumatic Stress Disorder (PTSD) over a lifetime, regardless of the child's gender or sexual orientation. The significantly higher suicide risk for gender-nonconforming youth comes as a surprise to none of the researchers in the field (e.g., Dorais & Lajeunesse, 2000). The pressure to conform to gender norms and the ostracism to which these children are subjected are among the most significant challenges they face (Yunger, Carver, & Perry, 2004). As Zucker (2004) states: "In boys who had GID, behavioral difficulties ... increased with age. This was interpreted as being consistent with the influence of social ostracism, which becomes more pronounced over time" (p. 555). Although young boys and girls are submitted to various pressures to conform, these pressures differ according to the child's sex.

Different for Boys

For pre-pubescent children, studies tell us that gender-nonconformity in a girl does not draw as negative a reaction as it does in a boy (Haldeman, 2000). As Moore (2002) illustrates:

> Contemplate for a moment twin images: one, a 5-year-old boy wearing a pink dress and faux pearl necklace; the other, a girl of the same age wearing a cowboy hat, boots, and leather chaps. Which one will have more trouble in kindergarten? At the park? With the neighbors? (p. 5)

In a North American context, the rules relating to gender expression for boys are recognized as being more stereotyped and more intransigent than for girls; boys are subjected to instant and severe sanctions for not abiding by these rules (D'Augelli, Grossman , & Starks 2006; Maccoby, 1998). Moreover, three (Cohen-Kettenis & Pfäfflin, 2003) to five (Zucker & Bradley, 1995) times more boys than girls are referred to gender specialists. Many attribute this difference to the gap between the level of social tolerance of atypical behavior in girls and in boys (Wilson, Griffin, & Wren, 2002).

Impact of a Child's Gender-Nonconformity on the Parent-Child Relationship

Parents have long been held responsible for the development of a non-normative masculine expression in their child. Numerous hypotheses focusing on parents' mental health, parenting styles and family dynamics have been scrutinized for almost a century, yielding no clear or agreed-upon results (Wren, 2002). Despite the lack of scientific confirmation, parents who consult with professionals about their child's gender expression are still at risk today of being held responsible for their child's gender-nonconformity (Tuerk, 2004).

Until very recently, however, the parents' experience of raising a gender-nonconforming child has not been the object of scientific inquiry. According to Menvielle and Tuerk (2002), who developed a support group for parents of gender-nonconforming boys, parents suffer secondary stigmatization that appears to contribute to a sense of isolation and shame. Parents who come to the group suffer from feelings of "guilt, sadness, anger, and anxiety about the future. They may lack self-confidence and seek advice on how to manage the child" (p. 1010). The authors argue that the more parents feel supported and are able to confront their own responses, the more they become able to contribute positively to their child's "long-term adjustment, self-esteem, and social integration" (p. 1010). Based on interviews with parents of transgender adolescents, Wren (2002) identifies two key elements that contribute to maintaining the parent-child relationship, as parents journey toward an acceptance of their child's gender identity. The first is that parents be able to identify signs all along their child's developmental pathway that confirm for them the inevitability of a transgender outcome. The second is that parents attribute their child's gender identity to biological factors rather than to psychological or family dynamics on which they feel they could have acted. Many experts therefore recommend an intervention to help gender-variant children that does not involve attempts to influence their gender expression or identity. Rather, they suggest offering appropriate support to parents in order for them to better support and protect their child (Hill, Rozanski, Carfagnini, & Willoughby, 2005).

Studies inform us that fathers struggle more than mothers in their acceptance of a gender-nonconforming son, which can contribute to a destabilization of the father-son relationship (Landolt, Bartholomew, Saffrey, Oram & Perlman 2004). Fathers, more than mothers, encourage the development of stereotypical masculine behavior in their son (Lytton & Romney, 1991) and have less tolerance for atypical behavior (Beard & Bakeman, 2000). This lack of tolerance may contribute to a higher risk of physical and verbal abuse from parents and from fathers in particular (Corliss, Cochran, & Mays, 2002; Landolt et al., 2004; Menvielle & Tuerk, 2002). Mothers are more disturbed by a son's gender-nonconforming behavior than a daughter's, but tend to be more circumspect than fathers in their response (Langlois & Downs, 1980) and tend to preserve the mother and son bond (Landolt et al., 2004). According to some experts, there are two main reasons parents consult a mental health professional for their gender-nonconforming child: first, the belief that their child's gender-nonconformity is predictive of a future homosexual orientation that can be corrected with early intervention, and second, a desire that their child conform to his gender role in order to protect him from being victimized (Meyer-Bahlburg, 2002; Zucker & Bradley, 1995). Several studies, however, have indicated that the negative outcomes seen in sexual minority and gender-nonconforming youth can be mitigated by parental acceptance of the child's or the youth's difference (Ryan, Russell, Huebner, Diaz, & Sanchez, 2010; Travers, Bauer, Pyne, & Bradley, 2012).

LISTENING TO PARENTS' VOICES

This study is among the first that gives voice to parents of gender-nonconforming children. Five parents were interviewed. The interviews took place between April and August 2010. Each lasted from one hour to one hour and a half and was semi-structured, using minimal prompts that allow for the parents' experiences to emerge with the least interference and guidance from the interviewer. Two couples and a single mother were interviewed. A summary table providing basic information about the participants and their families is included at the end of the chapter. Each of the parents had expressed varying degrees of struggle in regards to accepting and supporting their child's gender-nonconforming behaviors. For some, acceptance had been immediate; others were engaged in a process, challenging their hopes and dreams for their son, learning and adjusting their feelings and behaviors all along the way. Regardless of their starting point, the common denominator for these parents is an overwhelming preoccupation with their child's well-being. The portrait emerging from earlier research literature paints parents of gender-nonconforming sons as reacting negatively to their child's atypical gender expression and attempting to discourage a possible emerging homosexuality or transsexuality (Meyer-Bahlburg, 2002; Zucker & Bradley, 1995). In this study we begin to observe that parents' attitudes, feelings and behaviors follow a more complex and nuanced pathway.

Parents' Feelings

Of the three dimensions studied, "Explanation," "Feelings" and "Behaviors," "Feelings" emerged as the most potent by far, and the one containing the greatest amount of information shared by parents.

Parents' fears for the child

Parents report a significant amount of anticipatory anxiety related to the rejection they expect their son will experience and its impact on their child's development and adjustment, throughout adolescence and adulthood. It is striking that the concerns are so clearly expressed by all the parents interviewed; however, to the best of their knowledge, none of the children has yet experienced any significant rejection from either peers or adults. As Anna explains: "My kid has never been targeted because of his difference. That doesn't stop me from … worrying that he will be; it'll happen." Parents will bring their children for an assessment at one of two critical developmental crossroads: the start of elementary school or the onset of puberty (Menvielle, 2012). Parents like Patrick and Evelyne make it clear that they consulted professionals not to change their child's sexual orientation or gender identity but rather because they felt their child was unhappy; they also hoped to prevent the gender-variant behaviors from exposing him to dangers outside the home. Evelyne voices clearly her present and future concerns for her child.

> My child is starting school. … He'll be more often outside than at home. That was my first goal [in seeking professional help]; I don't want him to be isolated. You know, we hear so many horror stories, teenagers who run away and then commit suicide … because they're tired of experiencing this and of getting bullied.

All the parents interviewed emphasized the importance of their child feeling supported at home and within their peer group. Because most gender-variant boys like Anthony socialize principally with girls (e.g., Zucker & Bradley, 1995), Anna worries that her son will soon face rejection from his female friends:

> What I'm worried about right now, actually in terms of his age, is that … his friends are girls. The friends whose house he sleeps over at are girls. The friends he wants to come sleep over at our house are girls, with one or two exceptions. Basically, his friends are girls and soon they will be getting to the age where that can't happen anymore. So that is a stage that I have decided to worry about in advance without being able to do anything!

Anna realizes the importance of a peer support or social network for her child. "I worry about whether he will be secure enough with himself and have enough of a support network that he needs to get through those terribly difficult years, that'll be even more difficult because he's who he is." The concern that her child may be the target of hurtful comments and rejection from adults is also quite present for Laurie: "Adults have prejudices. Especially men, their sons have to be very manly. That's still true. … I realize more and more that Roberto is different and that some people won't accept that." Parents are often also keenly aware that there may be negative consequences to not accepting and supporting their child. Regarding Anthony, John states:

> He wouldn't like sports camps, he doesn't like team sports. He's a bright kid and he's got lots of talents … I guess to keep him motivated, confident, that's what my concern is. There's an evil world out there too, which, you know, there's all the questions of drugs, sexually transmitted diseases and all sorts of stuff like this, like violence, that are going to be issues to deal with, so I guess that my primary thing is to make sure he knows he has our support and that he can talk to us.

These parents fear for their children outside the home whereas home is felt to be a place of safety and understanding. As Evelyne shares: "[My wish is] that he be able to deal with the outside world. Because at home, that's not a problem, we're all equipped to deal with him, we don't judge him. We love him as he is, no problem. But he's not at home twenty-four hours a day."

These parents are often described as "protective" or even "overprotective" in the scientific literature (Cohen-Kettenis & Pfäfflin, 2003; McConaghy & Silove, 1992). However, given the overwhelming evidence confirming that these children are in fact at much greater risk of suffering at the hands of their peers and adults, this perception of the parent as overprotective deserves to be revisited. What seems evident is that these parents are vigilant, anticipating the risks to their child and attempting to develop protective strategies to counter these risks. Roberto still likes to put on girls' clothes when he's visiting a home where there are girl-themed dress-up clothes with which to play. Because of this, Laurie prefers to have him play at home with his friends rather than supporting visits to friends' houses, especially without her there: "I'm pretty protective. He's not often been to friends' houses. … I prefer that things happen here at home. … All the children are beautiful. Sometimes it's the parents, geez …".

Parents feel it is their responsibility to protect their child as long as possible from the awareness that he is judged negatively by others for his gender-variant expression. John took Anthony shopping for sneakers and gently steered him away from the pink shoes he wanted, to the more gender-neutral white shoes. As he says, "It didn't bother me if he wanted those that were pink but I decided he'd get some kind of social reaction at school, and that might make him feel uncomfortable." Laurie states clearly that her concern is for her son, not herself:

I feel like if tomorrow morning he dressed as a girl and he went [to school] … I'm not ready for the repercussions; I'm not talking about repercussions on me, I'm talking about the teasing and the "this and that" he'd experience.

These parents are fully aware that their child's gender expression will draw negative reactions to him. They therefore attempt to protect him in various ways, all the while knowing they may only be delaying the inevitable: either they impose certain limits on the child's behavior or society will do so in ways that are likely to be more hurtful to their child.

Inner conflict regarding limit setting

One of the more unexpected facts the data reveal about these parents is that they each decide to limit their child's non-normative gender expression at one time or another, to one degree or another, and struggle with complicated feelings associated with these decisions. They experience a conflict between their desire to allow their child's interests and tastes to blossom fully and their responsibility to protect him. They are keenly aware of the likelihood that their child's spontaneous expression will place him at risk for rejection and even violence.

Laurie expresses relief that Roberto is reaching an age at which she'll be able to explain to him the importance of not talking about some of his interests outside the home. She shares with the interviewer what she could instruct him to say: "See Roberto, it's best you don't say it … don't say: 'Oh, you have a nice dress, I'd love to have one like that!' Spontaneity like that … could make boys who are around say: 'Hey, what's that?!'" She makes a point of explaining her motivation to limit his behavior: "It's more from a place of love, a feeling of wanting to protect [him]." On the other hand, aware of the importance of letting her son express himself, she talks about restricting his desire to wear a dress at a friend's house but states: "He has a place to express himself here [at home]."

As parents attempt to influence their child's choices, they also struggle against the overwhelming conditioning of gender stereotypes to which their child, along with all others, is subjected. In this case, Anna works hard to maintain Anthony's self-expression through his clothing options; she counters the belief that certain colors are not appropriate for boys by pointing to his father's clothing choices: "Once, in daycare, he came back and said: 'Purple is for girls' and I said: 'No, it's not; Daddy has a purple turtleneck, you can both wear your purple turtlenecks.'" Parents notice that their children quickly assimilate prevailing gender norms. Many respond the way Anthony did after he received a negative reaction from boys in his class for bringing in his pink princess shoes. John tells us: "He never did it again but he didn't stop playing with them … he just did it at home. It doesn't work at school,

I guess." Anna and John are among the many parents who choose to give their son much of the control over where and when he will express his gender specific interests. However, these parents continue to carefully monitor the world's response to their child along with their child's moods and reactions as he ventures out into the world expressing his difference. These parents stand ready to adjust their position as needed and seem careful not to confuse their own needs with their child's. As Anna states, "I'll try to support his right to wear a pink t-shirt in the world, but if he feels uncomfortable or whatever—because he's not my figurehead going out in the world for the rights of non-traditional boys—then the t-shirt can go in the drawer!"

Explanation: "Why Is My Child Like This?"

For these parents for whom the question even arose, there seem to be no simple, single, permanent explanations for their child's difference. Their comments reflect their level of involvement in searching for an answer, a search complicated by the state of scientific inquiry which seems to evoke more questions than it answers (Zosuls, Miller, Ruble, Martin, & Fabes, 2011). It is striking to note that they each expressed directly and indirectly a number of hypotheses regarding their child's gender expression. No single hypothesis or belief seemed sufficiently salient to fully satisfy these parents. As an example, speaking of her son, Roberto, Laurie states: "He was born this way," evoking the essentialist idea that something in his biology is determining his behavior. Later she says: "It has an impact that he grew up a lot in a feminine world; he's had many more feminine [role models] around him," evoking the belief that his enactment of gender is determined by his immediate role models. The degree of interest in answering the question: "Why is my child like this?" varied significantly and seemed related to the degree to which parents struggled with accepting their child's atypical gender expression. It may be that answering the question will become more relevant for some of the parents if the child persists in his non-traditional gender expression as he approaches puberty.

The "biological" explanation

Subsumed under this general theme we find different types of hypotheses considered by the parents. For some, the "born this way" hypothesis is associated with the belief in a natural variation in the types of personalities and preferences with which we come into this world. For others like Patrick, one of the parents who has struggled the most with his response to his child's gender expression, Justin's gender-variant expression is the result of an illness: "In my mind, he's ill. He's different, he's ill. It's a strange word 'different;' it may be better to say than 'ill;' but if he was born like this but he's not ill [then]. ..." Patrick and Evelyne are two parents who've struggled to make sense of and support their child's gender-nonconforming behavior. They consulted several mental health professionals in their search for guidance regarding their son's gender-variant expression, eventually meeting with a well-known gender specialist. When asked to talk about why they were consulting him, Evelyne answered, "The only thing I want is for my child to be happy and well. If he's going to be different, then he'll be different and I want him to be equipped to confront others and to accept his difference!" Parents like Patrick and Evelyne make it clear that they consulted professionals not to change their child's sexual orientation or gender identity but rather because they felt their child's gender expression might be the result of an illness. They observed he was unhappy and they hoped to prevent the gender-variant behaviors from exposing him to dangers outside the home.

At the other end of the spectrum, we find Anna, one of the parents who, from the start, struggled the least with her son's atypical gender expression. Interestingly, the question never arose for her, as from the start she clearly saw society as "ill," not her child: "My kid's a wonderful kid and the problem is in North America in this period of time or whatever." For some parents, it seems the "why" question is answered by pointing to society's limited cultural norms for boys.

The "homosexuality/transsexuality" explanation:

Although these parents all understand that their child's gender-variant behavior might represent an early manifestation of homosexuality or transsexuality, none of them felt this was a foregone conclusion. As John explained: "How else he develops in terms of his own sexual identity ... whether he's gay or bisexual or heterosexual ... whatever, that's not important to me." Interestingly, none of the parents expressed the belief that anything could be done now or later to alter their child's sexual orientation if he were gay. For many parents the possibility that their son might some day come out as gay is much less of an issue than managing the child's current gender-variant expression. As Laurie shared:

> Homosexuals, there are some who are very effeminate and very caricatured. Others are very manly. ... For sure the ones who are effeminate, all over the place, we notice them more. ... I'd rather [Roberto] be simple. I don't want him to have a hard time; I don't want him to be sad, that he fall into depression issues.

Laurie worries about the consequences on Roberto's mental health that come from being "noticed" more, from standing out in regards to his gender expression. She knows that this is what places him at risk, more so than the possibility that he may one day express a romantic and/or sexual interest in men.

The "gender influences" explanation

These parents also search for answers in the types of male-female interactions to which the child was exposed. Their own modeling of gender-appropriate behavior seems to be one area of concern. As a single mom, Laurie worries about her son growing up with no male role models in the house: "He's born like this but at the same time there are things like there are no men who pee standing up [at home], no man shaving. … I'm his only model." Later in the interview however, Laurie expresses relief that her son is mostly surrounded by women at home as well as in her extended family, as she worries about men's judgments and attitudes toward her son. "For a man, his child has to be his strong one, his tiger. … For them, my son has a weakness." Then speaking of the father of two girls with whom Roberto plays: "It would be worse if his two daughters were boys, in the sense that [he might feel] 'Is it contagious … ?' I know that's there."

Anna recognizes the importance of having men in Anthony's life but only as long as they support and validate her son's gender expression:

> Having supportive men for a boy; having men around who just [say,] "You're who you are"; I feel that's been wonderful. … I feel that Anthony has the kind of father … [who] totally supports him in who he is with Barbie and all that stuff and doesn't try to get him to play baseball. And then having a teacher like Ryan [who is supportive]; then again I feel, underneath my worries and my whatever … [that] this gives Anthony a base.

It seems these parents welcome the presence of male role models for their sons but only to the extent that they can support the child's atypical gender expression.

Parents' Behaviors in Response to Their Child's Gender Expression

The parents interviewed express clearly their understanding that the protection they can offer their sons will extend only so far. They are fully aware that for their child to become autonomous and fulfilled, they must, like all children, be encouraged to gradually step out of the safety of the home, explore relationships and learn to negotiate their place in the world. These parents prepare their children by nurturing their strengths and resilience, and by deciding when it is in the child's best interests to limit or support certain forms of self-expression.

Developing strength and resilience

These parents carefully consider the choice of environments that will nurture their child's abilities and strengths. Anna explains, "I think he does need security. That's why he's at a small school, an alternative school. We're trying to give him environments that he likes; so for camps, he's gone to artistic camps like arts and music camps, because that's what he likes." Evelyne thoughtfully concluded her interview by stating, " I want him to feel good within himself and I want him to be able to stand up to the world." This sentiment is shared by all the parents in the study. As Laurie states: "[I] try for him to be strong because I'd like that, I'd like him to be strong." Of course, these statements could be made by any parent but are particularly poignant coming from parents who acknowledge the added challenge of preparing their sons for a world hostile to gender-nonconforming individuals. John genuinely values and supports Anthony's non-traditional interests and sees them as a source of strength for his son: "I want him to have confidence in himself. The rest is fine, I mean, I'm actually happy that he can knit well. I can't, I couldn't … he dances well, he's got musical talent, which I don't have. So I'm very, very pleased with these things. It's great!"

Overall, these parents seem convinced that not supporting at least some of their son's interests will hurt him and increase his vulnerability should the judgment and rejection he experiences also come from within the home, a place parents seem quite invested in making safe and supportive. Patrick talks about his Justin's interest in dance and music: "But he loves music. That, I tell myself, has no [gender]. He loves music. He loves dancing. Where the girls take dance classes there's a bunch of boys who dance. He'd like that." Evelyne plans to send her son to a school with a strong emphasis on the performing arts: "[When Justin plays with his sisters], they create dances, choreographies. … He dances and he's really good, too!" Speaking of Justin's integration into this school, Evelyne says: "I think he would fit really well there. He's more artistic than athletic." These parents deploy considerable energy toward accepting their son's difference and supporting the development of strengths and resiliencies. They work hard at finding ways to encourage his autonomy and at finding environments that will accept his difference.

Limiting and permitting

When these parents feel it will not significantly curtail their child's development and well-being, they will sometimes steer him toward gender-neutral options for play or clothing choice. Regarding the choice of activities, Evelyne comments: "Well, now we've solved the problem of 'boy games' and 'girl games;' we go to the park a lot. He loves playing in the park; we go outside and play in the park, ride bicycles. He loves it!" Regarding clothing options, Anna shares this anecdote:

> He wanted the little pink Dora sneakers. … We worked on getting his attention diverted and convincing him he wanted different sneakers instead, because sneakers are expensive and they are difficult to get. And I didn't want him getting Dora sneakers and then somebody saying whatever and then there would be an issue around

sneakers. ... That was some caving on my part to social pressure so there's a kind of judgment call thing.

Parents are vigilant and anticipate how receptive various environments will be to their child. They cannot take for granted that their child will be welcome everywhere. The same parents who will purchase a pretty pink dress for their son to wear at home, and maybe with extended family members or friends, will insist he leave any sign of his difference at home when it comes time to return to school. These parents go to great lengths to explain to their child the reasons for restricting their gender expression in certain contexts while attempting to preserve their self-expression.

The following anecdote illustrates the complex set of priorities with which parents are confronted, as they feel at times compelled to both limit and support their child's behavior. In kindergarten, Roberto had wanted to do ballet and wear a pink tutu, a costume item reserved for girls. Laurie watched the movie *Billy Elliot* with him; She did so preventively, assuming he would someday feel marginalized by his interest. *Billy Elliot* is the story of a young boy who resists his Dad's wish for him to take up boxing, in order to follow his dream of studying ballet. Roberto had practiced a dance choreographed by Laurie's mother and, unbeknownst to Laurie, had performed the routine in class. After stating in a rather frustrated tone that her mother didn't think about the potentially negative outcome for Roberto, Laurie describes what ensued: "They stopped the music in the middle [of the routine] because some in the class were saying 'What's that? Ballet? Guys don't do that! What *is* that dance?!'" The teacher, in Laurie's opinion, was unable to intervene effectively to limit or neutralize the negative feedback from Roberto's classmates. Laurie then explains that if her son had been a bit older, she would have said to him: "Look, Roberto, you can do ballet here [at home]. At some point we'll sign you up for ballet classes. ... And there, there'll be lots of others like you. But right now, when it's about school, you'll [need to be like the others]." Remarkably, when Roberto told her later on that he no longer wanted to do ballet, she responded as follows:

> Look, Roberto, ... if you don't want to do it anymore because you're not interested anymore ... that's fine; but if you don't want to do it anymore because others are saying 'What's that?!' ... You saw *Billy Elliot* who becomes a great dancer! It's just right now, they ... There are others like you; there are others like you in your school; there are others elsewhere. At some point everyone [with your interests] comes together!

Laurie fights for him to hold on to his interest in ballet and is quite moving in her struggle to reassure Roberto that his interest in ballet is legitimate. As much as she feels his interest places him at risk, she attempts to reduce his feeling of isolation and marginalization with the promise that there are other boys like him and that he will someday meet them.

IN SUMMARY

Two main areas of concern emerged from the parent interviews: The first, their fear for their son at present and in the near future, as he ventures out into the world, and more specifically, as he advances in grades at school. Parents anticipate that their child will experience rejection and be the target of teasing and bullying. They worry that these experiences will increase his vulnerability to depression and suicidal feelings, that he could run away, turn to alcohol and drugs as a means of escaping an intolerable situation, and develop a sense of self-hatred or low self-worth. Without necessarily being familiar with the overwhelming empirical evidence supporting their fears, these parents identify clearly the present and future risks to their son's development. The second major concern expressed relates to the complex, moment-by-moment decision-making process in which parents are engaged as they monitor the child's expression outside the home. These parents must constantly weigh their son's need for spontaneous self-expression against the risk of his experiencing rejection and ridicule from peers and adults alike. Whether or not they are fully aware of the reasons motivating their decisions, their statements reveal deeply conflicted feelings associated with curbing their son's expression, interests, tastes and preferences. They attempt to mitigate the potential negative impact on his sense of self, his self-esteem and his self-confidence in various ways, such as explaining their reasons or attempting to distract the child, interesting him in more gender-neutral activities or choices. They express their commitment to developing their son's strengths and resiliencies as a protection against the rejection and bullying he is expected to experience eventually outside the home; they do so by validating many of his gender-nonconforming behaviors and preferences, whenever and wherever possible. A study of 42 parents of gender-variant children and teens by Hill and Menvielle (2009) arrived at similar conclusions:

> A central feature of their [the parents'] experience is the struggle created by the pursuit of contradictory goals: the wish to support their child's self-expression with its concomitant increase in social visibility against the need to maintain personal safety through monitoring, censoring, and social conformity. Such unavoidable tensions and dilemmas are part of the daily lives of these youth and parents. (p. 267)

It seems day-to-day reality for these parents finds their child exploring, choosing, changing and expressing tastes, preferences and talents. They appear to be in tune with the fluidity and the exploration in which their son is engaged. At some point, however, they are each faced with the limits, great or small, they feel they must impose on their child's expression, a dynamic Diane Ehrensaft (2011) refers to as "walking the gender-creativity tightrope" (p. 116). And as they steer their son away from wearing and drawing pretty outfits, singing his favorite female pop idol's song, pursuing his love of ballet or figure skating, they may wonder anxiously, if, in attempting to shield him, they are stifling the seeds of a next Calvin Klein, Pavarotti, Baryshnikov or Elvis Stojko.

RECOMMENDATIONS

Inform, Empower and Support Parents and Children

While far from exhaustive, here is a short list of ideas for families and professionals interested in supporting gender-creative children that emerged from the issues broached by the parents in this study: create community, expand the safety zone, transform school environments and challenge your own biases.

Create community by finding opportunities for parents and children to socialize with other families in order to reduce their sense of isolation. These should be safe spaces where every family member can drop their guard and no longer feel they need to monitor their behavior or their safety. Several opportunities have been cropping up throughout North America in the past decade or so in the form of summer camps, arts schools and formal and informal yearly conferences and gatherings.

Expand the safety zone. Parents evaluate home as being a place of complete safety and at the other end of the continuum, school as the greatest source of potential danger for their gender-nonconforming child. Parents should be supported in finding additional public and private spaces for their child to be themselves: Extended family, neighbors, friends' homes, day camps, activity clubs, extracurricular classes are often more contained and more manageable spaces than is school. The adults in charge of these spaces can frequently be approached and encouraged to transform the space into one that is inclusive of all children's gender expression. If parents meet with resistance to this idea, they can still insist that the people in charge be alert and protective of the gender-nonconforming child in their care.

Transform school environments through existing frameworks. Schools are often already involved in the implementation of anti-bullying and anti-violence initiatives; parents can find out who the key individuals are in a given school and approach them to make sure gender expression and gender identity are included topics in the school's efforts.

Challenge your own biases. Counselors and therapists must challenge their own biases and become informed regarding the development of gender, gender expression and gender identity if they wish to be of help to these families. Provide parents with reliable, normalizing information regarding gender-nonconformity in children. Provide a space for them to talk about their fears and their dilemmas, a space in which they feel heard and validated. In other words, model the space they are attempting to create for their own children.

Expanding the Gender Playground

In order to support these families, the prevailing beliefs regarding gender norma-tivity must be challenged in their entirety. Not only to create a space for gender-nonconforming children to develop and flourish, but to create such a space for all children. The same culture that condemns the young boy's dream of doing ballet in a pink tutu sends a clear message to all boys and all children that they are expected to limit the exploration of their creative self. All those involved in the lives of young children need to be empowered to push against attempts to restrict any child's creative self-expression. Ideally, this can occur when children are at a young age and look to the adults for approval regarding their exploration, when they begin to map out the gender playground in which they will allow themselves to play. For every child, the concern should be to make the playground as large, inviting and varied as possible, offering all children an infinite number of options for play and self-discovery. In this way, the gender-variant child will be supported. As important, it may then become possible for the boys who naturally gravitate toward basketball and hockey to continue to do so but in this new playground to also feel they can join the school choir, pursue their interest in oil painting or share with their friends how they cried at their grandmother's funeral.

Table 1. Participant Descriptions.

Alias	Age	Marital Status	Cultural Background	First Language	Education	Child's Alias	Child's Age
Laurie	40	Single	Caribbean / Caucasian	French	High School	Roberto	8
John	47	Married (to Anna)	Caucasian	English	University	Anthony	8
Anna	45	Married (to John)	Caucasian / Jewish	English	University	Anthony	8
Evelyne	44	Married (to Patrick)	Caucasian	French	High School	Justin	6
Patrick	41	Married (to Evelyne)	Caucasian	French	High School	Justin	6

NOTES

1. Although a small percentage of gender-nonconforming boys may eventually identify as "transgender," we cannot generally distinguish these children from those who will keep identifying as male. The decision was therefore made to refer to these children as boys in order to broaden the discussion and include all male-bodied children who do not fit narrowly defined gender stereotypes.

2. This study as well as the studies referenced in this chapter speak to a present-day North American and Western European outlook on childhood gender-nonconformity. Many cultures elsewhere in the world operate from different and much broader perspectives on this topic (e.g., Bartlett & Vasey, 2006).

CHAPTER NINE

Ten Fingers, Ten Toes, and Potentially Trans

The Everyday Revolution of Gender-Diverse Parenting

ARWYN DAEMYIR

INTRODUCTION

While resources are starting to become available in support of children who have already asserted their gender-nonconformity, creativity, or transgender status (see Ehrensaft, 2011), little conceptualizing has been performed on preventing the damage done to these children before their "coming out" process. This chapter seeks to fill this gap, and describes an approach, termed "Gender-Diverse Parenting," or GDP, which I will claim may improve the environment in early childhood to reduce the trauma done to transgender and gender-creative children, and increase transformative "gender justice" (Travers, 2012) for all children. Although potentially revolutionary, GDP is not a radical alternative to a neutral default. Rather, I show here how current parenting practices are actively harmful and intrinsically (though often invisibly and sometimes unintentionally) biased in favor of children who are willing and able to conform to the gender expectations based on the sex assigned to them at birth. I offer these challenges to the status quo not to destroy, and certainly not to insult, but to nourish and create space for children and the adults they will become to flourish as who they are.

I am a theorist situated outside the academic sphere; a scholar and practitioner of Gender-Diverse Parenting with my white middle-class family (which includes at least one gender-creative child); and, like so many queer women of my generation, a former "tomboy" and gender-creative child. I was born toward the end of the 1970s "unisex" era (1965–1985) of children's clothing (Paoletti, 2012), and as such was raised largely in hand-me-downs from my older brother: rainbow turtlenecks and pink overalls, blue corduroys and white blouses. I was granted the freedom to decide what being a girl meant to me, but never the freedom to discover whether I was even a "girl"; I received glimmers of acceptance from my parents about non-straight sexualities before "coming out" as bisexual, but the possibility of me or any of my peers being transsexual or transgender was never mentioned. This foundation, for good and for ill, has helped shape much of my thinking around what might be possible when it comes to parenting and gender.

I present GDP as an alternative both to traditional parenting and to the "gender-neutral," "unisex," or "gender-free" parenting I experienced growing up. Traditionally, normatively gendered items (clothes, toys, decorations) are offered to children, and in some cases, only these "gender-appropriate" items may be allowed. Consequently, a child is steered into accepting and performing their birth-assigned gender, either "boy" or "girl." Parents may believe they are responding to "natural" and absolute gender differences, or they may actively seek to create these differences as a reflection of their valuing of difference-sexism (Kane, 2012). On the other side are gender-neutral, gender-free, or unisex parenting (which I will collectively call "oppositional" practices), wherein highly gendered clothes, toys, and colors (e.g., frilly shirts, dolls and trucks, pink or "camo" anything) are removed from a child's environment and replaced by gender-neutral options, in an effort to steer the child into de-gendered, "genderqueer," or androgynous ways of being.

This chapter has two aims. The first is to challenge approaches to parenting and early childhood education that undermine or actively oppose the full humanity and personhood of women/girls and sexual and gender minorities, which both traditional and oppositional parenting practices do (traditional parenting does so by design and intent; oppositional parenting does so by failing to challenge the positioning of parents as authors of their children's gender). Second, it aims to propose alternatives which do not merely strip away problematic elements of sexist culture, but include positive practices which are actionable, immediate, and accessible. However, these specific practices do and must arise from the theoretical, from collective and individual lived experience, from our passionate longing for a better world for our children. No approach to parenting which is based on a list of forbidden or mandated behaviors can be sufficiently adaptive and culturally competent to be transformative in the ways transgender and gender-creative children need. These children need not merely access to clothing and bathrooms and sports teams, but a radical shift in their cultural milieus: a psychic and social creation of space and welcome, where the old unwanted restrictions will fall away and expansive inclusive possibilities will grow in their place.

To these ends, this chapter is organized into four main sections. We will begin with explaining the need for Gender-Diverse Parenting, by asserting its foundational precepts, including the prevalence of transgender and gender-creative children, and following the logical ramifications of these assertions. This will lead to the conclusion that parenting around gender must be fundamentally reconsidered for all children, not only those already identified as transgender or gender-creative. Next, we will examine what constitutes GDP, identifying it as epistemological rather than prescriptive or proscriptive, as a means to engage in transformative gender justice rather than as an end goal in itself. We will then explore what it means to undertake GDP, considering both the ramifications within the family and for the child, and exploring specific ways the approach may be implemented. Finally, I identify areas within and around this topic that are in need of future expansion and examination and suggest potential roles of educators, clinicians, researchers, and parents in promoting Gender-Diverse Parenting to a broader audience.

WHY ALL CHILDREN NEED GENDER-DIVERSE PARENTING

As outlined in Diane Ehrensaft's chapter in this volume, transgender and gender-creative children both exist and matter. This is obvious reason enough to change our approach to parenting once a child has "come out" to us. As we will see through the following points, however, it is also sufficient justification to implement Gender-Diverse Parenting, even if GDP were not also beneficial for cisgender, gender-normative children. The first point, which most persons-on-the-street, gender essentialists, and transgender rights activists could likely agree on, is that gender is real, intrinsic, and, mostly, immutable.[1] One's understanding of one's gender might change over the course of a life, and may even evolve and expand and settle. And yet there is nothing any person can do to change one's gender, much less can any outside force.

Secondly, we can recognize that gender is innate, and present from the beginning of life. Put simply, whether or not a person knows what their[2] gender is, before they even have a concept of a category for "gender," some part of them inside is already gendered, already awaiting their growing discovery of it as they learn and mature and live. The people around the individual tell them what gender means to their culture(s); although culture constructs meaning from gender, however, culture does not create anyone's gender to begin with.

Now we move into the more contested assertion that genitals are not gender. While I do not make the now-common distinction between sex and gender, as I find that this distinction reinforces cisgender ways of being as more "real" than transgender ones, it is imperative that we recognize that an individual's gender cannot be determined by an examination of their genitals, either in adulthood or, more to the point, at birth. Intersex or "ambiguous" genitalia and the reported experience of transgender adults challenge the prevailing belief that genitals are at all indicative of a person's authentic gender. Instead, we must rely on subjective testimony to know a person's gender; that is, we can only know when a child (or adult) tells us.[3]

From these three points, we can conclude that we cannot know ahead of this self-pronouncement which children are going to be transgender and which cisgender, much less which will prefer a more gender-typical gender performance and which a more creative one. It could be argued that the population of transgender and/or gender-creative children is so infinitesimal that these minorities ought not be taken into account when constructing parenting paradigms. My two-pronged response to this is that transgender and gender-nonconforming individuals are a much larger minority than often conceived of, and that their existence, however much a minority, matters for itself. Further, as feminists at least as far back as Adrienne Rich (1980) have noted (though often at the last moment eschewing the logical trans-inclusive conclusion in favor of a transmisogynist gender essentialism), the assumption that a gender, gender role, and gender performance should be assigned based on genital appearance at birth is harmful for all children.

There are many arguments about the prevalence of the transgender and transsexual population, with reported numbers as low as 1/100,000 to as high as 1/200. Olyslager and Conway (2007), however, say the rate of transsexual women "appears likely to be on the order of at least 1:100 (i.e., 1%) or more" (p. 23), and point out the flaws in several of the lower-prevalence figures. These rates, further, are consistently seen as lower than that of transsexual men, and do not include the wider transgender umbrella (which includes people who are neither men nor women, or some configuration of both, or exist as another gender altogether), a population even more poorly counted than transsexual women and men. Regardless of the accuracy of these specific rates, some sizeable minority of the population persistently expresses a transgender or transsexual identity. And key for our purposes, given the innate and immutable nature of gender, and that most reports even from those who transition as adults express a persistence from the start of life (even if the individual was not able to identify the feeling until later), we can conclude that the prevalence for the infant population is the same as for the adult population, and therefore around or above 1% of all babies born are/will be transgender.

Given the contradictory nature of most gender expectations, I think it's safe to say that no child, no person, conforms entirely to the gender expectations of their society, nor can they. Yet, we label a large minority of children, especially male or assigned-male children, "gender-nonconforming" because they actively seek out and engage in gender-expectation-defying behavior, dress, or activities in ways deemed overly outside of the norm. Sometimes this is transitory, sometimes permanent, sometimes indicative of a more lasting queerness (such as a non-heterosexual orientation), sometimes a response to an overly restrictive gendered environment, but regardless: in every sort of family in every culture around the world, whether they are made welcome and comfortable or not, we find gender-nonconforming children.

We do not have to look far to find evidence that current approaches to parenting do not well serve transgender and gender-creative children.[4] We also know that parental acceptance is protective against many of the adverse outcomes of living in a cissexist society (Travers et al., 2012). But, as Hill and Menvielle (2009) identify, parents of gender-variant children must go through a turbulent period of "struggling" to accept that their child deviates from the cis-heteronormative path assumed for them; during this period, children may experience episodes of having their gender identity or preferred performance suppressed, derided, or denied, which, even should a parent later abandon this unfortunate attempt, may leave a child damaged, and certainly takes energy away from their primary developmental work in order to defend or protect their "true gender selves" (Ehrensaft, 2011).

In traditional parenting, the question for parents around gender can be phrased as: "Did I do a good enough job inculcating in my children cis-heteronormative gender roles?" For children, it is: "Can I live with myself in the cis-heteronormative gender role I have been assigned, and if not, am I able to rebel enough to create space for my individuality to manifest?" I do not assert that this is a conscious question for the majority of parents (and indeed, do not doubt that many would be horrified if made aware of it), but rather that it is the question, so basic as to be unspoken, driving the majority of parenting practices, which are functionally sexist, cissexist, and heterosexist; that is, which devalue women, transgender individuals, and non-heterosexual individuals. The cis-heteronomative gender roles, as damaging as they are, are taken as inviolate, to, at most, be rebelled against; questioning the appropriateness of placing them upon children in the first place is rarely done.[5] Children are left to rebel or accept, but are not encouraged to actively engage with gender exploration; whether they ever come to know and understand their gender and gender's place in their social milieu is left to chance, later in their lives.

The approach of Gender-Diverse Parenting, the need for and shape of which I hope are becoming clearer, is similar to the one taken by affirming parents of gender-nonconforming or transgender children, as described by Pyne (2012). In his study of how these parents relate to their children, "participants refused to problematize their child; they searched for affirmation for their child; they relinquished parental authority; and they held open possibilities for their child's future" (p. 35). I contend that all children would be better served by this approach, which legitimizes their subjective authority (that is, their ability and right to speak to their own gender). Pyne (2012) goes on to tell us:

> Social theorist and political philosopher Axel Honneth has written extensively about modern social conflicts, proposing that all such conflicts are primarily struggles for recognition. The experience of social injustice, he contends, corresponds to the with-holding of legitimate recognition, as human subjects require a context of recognition to thrive. (p. 66)

Gender-normative cisgender children are offered some gender acknowledgment because they are able and willing to go along with the norms of their assigned gender. However, they are still in many ways unseen, through the deprivation of this process of parental recognition. Their own genders and gender performances are valorized only to the extent they reify and reinforce the norms, but are not in and of themselves authenticated.

We can now see how traditional parenting creates unnecessary harm, both directly and indirectly, to gender-normative and gender-creative and transgender children alike. Some gender-creative and transgender children may be unable or unwilling to express their need for parental recognition in ways sufficient for their family to acknowledge, and thus are denied this essential process. Gender-normative children are denied autonomy and authenticity when their families rely on their willingness to accept as "good enough" the gendered ways of being they have been assigned. Gender-creative and transgender children are harmed when placed into an environment in which their peers are ignorant of gender's diversity. And gender-normative children are made to perpetuate sexist beliefs and norms that remove the possibility of their full humanity.

We are obligated, morally and pragmatically, to reduce unnecessary harm to our children. Therefore a new approach to parenting is required for all children and all families.

DEFINING GENDER-DIVERSE PARENTING

Based on these above-noted failures of traditional approaches to parenting, then, it is possible to reach toward an approach that would address each of these and in so doing define Gender-Diverse Parenting. GDP is an epistemological approach to parenting which includes four defining features: a) the subjective reports of trans-gender lived experience are respected and held as valid and true; b) the provisional-ity of gender assignments is made explicit; c) the authority over and authorship of gender are relocated from the parent/caregiver to the child; and d) an environment is provided in which every child is able to express their authentic gender identity and to construct a gender performance that combines their innate preferences with the specific codes and mores of their culture(s).

What does it mean to assert that GDP is an epistemological approach? GDP rests on the belief that gender is both knowable and subjective: that is, gender falls within the field of what can be known (if we can assert to "know" anything, and do not fall into the skeptic's vat of being unable to prove we are not all disembodied brains experiencing remarkably realistic simulations); one's own gender can be known only by first-person experience, where experience is a convincing, if at times confusing, combination of perception, introspection, memory, and reason; and that another person's gender can only be known by direct, honest testimony.[6] Further, GDP must be seen as an ongoing engagement rather than a single stylistic choice: a method of coming into knowledge of gender (the parent of the child's gender, the child of their own gender, and also the child's knowledge of society's understanding of gender) rather than a goal to which to aspire (Steup, 2012).

To enter into "Gender-Diverse Parenting" as a means to its own end confuses the process with the product; there is no way to measure the "success" of GDP by looking at the child and their gender and gender performance. To do so is to replace the cis-heteronormative gender boxes with their opposite, which is perhaps a marginal improvement but is neither fundamentally transformative nor just. As Julia Serano (2007, p. 359) says, "Whenever we assign values to other people's genders and sexualities ... we are automatically creating or reaffirming some kind of hierarchy." Instead, GDP is a means to the end goal of transformative gender justice for all: its "success" can be measured not in the gender-creativity of a child or a generation, but rather in the gender (in)justice experienced by the child within the family unit and within the society at large.[7] The point is not to change the yardstick by which we measure parenting, but to change the process, to look at children for themselves, to value and center their subjective experience.

Parents practicing or drawn to GDP are not necessarily responding to an inherent creativity or nonconformity in their child but are actively engaging in the subversion of gender normativity. This may be because they themselves are living queer, trans, or gender-non-normative lives (Walks, 2012), or are otherwise interested in transformative gender justice as part of a larger radical agenda (e.g., Witterick & Stocker, 2012). It is an active, preventive philosophy rather than a reactive one, and yet it distinguishes itself also from previous attempts at oppositional gender-neutral parenting with its expansion of possibilities, rather than the reduction of them (as documented by Paoletti, 2012). In contrast to both gender-neutral and traditional parenting styles, described in the Introduction to this chapter, GDP relocates the "author-ity," that is, the right to write one's life, over gender and gender expression from the parent to the child, regardless of whether the parent seeks to cultivate or impose a traditional gender presentation or a divergent one. Parents who practice GDP do not abdicate their rights and responsibilities, but rather reframe them. Traditionally, parents guide a child into an assigned gender and educate them about "proper" gender performance. However, this always overwrites a child's own narrative and, particularly in the case of transgender or gender-creative children, imposes damaging barriers to the expressions of their authentic selves. GDP also calls for guidance and education, but in different ways. With GDP, parents and caregivers guide a child through the process of exploring gendered possibilities, educate the child in the various meanings (and lack thereof) of gender codes and performances in their specific cultural environment(s), and finally, encourage developmentally appropriate independence and autonomy with regard to gender.

DOING GENDER-DIVERSE PARENTING

The exact ways a family engages in Gender-Diverse Parenting will vary, in accordance with the particularities of their cultural environment. However, several characteristics of these choices are generalizable.

The key feature of Gender-Diverse Parenting, and what sets it apart from the "gender-neutral parenting" I was raised with, is the always provisional assignment of gender. This involves leaving room for a child to announce their own gender identity as they come to understand and recognize it. In the case of traditional parenting with its strictly assigned binary genders, children may speak up and assert a gender identity other than the one assigned and expected, but typically this takes extensive effort on their part. This effort may be one source of increased levels of stress and stress-related morbidities found among transgender and gender atypical children (Roberts et al., 2012). In an environment in which Gender-Diverse Parenting is practiced, the child is placed in a position of power to declare their gender; when a gender and pronoun are assigned, this is done with an explicit articulation of its provisionality, and the parents or caregivers are conscious that this is "a guess" about which they may be informed to be in error. This movement of the source of knowledge of gender identity from the caregiver(s) to the child(ren) is what allows all the other features of Gender-Diverse Parenting to be meaningful. In this way, not only are transgender children able to assert their gender freely, without first fighting against a gender imposed on them, but cisgender children are also able to construct their identities. Rather than "I am told I am a girl, so I guess I must be" (and also passively receiving the lists of meanings of what "girl-ness" entails), in the case of Gender-Diverse Parenting children finally have the chance to have an active, interrogative, and positive relationship with their gender, as in "I might be a girl; am I? Yes! Now, what does that mean to me? What type of girl am I (today); what type of girl do I want to be?" Rather than confusing children about gender, this approach to parenting allows children to develop a deeper, more nuanced understanding of gender than they would otherwise be allowed.

Of course, in order for children to identify their innate gender and construct their desired gender performance they need to have an awareness of what is considered possible in their sociocultural environment. Thus, another feature of Gender-Diverse Parenting is an introduction to a diversity of gendered ways of being. While traditional anti-sexist parenting seeks to provide usually "strong" representations of women and girls to counter the nonexistent or in-distress female characters of much media (Kane, 2012), Gender-Diverse Parenting expands this concept to varying genders and also gender performances.

The specifics of this introduction, including the categories, labels, terms, and potentialities for genders and gender performances, depend largely on the sociocultural environment in which the family is situated, and may include a mix of one or more "contradictory" cultural schemas. But in every population group, every culture, and every language are found words for both typical and atypical experiences of gender. Parents or caregivers doing GDP present as full a range of the gender diversity as they can from the cultural contexts that make sense to them, not only to teach gender-normative children about "diversity," but to allow children who may be atypical to identify the words and ways of being that best reflect and represent their authentic core, or "true gender self." Again, instead of creating confusion for children, encountering gender diversity provides them with more information that they can use to construct their understanding of gender, rather than being limited to a nursery story of "blue boys and pink girls, strong dads and nurturing moms" that is proved false even by a cursory observation of the world. Such a falsely simplistic narrative creates cognitive dissonance when its invalidity is discovered. An observant child might ask about other errors or even lies imparted by their parents. It may be more likely that such questions are left unasked, observed disparities are left unexplained, and opportunities for learning and learning to think differently are lost. This can contribute to and validate children's mutual and often violent policing of gender and gendered norms on the playground, which occurs with epidemic frequency and which we erroneously call "bullying" (see Stein, 2003, and Moy, 2008, for critiques of framing gendered violence and sexual harassment as "bullying").

Examples of how parents and caregivers can introduce a diversity of gendered ways of being include:

- seeking out alternative children's books, more of which are becoming available at an ever-increasing rate these days;[8]
- making sure the family's social circle not only includes but discusses diversity, not in a tokenized way, but in a way that recognizes and honors each person's distinct take on gender;

- finding diverse role models, people our children can look up to in the areas of their passion who exist outside gender norms;
- imaginative play (more on this below);
- and, because there are many otherwise wonderful and creative books that nevertheless fall into sexist tropes, "gender-switching" normative media: that is, swapping out "he" for "she" in adventure books, or naming the stay-at-home skirt-clad character the "daddy," or referring to the bemittened bunny as "ze."

We can also encourage playing with gender roles and pronouns. Play is a fundamentally important part of a child's development. Through play, children learn about themselves, the object or act they're engaged with, social and cultural limits, and the intricacies of human interaction. There are few topics more important and pervasive than gender. Therefore, parents and caregivers who encourage children to play with gender and gender roles are helping them understand their own gender, others' genders, and the role of gender in their society. Couching it in the slightly distanced form of imaginative play allows children to experience a variety of gendered ways of being without destabilizing their own identity, whether cisgender or transgender. (Certainly, children who play at being kittens are not made permanently unsure of their internal sense of species.) And yet, that first-person engagement with a variety of gender experiences allows children who do not fit in the culturally supported cisgender, gender-normative paradigm to discover or create the roles, labels, and pronouns that offer the sense of "belonging" and "self" that is a cornerstone of healthy development.

When children have had autonomy in gender identity, when they have grown knowing a diverse variety of potential gender identities, when they have been allowed to experiment and experience a wide array of genders and gender performances, and when they have been encouraged to construct their own, authentic gendered expressions, the last step is for parents to accept those identities and performances whatever they may be. Progressive styles of traditional parenting tend to promote acceptance of a "fully formed" or "out" gender-creative, gay/lesbian, or transgender identity in children, but these prior steps tend to be skipped. Without parental encouragement, assistance, or support, however, the odds of a child escaping the normalizing influence of kyriarchy are low. However, given an environment in which potential gender variance is welcomed, whatever identity and performance are eventually expressed need and deserve to be validated and accepted. While traditional parenting too often fails at the acceptance of creative, atypical, non-normative, or transgender identities or gender performances, progressive parents, those most drawn to

Gender-Diverse Parenting, may have the opposite problem. The latter may have difficulties accepting gender identities and performances that are more in line with normative gender expectations. This is the parental version of what Serano (2007) terms subversivism: "the practice of extolling certain gender and sexual expressions and identities simply because they are unconventional or nonconforming" (p. 346), and she goes on to demonstrate its failures for an adult population. There are additional pitfalls to subversivism for the juvenile population, however, because although the emotional and social costs for the lack of parental acceptance and validation are greater in transgender or gender-creative children, the developmental need for them is no less for cisgender, gender-normative children. Thus a key feature of Gender-Diverse Parenting and a primary challenge for all parents and caregivers is to accept whatever gender and gender performance preferences their child expresses, and furthermore to accept their validity in the moment without necessarily forming an attachment to these as permanent, persistent fact. While not dismissing gender typicality or gender-creativity as "just a phase," parents practicing GDP work to accept and honor their child's stated preference and identity without forcing the child to be making a decision now that will be held true for their entire lives, although it may prove to be so.

GETTING TO GENDER-DIVERSE PARENTING

We have so far discussed why we need to replace current parenting practices; discussed what practices, which I have collectively termed GDP, might better instill a deep and complex understanding of gender in our children; and explored how this will allow all children, transgender or gender-creative or otherwise, to flourish. Now, I wish to discuss how to support and spread this change in consciousness, because although individual children do and will benefit from having the right and ability to assert their own gender, from getting to play with gender, from having access to a rainbow of gendered toys and clothes: only when a critical mass of people adopt not just these practices, but also the philosophies and precepts supporting the practices will our culture change in the ways our transgender and gender-creative children require. Assuming I am addressing a sympathetic audience, I can ask: How do we do this? What actionable steps can we take to promote a cultural change? I believe there is a role for every reader to play in getting GDP widespread acceptance:

Researchers: we need papers to cite when we are speaking to policy makers, but we don't need any more research in which the gender-nonconforming child is a subject (nor even "participant"). We need to ask questions based in a centering and humanization of transgender lived experiences. These questions may include: What supports will help parents, particularly in marginalized or oppressed communities, defy sexist gender norms in their parenting? What will help them weather any social reprisals they may experience? What curricula can be introduced in schools to reduce rates of gendered violence? What work is already being done in communities that is supporting gender expression and gender authority for children?

Clinicians: if you work with transgender and gender-creative children and their families, you have the opportunity to encourage the framing of gender assertion as the proper role of every young human (and as with many developmental stages, this is one that, if not engaged in, in childhood, may be circled back to; keep in mind, perhaps, that the parents you interact with may need validation for their own gender journeys as well). If you work with a more general population of parents, there may be ways, without violating parental autonomy, to encourage an exploration of GDP as a healthier approach to gender in parenting; how this might be best accomplished I leave to clinicians to discuss and discover together. As clinicians, particularly those with doctorate-level letters after your names, you are seen as "experts," and thus it is in your power to validate parenting approaches in the popular mind (whether you believe that power to be your right or not).

Educators: although your primary concern may be students who are presenting as gender-creative or transgender, you can remember that perhaps several times that number of students are hidden, and so it is not only the visibly transgressive children and teens who need support and acceptance from their peers and teachers. Most of the students you work with will also likely one day become parents: In what ways can you influence now the parenting around gender they will engage in? When you talk about gender-creative and transgender students' futures, do you allow space for their choosing to become parents? How might you encourage them to rethink the ways they were parented, not to incite hatred for their parents' failures but to use that experience to bring them to more accepting approaches? Are there ways you can connect your "out" students with younger children as mentors, or to struggling parents as helpers?

Theorists and academics: at all times, we can center lived experience, and amplify authors and writers (whether granted "validity" by virtue of publication or not) from the communities about which we theorize. Do not only listen to parents, nor even only to those who were transgender or gender-creative as children, but listen as well to those who are transgender or gender-creative children now. Their language may be immature, but their ideas are often sophisticated and innovative beyond our own. They deserve to be listened to, and not just to improve our arguments but for themselves.

Parents: we have so much potential to create, or squash, space for our children. We are so often overwhelmed by the demands of daily life that feeling obligated to add on another "cause," no matter how worthy we find it, can send us to tears, or drink, or defensive anger. And yet, I encourage you to think about Gender-Diverse Parenting not as yet another thing for you to do, but as a reconceptualization of the important work you already do every day. Although mentally making this shift will likely be difficult, the act of putting it into practice may surprise you with its ease. Gender-Diverse Parenting has much to offer your child(ren), but it has so much to offer you, too. How much more time would you have if you weren't trying to control your child's gendered expressions, if you weren't fighting over their clothes, and their toys, and their hair, and the games they played? How much more energy would you have if you weren't worried about who they were going to grow up to be, because you knew that all authentic gendered ways of being were okay? How much more room for love would there be if you let go of the fear that you weren't doing enough to shape their futures? How much more could you enjoy this moment if you offered yourself and your child compassion and acceptance for who you are, and who they are, and knew that each of you was doing the best you could? How much more would you feel capable of if you were on the same side as your child, knowing that even if you faced a hostile world you were doing it together? How much more freedom would you have if you stopped channeling the hatred of the gender-non-normative from an uncaring society onto your child?

If I could offer a suggestion to the parents reading this, an assignment if you will, it would be first to stop enforcing gender norms. Stop doing the work of a culture that actively seeks to dehumanize you and your child(ren). And then, as you're able, find support for this shift. Even if your child isn't gender-creative or transgender, we all can benefit from bouncing ideas and sharing experiences with other parents seeking to stop perpetuating gender bigotry. Talk with your neighbors, find sympathetic groups online, read works by gender-creative and transgender writers.

There is much work to be done to support openly gender-creative and transgender children, and you will find abundant examples throughout this book. It is, of course, necessary work; it is also, however, reactive, trying to play catch-up to save a population already under attack. Without abandoning that important pursuit, I want us to take a moment to imagine a world in which it has largely been made unnecessary, in which children from before birth are offered space and guidance to become authentically themselves, in which they start out knowing they are accepted and welcomed exactly as they are.

NOTES

1. However, what those groups mean by real, intrinsic, and immutable can be very different, indeed, diametrically opposed. Gender essentialists use this supposition to deny the realities of transgender embodiment and experience in favor of a "real" pre-transition gender; transgender rights activists use it to affirm the gender that was underlying the whole time.

2. I use the singular "they/their/them" throughout this chapter when a specific gender is not being referenced. I do this to avoid the sexism of the generic "he," the exclusion of non-binary genders of using only "he/she," and the confusion of attempting to alternate between all possible singular specific pronouns.

3. To follow this logical aside for a moment: Does this mean we, lacking a sufficient fluency in canine communication, cannot know a dog's gender? Or does it instead mean that a dog cannot be said to have a gender? I will leave the debate to the philosophers, and suggest only that for human purposes, until we are able to communicate meaningfully with another species as sentient and introspective as we are, perhaps it doesn't matter. Rather than "gender is between the ears and sex is between the legs," perhaps it's more meaningful to say that "gender is human, and sex is not-human." Not to assert that nonhuman animals lack a gender, but rather that we lack a way of knowing it (because another's gender can only be known by direct testimony), and that in any case where gender is knowable (humans), sex as a category is irrelevant. Sex is a pseudo-objective categorizer to be used in cases in which gender testimony is impossible, and as Roughgarden (2004) thoroughly documents, such categorizations are far more muddled than popularly believed.

4. According to the national survey report Injustice at Every Turn (Grant et al., 2011), "57% [of transgender adults] experienced significant family rejection," which contributed to the risks of outcomes such as homelessness, HIV infection, and suicide. The good news is "family acceptance had a protective affect [sic] against many threats to well-being"; the bad news is less than half of transgender respondents reported this acceptance. Also particularly telling are the rates of homelessness among transgender and gender-nonconforming youth. In another survey (Travers et al., 2012), 65% of trans youth without strongly supportive parents experienced inadequate or insecure housing (defined as homelessness, "couch surfing," or "great difficult[ies]" securing housing payments). These parents' approaches have insufficiently prepared them to weather a significant disruption to their ideas and expectations of who their children are and what their lives will be.

5. There exist some minority movements to reject and replace the sexist gender roles and to a lesser extent heteronormative gender roles (Kane, 2012), but even here the assumption is rebellion is still necessary. So too is this assumption found in the otherwise revolutionary work of Ehrensaft (2011).

6. Mental health professionals who specialize in "reparative" therapy as they attempt to "cure" transgender individuals, therefore, rely on a belief either that transgender people are lying or mistaken (dishonest testimony); that gender cannot be known by subjective means, which also is the essentialism that biologist Joan Roughgarden calls "a mistake" (2004, p. 23); or that gender is not knowable (in which case, one wonders what the point of their job is, exactly). This mirrors the failed trajectory of homosexual reparative therapy, denying as it does the authority of the individual over their own identity, and ignoring the nonpathological

possibilities inherent in the "unrepaired" population. The complicated relationship between homophobia and transphobia and reparative approaches to gender-nonconformity is compellingly explored in Bryant (2008).

7. I caution here, however, against measuring the parent(s) by the "success" of GDP, as it, like all parenting, takes place in a broader context, and as such the child(ren) will be influenced not only by the parents' choices and their own desires but also by a society steeped in gender injustice. To place the full burden of gender revolution on parents (most often on mothers specifically) is to replicate the "mother-blame" endemic in wider kyriarchical culture.

8. Children's books which present a broader spectrum of gendered possibilities include *10,000 Dresses, Backwards Day, Adventures of Tulip, Birthday Wish Fairy, Princess Boy, The Paperbag Princess, Mama, Mommy, and Me, Daddy, Papa, and Me*, and many others; it is beyond the scope of this chapter to provide an exhaustive survey. Although racial/ethnic and socioeconomic diversities are as yet highly limited in these selections, I find it hopeful that there are options available that are starting to reflect the amazing diversity of gender.

CHAPTER TEN

Parent-Initiated Gender-Creativity

Raising Queerlings

MICHELLE WALKS

It's very sad to me. I am very sad to see Sage grow up in the world; and he's [in] such an innocent place right now. He doesn't understand gender. He doesn't get it. And it is so wonderful to see him play with his dolls, pretend to be Angelina [the Ballerina] all of the time, and Alice in Wonderland, and Dorothy. He always picks the female figures, but he doesn't even know they are females. ... And I know it's going to leave him, and I'm going to be sad. And eventually he is going to be teased. He is going to be teased about his long hair. Teased for being Angelina, or whatever.

[... And] I feel pressure to cut his hair, 'cause he has bangs. It's 'cause he has bangs and long hair that he looks particularly girly-girl. You know? If you have all of it long, a lot of boys do that, but not many have bangs and a bob. [Laughs] It's like a bob. He prefers to wear girly clothes, so I know, people must think that I am really trying to screw my kid up big time. Not only am I raising him in a two-mom household, but I'm actually trying to make him into a girl! [Sighs.] But no, I actually don't give a ——. I actually think it doesn't matter.

So, in terms of gender and mothering, I just wish that people would leave me alone with the gender crap. Why can't we be whoever we are, whatever that is? Why do we have to focus on butch, femme, male, female—all those things? (Bryn[1,2])

Since the 1970s research has been conducted on and with lesbian, gay, and bisexual (LGB) parents. Most of this research has aimed to prove competency of LGB parenting and compared it to that of heterosexuals (as noted in Epstein,

2009a; Lewin, 1993; Moore, 2011; Owen, 2001; Stacey & Biblarz, 2001). Believing that research on LGBT (lesbian, gay, bisexual, and trans) parents had reached saturation, my research aim was to investigate butch lesbians,' transmen's, and genderqueer individuals' experiences of pregnancy and infertility. During my first interview with someone who had experienced a pregnancy (*Bryn*, see above), I realized that I had discovered experiences that had yet to be researched or talked about much. While numerous studies over the past 30-plus years have concluded that LGBT-parenting is "just as good as" or "the same as" the parenting of heterosexuals (as noted by Epstein, 2009a; Lewin, 1993; Moore, 2011; Owen, 2001; Stacey & Biblarz, 2001), this research has not acknowledged the diverse reality inclusive of *queer* parenting. Instead, the mission of most of this research was to legitimate and show the aptitudes of LGB parents (Epstein, 2009a, 2009b; Owen, 2001; Stacey & Biblarz, 2001). What it failed to do was acknowledge that parenting by LGBT parents is quite diverse. Therefore, it is time to recognize the different approaches that queer parents bring to parenting (as has been exemplified in Epstein, 2009b).

In doing so, this chapter focuses on queer parents who explicitly *fail* to meet normative ideals of parenting because they challenge patriarchal hetero- and homonormative and cisgender ideals. Before getting to the experiences, I examine the neoliberal social context of the research, and Judith/Jack Halberstam's theory of *The Queer Art of Failure* (2011), and then I review the research methods used in the research. Then, I discuss the actual experiences of *raising queerlings*. In the end, it is argued that *raising queerlings* is not an act exclusive to people who by their gender or sexuality identify as "queer," but rather I invite all people to engage in parenting that "fails" to uphold the *status quo*.

SOCIAL & POLITICAL CONTEXT OF RAISING QUEERLINGS

I chose to locate my research in British Columbia, not just because it is the province in which I was born and raised, but also because I recognized its unique welcoming political and social climate for queer individuals and families. British Columbia, and East Vancouver in particular, has earned a particular respect and notoriety for being a lesbian (and queer) mecca, especially for those interested in parenting. In 1986 this was illustrated by "a small group of lesbians, calling themselves the Lavender Conception Conspiracy, [who] were meeting together to share information and to support each other in their desire to become parents" (Epstein, 2009a, p. 16). More recently this has resulted in one East Vancouver midwifery practice offering information sessions specifically for lesbians and queers, focused on alternative conception as well as queer (family) legal rights. Those living in East Vancouver are aware of its uniqueness, and the privilege that comes with living there. *Quinn* noted, "I mean I live in East Van[couver] and work at a university! I mean, an elderly lady has not screamed at me coming in the bathroom for years! I'm aware that I'm in an East Van[couver] bubble." The visibility of lesbians and other queers in East Vancouver, and BC more generally, has likely been both a cause for and an effect of the central role that BC has played—along with Ontario and Québec—in making Canada unique in terms of "the legal and policy changes … achieved in the areas of relationship recognition, adoption, second-parent adoption, and birth registration" (Epstein, 2009a, p. 21).

Since the mid-1990s, legal rights relating to queer reproduction and family have been revised a number of times in British Columbia. Three particular policy updates exemplify these changes. The first occurred in 1995, when a Human Rights Tribunal decision made it illegal for physicians and clinics to deny lesbians access to fertility services in BC (Luce, 2010). The second change happened the following year, when it became legal in BC for any one or two adults—regardless of sexual orientation or marital status—to adopt children (Kelly, 2011; Luce, 2004, 2010; Owen, 2001). Third, in 2001, a BC Human Rights Tribunal ruled that it was discriminatory to prevent the naming of two women on their child's Registration of Live Birth or birth certificate, if their child was conceived using the sperm of an anonymous donor (Kelly, 2011; Kranz & Daniluk, 2002; Luce, 2010). Additionally, provincial and federal changes to the definitions of "spouse" and "common law" to be inclusive of same-sex couples, in 1997 and 2000 (Kranz & Daniluk, 2002; Luce, 2004, 2010; Owen, 2001), and the legal recognitions of same-sex marriage—in BC in 2003 and Canada in 2005—were monumental in legal recognition of queer families.[3] Despite these changes, British Columbia is not a place of total solace for queer individuals and queer-parented families. The polarization of public respect, understanding, and acceptance of queer-led families has been expressed in national statistics and school boards, and in response to Pride celebrations throughout BC.[4] Likewise, an Angus Reid poll found that in 2006 only "61% of Canadians wanted same sex marriage to remain legal" (Angus Reid, 2010). Moreover, the larger neoliberal context works to quash anything "queer" and outside of the normal.

Neoliberalism appeals to our cultural love affair with capitalism, and has relied on a discourse that is often recognized as neutral and normal (Craven, 2010; Griffin, 2007). This has inevitably impacted its success (Craven, 2010; Griffin, 2007). Anthropologist Christa Craven explains that

> *neoliberalism* [is] a political philosophy that rests on the idea that shifting away from government responsibility for ensuring personal liberties toward a 'free,' or unregulated, market will ultimately resolve social inequalities. Thus the state's role has moved

beyond protecting the freedoms of individual citizens to safeguarding the ability of corporate entities to compete within the market. The notion of what freedom means in the context of citizenship has also changed. Although neoliberalism still promises citizens 'freedom,' it is defined almost entirely by their ability to participate in financial markets. (2010, p. 9)

Further, Penny Griffin reveals that "neo-liberal discourse (re)produces meaning through assumptions of economic growth and stability, financial transactions and human behavior that are intrinsically gendered while presented as universal and neutral" (2007, p. 220). Thus, under the guise of a political and/or economic philosophy, neoliberalism affects people's behavior, identities, social relations, definitions of personhood, and "particular definitions of successful human endeavour" (Griffin, 2007, p. 226). One particular way that neoliberalism is embodied is through hetero- and homonormativity (Duggan, 2003; Griffin, 2007; Halberstam, 2011).

While heteronormativity is a practice of seeing, comparing, and expecting everyone to be heterosexual, homonormativity is the practice of "normalizing" being gay or lesbian, and thus not presenting one's self as a threat or challenge to heterosexuality (Duggan, 2003). Homonormativity has proved to be effective in gaining rights like marriage—an institution that acts to normalize the relationships of gays and lesbians through the (perceived) demonstration of commitment and monogamy (Duggan, 2003; Ettelbrick, 2007). Duggan explains that homonormativity acts to "[depoliticize] gay culture [by anchoring it] in domesticity and consumption" (2003, p. 50). Thus, Duggan asserts that homonormativity "is a politics that does not contest dominant heteronormative assumptions and institutions, but [rather] upholds and sustains them" (Duggan, 2003, p. 50). In *Why Are Faggots So Afraid of Faggots?* (2012) Mattilda Sycamore notes,

> We [the contributors of *Why Are Faggots So Afraid of Faggots?*] wonder how our desires have led to an endless quest for Absolut vodka, Diesel jeans, rainbow Hummers, pec implants, Pottery Barn, and the perfect abs and asshole. As backrooms [of gay night clubs (that are used for casual sex)] get shut down to make way for wedding vows, and gay subculture morphs into 'straight-acting dudes hanging out,' we wonder if we can still envision possibilities for flaming faggotry that challenges the assimilationist norms of a corporate-cozy lifestyle. (p. 1)

Duggan similarly explains that through neoliberalism and homonormativity, "we [queers] have been administered a kind of political sedative—we get marriage and the military, then we go home and cook dinner, forever" (2003, p. 62). Through this statement, Duggan succinctly exemplifies homonormativity using a 1950s perfect family ideal—through marriage and domesticity LGBT folks are not a threat to the *status quo*. They are not queer; they are pacified and normal.

For gay and lesbian parents raising children, it often seems safer to demonstrate that they are not a threat to patriarchal, heteronormative ideals nor to their children's well-being. As a result, gay and lesbian parents have fairly successfully proved themselves as capable, competent, and effective parents (Epstein, 2009a; Owen, 2001; Stacey & Biblarz, 2001). Moreover, this homonormative approach has often resulted in all LGBT parents being regarded as "sell-outs" to homonormativity, and deniers of their *queerness*. While Lewin (1993, 2009a, 2009b) demonstrates that being gay does not lie in opposition to fatherhood or being a lesbian with motherhood, I illustrate how queerness and parenthood are not mutually exclusive.

FAILURE, QUEERLINGS, AND GENDER-CREATIVITY

Three concepts are foundational to understanding the decisions and experiences of queer parents who purposefully raise gender-creative children: gender-creativity, queerlings, and *failure*. While failure is typically thought of as a negative thing, in *The Queer Art of Failure* (2011) Judith/Jack Halberstam points out the importance of considering perspective with regard to failure. Halberstam notes that failure is not a lack of success, *per se*, but rather that failure is found through the unsuccessful maintenance or contribution to the neoliberal, patriarchal, heteronormative *status quo*. Whereas failure is ordinarily feared, Halberstam illustrates that failure can actually result in joy. While failure can be unexpected and/or disappointing, Halberstam also points out that *failure* can be playful, liberating, creative, planned, and explicit, or likewise, implicit, spontaneous, and subversive. Halberstam explains that "we can ... recognize failure as a way of refusing to acquiesce to dominant logics of power and discipline and as a form of critique" (p. 88). While the examples in *The Queer Art of Failure* are mainly from popular culture media and history, I use this chapter to focus on one way that *the queer art of failure* is creatively enacted in contemporary everyday life—through the art of "raising queerlings."

My partner creatively came up with the term "queerling" for our son and other children who are raised by queers. Previously, others have used "queer spawn" (Epstein, 2009b), the children of or within queer/LGBT (parented-/headed-/led-) families (Epstein, 2009b; Moore 2011), and/or the children raised by lesbian mothers and/or gay fathers (Kelly, 2011; Lewin, 1993, 2009a, 2009b; Owen, 2001) to refer to those who in this chapter are called "queerlings." While my partner and I recognize that queerlings are not *necessarily* queer themselves in terms of their gender or sexuality, they are, from an anthropological prospective, culturally queer.[5] That is, they are raised in an environment of queerness, and this can lead the children to have some queer characteristics and/or politics. This does not mean that all children of LGBT parents identify as "queer" themselves (politically or due to their gender or sexual inclinations). Instead, children of queers also have agency enough not to identify, practice, or live as queer. That said, "queerlings" are not just any children raised by LGBT [or lesbian, gay, bisexual, and trans] parents; they are the children of *queers*—parents who embrace and engage in *the queer art of failure*. For example, many of these parents and children "revel in and cleave to all of [their] own inevitable fantastic failures" (Halberstam, 2011, p. 187), including through resisting gender boundaries.

While Halberstam (2011) referred to this as *queer*, she also recognized it as *feminist*. Moreover, queers are not the only ones to explicitly and implicitly challenge gender norms and *status quo* politics in their families. Not surprisingly, recent research and publications show that "feminist" parenting also aims to counter the patriarchal heteronormative *status quo* (Green, 2011; O'Reilly, 2004). As is illustrated by the other chapters in this book, there are obviously many heterosexual parents who also consciously raise gender-creative children whether because they are following their child's lead, or they are initiating it themselves. Whether we label these parents as queer, or feminist, or simply as supportive parents, it does not really matter. Their actions speak louder than words.

A feminist mother and researcher of other feminist mothers, Fiona Green points out:

> As in other areas of my life, mothering is a site where personal action is political and where general societal values are reflected in personal experience. I saw how mothering had become a location where my feminist activism could question and challenge, rather than support and replicate, patriarchy. (2011, p. 17)

Likewise, Green notes, people may engage in feminist (or queer) practice without even knowing their particular philosophy has such a label (2011, p. 13). Those I interviewed did not label their parenting as "queer," nor express a feeling of "failure" in their practice, but this does not stop their practice from being these things. Their parenting was guided by their hearts, and in so doing engaged with liberty, playfulness, creativity, subversion, and, thus, *failure*. I expect that this book will not just foster more awareness and understanding for child-led gender-creativity, but it is hoped will also serve as a catalyst for an increase in parent-led gender-creativity.

In *Gender Born, Gender Made*, Diane Ehrensaft explains gender-creativity as her "made-up category" that refers to and is inclusive of children who

> [transcend] the culture's normative definitions of male/female to creatively interweave a sense of gender that comes neither totally from the inside (the body, the psyche), nor totally from the outside (the culture, others' perceptions of the child's gender), but resides somewhere in between. (p. 5)

Ehrensaft goes on to explain:

> In this day and age, raising a gender-creative child is still never an easy matter, despite years of hard effort on the part of feminists, gay and transgender activists, and progressive gender specialists to make room for broadened expressions of gender as a healthy rather than pathological way of being. (p. 5)

While the children that Ehrensaft discusses are what I call "child-led" gender-creative, here I present another perspective, what I call "parent-initiated" gender-creative children.

With this in mind, this chapter uses some of the findings from my doctoral research, and focuses on examples of queer parents in BC who explicitly cultivate gender-creative children by challenging patriarchal hetero- and homonormative ideals. As gender-creativity and raising queerlings were not topics I set out to explore in my interviews, they were not discussed in every interview I conducted with parents. That said, discussions of parenting queerly came up in six of the eight butch lesbian and genderqueer individuals whom I interviewed (who had experienced a pregnancy). Of these, three (*Bryn*, *Quinn*, and *Tash*) spoke at length about fostering gender-creativity in their children, while there was more tension and apprehension in the narratives of *Joy*, *Lou*, and *Vanessa* with regard to their parenting queerly.

RESEARCH METHODS

Between February 2011 and April 2012 I conducted research on the reproductive choices and experiences of butch lesbians, transmen, and genderqueer (BTQ) individuals in British Columbia. The research involved interviews, questionnaires, and participant-observation. My research involved the use of three different anthropology-influenced research methods, with a goal of being able to triangulate (compare and contrast) the findings of the three methods. I conducted face-to-face interviews with various health care providers (HCP), as well as with BTQ individuals who had experienced either infertility or a successful pregnancy. I distributed questionnaires to and collected them from BTQ residents of British Columbia and HCPs who practice or reside in BC. I also conducted what is called Participant Observation, which included attending, watching, and participating at Pride events, family and family-friendly events, and LGBT events in the province, as well as walking around the neighborhoods of the interview participants to see what visuals (store signs, church signs, people, playgrounds) they might encounter on a daily basis.

Throughout my research in BC, I came to hear about and see how other queer parents raise queerlings. While my interviews were conducted with butch lesbians, genderqueer individuals, and a transman—people who are visibly queer—I am a queer femme who "passes" as straight often enough that I regularly had to "out" myself to the research participants as both a queer femme mother, and a partner to my son's trans-dad. After this disclosure, the individuals I interviewed seemed to be more at ease with the whole interview process, as well as quite comfortable talking about their gender-transgressive children (when that was the case), and about the challenges of raising their children in a heteronormative society. During my interviews, the research participants and I often shared our stories about having boys with longer hair; our challenges in acquiring appropriate clothing for our children that is not always blue or camouflage for boys and pink and sparkly for girls; and having our children often perceived as a different sex from what they are. While not all of the parents I spoke with shared these experiences or desires, the ones who did are the interviewees whom I found most interesting. It wasn't that all of the stories involved 'hard core' challenging of hegemonic gender values, but those that did interested me more because they contrasted with those we typically read or hear about in research on LGBTQ parenting—those that say that gay- and lesbian-led families are just like those with straight parents (Epstein, 2009a; Lewin, 1993; Moore, 2011; Owen, 2001; Stacey & Biblarz, 2001; similarly noted and critiqued in Epstein, 2009b).

FINDINGS

All three of the parents who highlighted explicit narratives of *raising queerlings* were conscious of the embodied femininity and masculinity of their children, and supported their children in expressing themselves in ways in which they felt most comfortable. *Tash, Bryn,* and *Quinn* each explained to me how they purposefully parented in ways that challenged heteronormative, patriarchal expectations of gender and children. What stood out for these parents was how their children's gender and bodily expressions contrasted with the cultural *status quo*, although none of the parents considered their children to be trans or explicitly genderqueer. All three of these moms[6] believed strongly—in part due to their own experiences growing up with a non-normative gender—that their children should be given the opportunity to be exposed to things of all genders, thus facilitating their children's comfort in expressing their gender(s) comfortably. At the same time, however, these moms also expressed concern for their children's well-being growing up in a culture in which dichotomous genders are privileged, as those who visually contest this dichotomy often face endless critique and challenges.

A variety of overlapping themes emerge in this chapter, but they all come back to one that is key for everyone, regardless of gender, age, or parenting status: we all want to feel "good enough." Whether as a child, as a child of a particular sex, or as a parent, we all feel pressures to be different and "better" in the eyes of society, and often this stems from a very narrow idea of what "good" is. Those I spoke with challenged these normative pressures, and instead insisted that we "fail" to meet that type of success. From what they said, I have compiled a list of new standards from which we can measure ourselves, as we "fail" to meet the heteronormative, neoliberal *status quo*. These standards include: respecting who people are (*Bryn*), not having gender norms socialized into us (*Tash*), not having to succumb to social pressure (regarding gender) (*Vanessa*), letting children be secure in whatever gender(s) they are (*Quinn*), and having freedom (*Joy*). Moreover, *Quinn* brought attention to the first—and no doubt the most pivotal—social sex and gender attribution that exists, that which occurs when our genitals are first categorized as "male" or "female."

In fact, *Quinn*'s way of addressing this very significant moment was the earliest example of explicitly raising a queerling that was given. *Quinn* told me of her desire not to have her child's sex announced upon their birth, as she felt it was not necessary to attribute the western cultural dichotomy of sexes and genders upon herself (as a new mother) and her child, especially in her newborn's first moments after being born. She, thus, informed her midwife of this.

> *The one thing [that was important to me] when the baby [was born, was that], "I really prefer that you don't do the 'it's a boy!' [or] 'it's a girl!' thing." And she [my midwife] was like, "I never do that! That's completely not my role. That's completely up to the parents to do or not to do." Like the whole, 'it's a boy!' [or] 'it's a girl!' as the most important thing, is so messed up in my mind. And then the whole 10-fingers, 10-toes thing, it's just as bad 'cause who really cares about fingers and toes? I'm like, I wanna hold the baby and make sure its spinal column is closed. That's all. I wanna hold my baby and check its spinal column. She [the midwife] said, "Absolutely, I never ever do that." And one of the newer midwives was not on the same page, one of the apprentices, and so she actually did it: "It's a boy!" Then I was like [sigh, in frustration and disappointment with being told].*

As *Quinn* articulates, her desire to "fail" to have "the announcement of the sex" of her newborn child—which, in fact is not uniquely queer and is becoming more common especially among feminist parents—also stems from a belief that a baby's health and parental bonds with the newborn are more important than the child's genital makeup. One could argue that this ("failure," and) belief—that other things in life are more important than a constant reinforcement of the cultural dichotomy of the (perceived) two sexes—is what underlies raising queerlings in general. Whether it is in following the interests and passions of the child, or keeping the child safe and healthy, the child's sex should not (or does not have to) be of primary concern when raising them.

For *Bryn*, who was at the time of our interview raising a preschool-age son, frustration with gender boxes concerned both herself and her son, *Sage*. When I asked her about the relationship between gender and mothering, *Bryn* replied with the opening quote of this chapter. What *Bryn* was saying was not that it did not matter that people thought it was weird or screwed up. Instead, she expressed that having longer hair, wearing particular colors of clothes, or having particular role models should not be based on someone's sex or gender. *Bryn* was committed to "failing" to meet the *status quo* perceptions of gender; she would continue to mother in a way that respected both who she is and who her son is. While she could sit back and feel bad about not meeting mainstream expectations, and being judged for being a bad parent, *Bryn* gave up on being "successful" in their eyes. Despite that, *Bryn* was concerned about *Sage's* future and bullying by other children. This was highlighted when she said, "And I know it's going to leave him, and I'm going to be sad. And eventually he is going to be teased. He is going to be teased about his long hair. Teased for being Angelina, or whatever." Teasing is a very effective technique of social pressure, especially with regard to gender.

While *Tash* did not say whether teasing played into her becoming "more of a girl" during her teens, my guess is that it did. Like many of those I interviewed, *Tash* grew up with mostly boys as friends, "until I was a teen, and succumbed to some of that pressure to be a girl, but I was not all that good at it. I've never been good at [being a girl]." After giving it a try for a few years, *Tash* reveled in her "own inevitable fantastic failure" (Halberstam, 2011, p. 187) and eventually decided that part of that was to become a "butch Mama." When she was pregnant, *Tash* convinced herself that she was having a son. When her daughter *Lucy* was born, *Tash* was surprised, and she remembers saying, "But I don't know anything about being a girl!" Despite this, she recognized the importance of supporting *Lucy* in being herself, even if "*Lucy* is a bit more on the girly-ish side and wants frills."

Tash was aware that *Lucy's* attraction to frills might be age-related—preschoolers in general love shimmery and "pretty" things—and also an effect of daycare and popular culture. In fact, our interview had started late because *Tash* and *Lucy* had been out searching for slippers for *Lucy* to wear at daycare; eventually they had come home empty handed.

And we were in [a cheaper-end chain store] today, and the woman just couldn't wrap her mind around it, 'no pink.' ... [The particular store] only has pink slippers. ... For girls they only have pink slippers with characters on them. Oh my god, everything is fucking pink! And I am getting so bitchy about it that Lucy is now repeating it, "Pink is not the only colour!"

[laughs] So, yeah, FYI. … But I'll be damned if I am buying something with flippin' Dora on it, and I'll be damned if I am buying something pink, [with] sparklies on them!

Moreover, *Tash* acknowledged the importance of both recognizing who *Lucy* is and giving her alternatives in terms of gender. Thus, *Tash's* decision to avoid pink, sparkly Dora slippers despite her daughter's girly-ness was thus not to crush any appreciation that *Lucy* had of pink, but instead was done to bring awareness of social pressures/norms, and to be political in terms of providing an alternative to what girls are expected to wear and be. Although *Tash* did not explicitly say it, I got the impression that this choice was not just for *Lucy's* benefit, but also for the awareness and exposure of all the daycare children and staff. If they can see one child enjoying being who she is, they may lighten up on the dichotomous gendered expectations for the other children (and themselves).

I want to roll with who she is, but I also want her to have a range, and not to have that [gender norm] socialized into her, 'cause she's kind of a crazy dresser. … 'Cause some of the kids at daycare, I mean—man!—they could be clones. The girls look one way, and the boys look another way. You know, they are so small, why don't you let them be who they are?

This comment of letting the kids "be who they are" recognizes, as Halberstam suggests, success in the "embrac[ing] of the absurd" (2011, p. 187); moreover, it was similar to both what *Bryn* had talked about, as well as *Quinn's* experience with her son *Levi*.

Quinn successfully "embraced the absurd" in how she spoke with her son about gender and sex. This came through her narrative about *Levi's* sense of self, as well as how she queerly taught him about what boys and girls are.

He's always been very secure about his gender, like I was always very careful from day one, to, you know, [teach him] what's a girl, and what's a boy. And I was very careful not to fall into the trap of those stupid stereotypes and stuff, "boys have penises, girls have vulvas" or whatever, stuff. And, so far it's worked out great. He's remarkably secure that he's a boy. Which is something that I never—I don't understand 'cause I never had that kind of confidence about a particular gender identity. But he's also like, well, most boys have penises but there are some exceptions. Like most times, "I before E except after C" or whatever it is, but sometimes there's an exception. Life is full of exceptions … [so] it's just normal to him [to have exceptions and diversity].

Regardless of his strong sense of himself as a boy, *Levi*—like *Bryn's* son *Sage*— loved having longer hair.

While *Bryn* was concerned for *Sage's* future with regard to bullying because of his hair, *Quinn* was able to tell me of some of the negative effects that *Levi* had dealt with. *Levi* was a few years older than *Bryn's* and *Tash's* preschoolers, and he had unfortunately experienced "gender policing" and bullying, both at school. Additionally, one of his family members repeatedly asked about when he would have his hair cut. *Quinn* told me that *Levi* loved his longer hair, and thus she gave him tools to support and empower him. She admitted and explained:

> *My mom pressures him to cut his hair. We talk about how Bubba and Papa have a more old-fashioned worldview. And he's down with that, and that it's a cultural thing. That there are cultures where boys grow their hair long, and some cultures where boys cut their hair all short, and we can choose to do what he wants to do.*
>
> *He was having a lot of intense gender policing at the beginning of grade 2—end of grade 1, and the beginning of grade 2. It was from the older boys, mostly. They would fly paper airplanes into him, and they'd say, "Are you a boy or a girl?" on them.*
>
> *And he went through a period where he was thinking about cutting his hair, and then decided not to, because cutting his hair would be like giving in to the bullies! And so since then he's been adamant that he's not going to cut his hair because people wanted him to, because that would be like them winning, which has been interesting to see. His hair has become such a symbol.*

Quite obviously, both *Quinn* and *Levi* participated in *the queer art of failure.* They "refus[ed] to acquiesce to dominant logics of power and discipline and [instead, they took part in] a form of critique" (Halberstam, 2011, p. 88). *Quinn* and *Levi* worked *together* to make sense of the world around them, and to challenge norms of what parenting and childhood are. They demonstrate that children are not innocent and lacking agency, and adults do not have to protect their children, at least in the traditional sense. Moreover, creativity and spontaneity are clearly present in their negotiations and *failures* of gender and mainstream (Canadian) culture.

In addition to *Quinn*, *Tash*, and *Bryn*, *Joy* also was engaged in this *failure.* With *Joy*'s daughter *Emma* being only 2 years old, *Emma*'s agency and personal preference were not visible in *Joy*'s narrative, the way that *Levi*'s, *Sage*'s, and *Lucy*'s were in their mothers' narratives. For *Joy*, *Emma*'s gender *failure* was a matter of finances as well as allowing *Emma* free movement. *Joy*'s narrative reminded me of my own growing up, and made me reflect on how much has changed in the past 30 years, from when gender in children's clothes (those for children under 10 years old) was not as defined as it is today (see also Paoletti, 2012). *Joy*'s attitude was reminiscent of what I think many parents experienced in the 1970s and 1980s, when children's clothing was not as gender specific; hand-me-downs were fairly common, passed down from girls to other girls, or brothers to sisters, and more rarely (but still existent) girls to boys (Paoletti, 2012; personal experience/ knowledge). This contrasts with the emphasis on having *the* right clothes (according to the wearer's sex and the current popular culture icons) today.

I don't spend a lot of money on Emma's clothes, and I have a lot of hand-me-downs. They are hand-me-downs from both girls and boys—including [Emma's brother] Henry—so I have actually had quite a few comments from both adults and other kids that she looks like a boy, and it's particularly because she has so little hair. She's often mistaken for a boy even if she's in pink. So the hair thing really matters, but I'm very conscious of that, and I'm not going to change it 'cause, that's quite frankly who I am and I'm not going to spend lots of money on her clothes—on either of my children's clothes. But I've begun to notice—well, I think that I am somewhat nervous about that, if I present in a particular way ... and then my female child is also sometimes in clothes that people would identify with boys, that I'm imposing that on her ... I'm just a bit worried about what people might say. I'd defend myself, but I mean, my choice of clothes for Emma is by far a function of her ability to move. I can't stand the way girls are often dressed in tight clothes or clothes that restrict their movement and she's an extremely active, athletic kids and I want her to have the freedom to do that. And, that means often wearing clothes that are "boys,'" or for boys, ostensibly.

While *Joy*'s practice may not seem that much like *failure* in terms of gender—at least for those of us who grew up, as I did, wearing hand-me-downs from our older brother(s)—she is consciously and actively countering the *status quo* of not just gender/sex (and movement) restricted clothing, but also of consumerism/neoliberalism.

Moreover, *Quinn*, *Tash*, *Bryn*, and *Joy* were not the only parents to speak about why they parented the way they did; in fact, two parents explained to me their practice of not explicitly parenting queerly. For *Lou*, her decision not to be "political" with their[7] adopted children, *Yannik* and *Zola*, stemmed from their childhood spent with their parents at anti-abortion protests. They felt that being outwardly political/queer with their children—besides using the men's washroom when in public with their son, which *Lou* did successfully passing as a man—was using their children as pawns, as they could not truly understand or consent to participating in being *queerly* parented. On the other hand, *Vanessa* expressed her desire to be more queer in her parenting of *Abigail*, but she already felt judged and critiqued by both LGBT and mainstream heterosexual parents.

In fact, it was not until my second-to-last interview—which was with *Vanessa*—that I made the connection between *queer* parenting, neoliberalism, and homonormativity. I had met *Vanessa* as a genderqueer individual before she was pregnant, and knew she was passionate about queer reproduction. Once I had the go-ahead for my research, I sent her my call for participants, with the expectation that she would not only pass it on to others she knew, but also volunteer to participate due to her interests and experiences. So, I was surprised when I did not hear back from her. Little did I know that when she was pregnant and as a new parent, she had been very affected by neoliberalism and heteronormativity. *Vanessa* explained:

As you know, I didn't agree [to participate in an interview] immediately ...

I think because I feel [that] externally I do present differently [than before being pregnant], and not completely by choice. I think that's why when I talked to [my friend] I said, "Yeah, okay, this does fit me because I feel like I've succumbed to a fair bit of societal pressure since becoming a mother, and the kind of relentlessness of it." And maybe a desire to fit in a little bit or to avoid conflict a little bit—maybe as Abigail gets older for her sake, but for now, for my sake. But I'm not happy about it, I don't like the idea that there are mornings that I get dressed and then I think, "Oh, I'm going somewhere," and so I change. That happens on a semi-regular basis, and so [sighs] it's still there. But for now I feel this pressure. And I may just be [laughs] too tired to fight it or something. I don't know ...

Vanessa went on to describe some encounters she had experienced in the local grocery stores, and the critiques she had experienced from others, that linked her gender presentation to being not a "good (enough) mother." Thus, to preserve her own mental well-being, *Vanessa* altered the way she presented herself, and began to engage in more implicit queer parenting than what she otherwise would have liked to. Her shift in gender identity and presentation was echoed by another person, *Helen*, who had been suggested as a potential participant. When I spoke with *Helen*, she admitted that while a few years earlier she would have qualified to participate in my research—at least in terms of her gender identity and presentation—she no longer identified or presented as "butch." This was, *Helen* explained, both a result of becoming a parent as well as "growing older" and having a professional career—quite similar to Kath Weston's research participant *Cynthia Murray* who rationalized that her "switching from butch to femme involved the sense that she was getting too old to be butch" (1996, p. 141). While it can seem that neither *Vanessa* nor *Lou* engaged in explicit *failure*, it is clear from their justifications and other elements of their interviews that they both actually did parent *queerly* in more implicit ways.

CONCLUSION

Amongst LGBTQ folks, there remains a split about whether to be recognized as different/*queer* or as the same as heterosexuals. In 1989, the late activist and academic Paula Ettelbrick's essay "Since When Is Marriage a Path to Liberation?" was first published. In it she wrote:

> Being queer is more than setting up house, sleeping with a person of the same gender, and seeking state approval for doing so. It is an identity with many variations. It is a way of dealing with the world by diminishing the constraints of gender roles which have for so long kept women and gay people oppressed and invisible. Being queer

means pushing the parameters of sex, sexuality, and family, and in the process transforming the very fabric of society. (2007, p. 306)

To Halberstam (2011) this pushing and transforming is "failure." For *Bryn*, *Tash*, *Quinn*, *Lou*, and *Vanessa* this is everyday life.

While to some *failure* can seem haunting, coercive, or malicious, it is none of these things. *Failure* and *queerness* are a politics that bring attention to the current state of affairs, regarding gender, sexuality, and what is considered "the norm" in our culture. Or, in Halberstam's perspective, it is to "fail" the *status quo*. With this consideration, the moms I interviewed succeeded remarkably.

As this chapter ends, however, I want to suggest something to think about, albeit it is essentialist beyond my typical comfort zone. Singer-songwriter Ani Difranco is quoted as having said, "Either you are a feminist or you are a sexist/ misogynist. There is no box marked 'other'" (Cochrane, 2007). In a similar way, I believe individuals are either politically queer or they support heteronormativity— there is no box marked "other." Certainly there are more implicit and explicit ways to challenge heteronormativity, but I think we can all take something from *Bryn*, *Tash*, *Quinn*, *Joy*, *Vanessa* and even *Lou*'s *queer art* of parenting, that is, unless we enjoy the fact that we live in a patriarchal, heteronormative culture.

ACKNOWLEDGMENTS

I would first like to extend my gratitude to those who participated in this research. Second, I must acknowledge the Social Science and Humanities Council of Canada (SSHRC) for my four-year doctoral award (752-2007-2363). The research would not have been possible without either of these, and I am therefore very grateful to the research participants and to SSHRC.

NOTES

1. This chapter is based on my doctoral research and dissertation (Walks, 2013), and mostly Chapter 5: Raising Queerlings.
2. All names of participants, their children, and partners are pseudonyms.
3. Due to "common law" relationship recognition in Canada, parenting rights are not tied to marriage rights, as they are in some parts of the United States (Epstein, 2009a; Rayside, 2009).
4. Examples include Kelowna Mayor Walter Gray's 1997 refusal to include the word "Pride" in the city proclamation for "Lesbian and Gay (Pride) Day" (findlay, n.d.; Gray, 2012; Holmes, 2012), some people considering Pride parades "too sexualized" or too politicized

(Fralic, 2012; Holmes, 2012), and one physician respondent who wrote on their questionnaire, "What child, if given a choice, would opt for such [LGBT/trans] parents? Does no one consider their innocent victims?" (*Dr. A.*). Other examples are given in my dissertation (Walks, 2013).

5. The word "queer" is understood and used in a variety of ways, even with respect to people's identities and (sexual and gender) practices. While gay and queer can be considered synonymous, they are often differentiated in terms of "respectable versus degenerate" (Holmes, 2012, p. 235), respectively. Being "queer" is about fluidity, creativity, and the unknown; it is about challenging the *status quo*. It is a "mode of inquiry and politics that seek[s] to contest normalizations, [and] desire[s] to render gender, sexualities and other identities and embodiment as fluid" (Browne, 2008, paras. 2, 3). "Queer" challenges neoliberalism and neoconservatism, not simply with respect to their heteronormative assumptions, but also in terms of recognizing and respecting people's diversities in their beings and in their needs.

6. While not all butch lesbian or genderqueer parents identify as "mom," those I spoke with did. The transman I spoke with had not experienced a pregnancy or birth, and identified as a "dad."

7. With *Lou*, I use the pronoun "they" as *Lou* did not identify with either "her" or "him" pronouns, and felt more comfortable using "they" with reference to themself.

CHAPTER ELEVEN

Transforming Challenges into Action

Researching the Experience of Parents of Gender-Creative Children through Social Action and Self-Directed Groupwork

ANNIE PULLEN SANSFAÇON, AUDREY-ANNE DUMAIS-MICHAUD, AND MARIE-JOËLLE ROBICHAUD

INTRODUCTION

The level of support given to gender-creative children by their parents or caregivers is strongly linked to these children's overall health outcomes (Travers, Bauer, Pyne, & Bradley, 2012). However, little is known about the experience of parents and caregivers who are supporting their children throughout the process of growing up as a gender-creative / gender-independent / gender-nonconforming / transgender child.[1] This chapter discusses a project geared toward gaining a better understanding of this experience, including the challenges these parents and caregivers face while negotiating the social environments in which their children grow. This chapter also addresses the issues of working directly with parents in order to facilitate mutual support, collective mobilization and action on the challenges identified in the research. In what follows, we describe the research process, briefly summarize the research findings and explore the outcomes of the project in terms of action and mobilization. This chapter is divided into four sections. The first section briefly summarizes the background literature on the topic as well as describes the project context. The second section describes the methodology used to gain insight into the parenting experience. The third section discusses the data emerging from the group meetings. In the final section, we summarize the research by highlighting the main outcomes. Recommendations for future practice and research conclude this chapter.

What Do We Know about Parenting a Gender-Creative Child?

While research remains scarce on this topic, it tends to illustrate that the support of parents is a key to the health and well-being of LGBTQ youth (Moller, Schreier, Li, & Romer, 2009; Ryan, Russell, Huebner, Diaz, & Sanchez, 2010). Indeed, it seems that youths who are supported by their parents demonstrate significantly lower rates of suicide, self-harm, poor mental health and depression (Travers et al., 2012). It therefore appears that parents' support is fundamental to ensuring their child's optimal development and positive experience of growing up in a world that is often intolerant of differences.

Research also shows that the experience of parents with a gender-creative child may sometimes be challenging. Indeed, parents, just like the gender-creative children themselves, are likely to face oppression and discrimination (Riley, Sitharthan, Clemson, & Diamond, 2011). This oppression may also be exacerbated by other differences such as their socioeconomic status or their cultural heritage (Mullaly, 2010; Saketopoulou, 2011). Apart from these few studies, there is a dearth of evidence about the day-to-day experience of parents of gender-creative children including their needs and the challenges they face. And yet, because parents play such an important role in their children's lives, understanding their experiences is essential and may assist in the development of services that respond more closely to their needs and those of their children.

BETTER UNDERSTANDING THE PARENT'S EXPERIENCE: METHODOLOGICAL CONSIDERATIONS

Without entering into a long description of the methodology, we believe it is important to describe how the research was implemented. This is because some of the outcomes of the research are directly linked to the type of methodology used. Because prior research has shown how oppression and stigma are very likely to be experienced by this specific group, it was essential that the methodology not only enabled the gathering of research data but also provided an empowering forum for participants wherein they could begin to act on their identified challenges. The principles of anti-oppressive research, which revolve around a research program that is empowering, that positions the issues of power as central and that is transformational (Strier, 2007), were fundamental to the design.

Thus, we decided to apply a Social Action methodology (Fleming & Ward, 2004) through developing an intervention with parents based on the principles and process of Self-Directed Groupwork (Mullender & Ward 1991; Mullender, Ward, & Fleming, 2013). We believed that combining both research and intervention models would provide us with a powerful tool to put into practice the principles of anti-oppressive research. Indeed, Social Action Research is "participatory" because it aims not only at exploring and understanding the people's experience, but also at involving them as 'knower' in the process of discovery (Centre for Social Action, 2012). Furthermore, Social Action methodology, as a research framework, has directly developed out of Self-Directed Groupwork, a social work with a groups approach used in intervention (Fleming & Ward, 2004). Therefore, in this research, we have used Self-Directed Groupwork as a specific means both to collect data, and to work with parents so that empowerment and transformation are possible. Indeed, Self-Directed Groupwork is known to be an extremely empowering approach and has been described as a powerful tool to enhance the loss of power related to inequalities which oppressed people experience (Croft & Beresford, 1989; Denney, 1998; Mullender & Ward, 1991; Preston-Shoot, 1992; Rimmer, 2005; Solomon, 1976).

Fleming and Ward (1997, p. 5) have identified Self-Directed Groupwork as having two main characteristics. First, the model was specifically designed to distance itself from a 'deficit' or a 'blaming the victim' approach (Mullender & Ward, 1991). Furthermore, it is based on a commitment to people having the right to be heard, to define the issues facing them, to set the agenda for action and, most important, to take action on their own behalf, all of which fit well the within the principles of Anti-Oppressive research identified above. To actualize Self-Directed Groupwork as a research framework, a group was organized within a local partner organization in Montreal where bi-monthly meetings were held over a period of 9 months. Participant recruitment was carried out through partner organizations likely to come into contact with parents of young people who are gender-creative.

The parent-participants were invited to bring their children (gender-creative or not) along to the meetings, where supervision and toys were available in a separate room. No intervention or data collection was undertaken with the children in the context of this research project because of possible ethical issues. The 'child care' service was only arranged in order to increase the group's accessibility for participants. The group was co-facilitated by two research assistants working under the supervision of the researcher. Data were gathered in the form of facilitator notes containing verbatim participant commentary, facilitators' reflexive diaries and tape-recorded team meetings where data were discussed and further meetings with parents were planned (see Pullen Sansfaçon et al., 2012, for further information on the methodology).

The process of Self-Directed Groupwork involves five stages of intervention and examines different questions in order to understand the participants' experiences. The five stages are known as 'what,' 'why,' 'how,' 'action' and 'reflection' (Centre for Social Action, 2012; Mullender & Ward, 1991). The first stages of the process help participants identify their experiences, their commonalities and differences, as well as identify the aims of the group. The 'why' stage is particularly important but often undervalued (Mullender & Ward, 1991); it enables participants to move away from a personal deficit model in comprehending the issues they face, and toward a model firmly rooted in theories of structural oppression. Thus, with its five key questions, the process of Self-Directed Groupwork aims to facilitate change. Combining both approaches—that is, a Social Action methodology with a Self-Directed Groupwork intervention—allowed for participants not to be only used as research objects or mere consumers, but also to be active agents of change and knowledge production (Centre for Social Action, 2012). In order to achieve a high level of internal validity, all notes and verbatim transcripts collected in the research were available to participants during the meetings and the final report was circulated to participants for comments prior to finalization and dissemination.

SUMMARY OF THE RESEARCH FINDINGS

As they emerged throughout the research process, the parents' experiences revealed a reality that was both rich and complex. In the group's facilitated discussions, several key aspects of these experiences were highlighted. In order to fully situate the outcomes of the project in terms of the various actions undertaken by participants as a result of their involvement in the group, the next section will outline some of the main findings that emerged over the course of the 14 parent group meetings.

Understanding and Defining Gender-Creativity as a Concept

Throughout the research process, participants discussed at great length their understanding of gender-creativity in children. Overall, they understood the concept as a "way of being" that is often fluid, that may change over time and that does not easily fit into a binary model of gender that contains only male and female as options for gender identity and expression. Despite the fact that parents frequently discussed challenges related to parenting a gender-creative child, they nevertheless had a very positive perception of gender-creativity.

The group was far from reaching consensus on the 'correct' way of labeling gender-creativity in children. Parents discussed various labels that can be used including "gender-creativity," "gender-nonconformity," "gender independence" and "gender variance." While gender-creativity was considered to be a positive label, gender variance was also discussed, but was met with a range of differing opinions. For some of the participants gender variance as a term was a helpful label because it relates to medical expertise and legitimizes their child's difference. This represents one way of receiving recognition:

> I prefer [gender variance] because it's medical. So people just shut up. Bang! That's it, it's medical.

Those who felt comfortable with this label seemed to express a need for some sort of outside validation and recognition of their children's experiences. However, validation purely in a medical sense was not without its problems; many participants also agreed that there was a contradiction between their use of this term and the way they understood the very nature of gender-creativity. Indeed, while parents clearly did not perceive their children's situation as an illness—"people are not ill, it isn't a mental illness" or "the whole idea is that it isn't an illness"—some mentioned that it was nevertheless important to obtain a diagnosis of gender variance because this helped them access services:

> We need a diagnosis. Schools require a medical attestation. Let's say a child has ADHD. He needs the diagnosis to get services. The same applies for transgender kids. Diagnoses bring out a budget, then services.

> You take away the diagnostic, you don't have the medical team.

Medical labels and diagnoses were therefore considered important by most participants due to the support that medicalization can bring. However, participants were aware of the paradox of using a medical label such as gender variance. Even if they did not perceive their children as being 'ill' or otherwise expressing a medicalized pathology, being 'gender-variant' helped them to access services. At the same time, most participants—even those who saw the utility in using a diagnostic term to secure their access to services—agreed that gender-creativity was not an illness.

In short, parent discussions showed that society in general lacks understanding with regard to gender-creativity in children, which leads to further difficulties in all areas of life. One parent expressed these situations as follows:

> Gender-nonconforming kids are like baby pigeons. They are around, but no one seems to be noticing them.

This statement was made during the first group meeting and illustrates a feeling consistently expressed among participants, namely, that gender creative kids and their families suffer from a lack of visibility. Parents felt alone in their experiences of invisibility, to which they attributed several different causes. First, the taboo surrounding gender binary transgressions in children seems to be strong and persistent, which probably leads to the invisibility of gender-creative children in Canada, as well as in many other parts of the world. Whereas all the participants in the group were accepting of their children as they are, society's lack of acceptance, due in part to fear of the unknown or a basic lack of interest in children's lives and worlds, was a cornerstone of many group discussions. Indeed, if people know anything about gender-nonconformity in children, these parents explained that it is often considered to be negative: something that makes people feel uncomfortable. In many discussions, the group identified some parallels between the lack of acknowledgment of gender-creativity and the status of certain forms of sexuality as an enduring social taboo. For example, one participant spoke of how making people aware of gender-creativity is challenging because homosexuality is still an object of disapproval for many:

> I can't convince people, because homosexuality [from society's perspective] isn't okay.

Emerging from the parents' experience was a clear link between the invisibility of gender-nonconforming children and the pervasiveness of sustained homophobic attitudes in society:

> For us, we know it; there's a distinct sexual orientation and gender orientation. For us it's clear, but for society it's the same.

For participants, society in general still tends to discuss homosexuality and transgenderism as being the same and this contributes to the invisibility of gender-creative children. Thus, heteronormativity contributes to the marginalization of gender-creative children, even if gender identity and sexual orientation are not the same thing.

The Parents and Their Child: Recognizing and Accepting the Child as Being Gender-Creative

During the group discussions, the parents often conversed about the process they had to go through when they realized their child was perhaps gender-creative. First, they were clear that while they could identify commonalities in their children's experiences, they agreed that gender identity development was a unique and fluid process. Parents agreed that their children are somehow going through a singular, similar experience that nevertheless needs to be understood with flexibility. One common experience among the participants was of their children expressing that they are in the "wrong" body. However, participants also noted how their children were going through a "back and forth" process; that is to say, their child's level of identification with the 'opposite' gender varied by degrees depending on the context. For example, a child could more easily and strongly express their identification with the other gender during the summer, far away from their school and peers, and return to a more gender-conforming self-presentation at the beginning of the fall term. This contextual, seasonal variability was directly attributed to pressures felt in gender-normative school environments. However, while their experiences varied, one thing was clear across the group: parents expressed that it was very important to support their child through these varying stages of gender exploration. During this exploratory period, participants all identified the importance of allowing children to experiment with their gender identity and expression.

It is important to note how these parents stated that they have never directly suppressed their children's gender expressions. Participants in this group were therefore fully supportive of their children's gender identities. For parents, it was important that they embrace their children's identities and support their development. Indeed, acceptance was one of the recurrent themes discussed by the participants. For these parents, it was impossible to understand why some parents do not accept their children as they are. The safety of their children was paramount and seems to be the main justification for these parents' affirmative parenting perspective. They felt responsible for their children's well-being and worried that "bad things" such as depression or suicide might be on the horizon if they do not accept the children as they are in the present. They also saw their support as essential in decreasing their children's feelings of being alone or rejected. The concept of "parental duty," i.e., a parent's duty to protect their child and ensure their well-being, seems to have underscored their acceptance. These parents also recognized that the process of accepting one's child as they are is not without its challenges. Indeed, many expressed "shock" when they first realized that their child was gender-nonconforming. In other words, there were some clear challenges associated with acceptance and support of their children. This is the focus of the subsequent discussion.

Specific Challenges to Parenting a Gender-Creative Child

While the group expressed the necessity of providing constant support to their children, participants also voiced that this is not always easy. For example, they discussed at length some of the difficulties their children go through and the impact of these difficulties upon their children's well-being. For example, sometimes children seem as though they are depressed, sad or lonely because of a specific experience they have due to their gender-creativity. Witnessing those behaviors and feelings among their children has caused parents much fear and anxiety. In the group's overall account, these feelings had a deleterious impact on their own well-being; some explained how they sometimes feel overwhelmed by their situation. Parents also experienced feelings of powerlessness because they felt that, as individuals, the remedial actions they could take were limited. Indeed, one can

protect one's child, but one cannot prevent their feeling hurt by a situation they encounter. However, these parents also recognized that children are resilient. Indeed,
participants acknowledged that their children were better able than they had first
thought to cope with the challenges they faced. Parents' feelings of powerlessness
were also associated with ambivalence, uncertainty and internal conflict regarding
what kind of support to offer. For example, on many occasions parents discussed
how difficult it could be to decide on the most appropriate way of supporting their
children, or to make decisions on their behalf, such as when accessing care.

> I'd be scared to do something and that she blames me afterwards.

> You have to be careful. It is not going to be good if you give her the hormones and
> then she regrets it.

Again, their experiences of decision making are packed with fear and anxiety. One
recurrent fear was that their children might blame them in the future for a decision
or action they had taken in the present, e.g., giving or withholding consent for their
child to take hormone blockers.[2] Indeed, while these parents agreed that affirmative parenting was the only way forward, the decision-making process around potential medical interventions (hormone blockers, or hormones to transition to the
other gender) or even a medical follow-up on their children (the very fact of seeing
a pediatrician about their child who is not considered 'ill') was altogether another
matter. On multiple occasions, these parents acknowledged that they felt unsure
about the best action to take. Given their understanding of gender-creativity as a
fluid process that may change over time—and how some children may never fit
within the gender binary—making decisions without knowing the exact identity outcome for their children was difficult. A general uncertainty about gender
identity development—e.g., some children might become transgender adults while
some others may identified as two-spirited—rendered the very idea and process of
decision making on behalf of their children both fraught with anxiety and tricky.

The participants also demonstrated their awareness of various social pressures
with which they must cope in everyday life. According to the participants, their
children face many challenges with regard to their immediate environment, such as
in their sibling interactions and the broader family relationships as well as in their
schools and communities. In the first instance, while most of the parents shared
that their children's relationships with gender conforming siblings are generally
harmonious, some also detailed specific situations wherein an immediate family
member did not accept a child's gender independence. For example, some parents
expressed difficulties emerging when one parent does not support the affirming
parenting style of the other parent, or when one parent particularly struggles to

accept the child as gender-creative. One participant illustrated this idea with a personal anecdote wherein she was constantly arguing with her ex-partner with regard to how they should raise their child. However, in the group overall there seemed to be a high level of acceptance among siblings and the immediate family. Therefore, while support was not automatically to be expected among immediate family members, participants seemed to identify this challenge as being on the whole workable, and were surrounded by supportive family members.

Another key challenge emerged in the school environment, which was a recurrent topic of group discussions. It is important to note that the majority of the participants' gender-creative children were school aged and, according to their parents, faced many issues at school. As discussed previously, because gender-creativity is still generally associated with sexual orientation it was unsurprising that gender-creativity was largely unknown, or seldom raised by school staff. For participants, the school environment was often problematic as there was largely no support for their children. When services *were* offered, they were not fully adapted to suit their children's needs. Thus, the lack of adequate in-school services was perceived by the group as a significant obstacle to their children's ease of participation in the school environment.

Apart from having to cope with school-based challenges, these parents also expressed how hard it was for them and/or their children to access broader services that met their needs, such as suitable health care. The first level of difficulty pertained to finding appropriate services—e.g., that can offer targeted support for them as parents, or for their children—or medical clinics and health care providers who are sensitive to and informed about the needs of gender-creative children. Group discussions highlighted the scarcity of specialized resources. For example, one parent shared that she had to go to three different hospitals before being able to receive adequate services that met the needs of her gender-creative child. In this particular case, the first two hospitals were not able to accommodate the child because of his gender-creativity.

> When he went to the clinic, the nurse refused to give the shot. The nurse made a call to talk to a doctor. It took three months to get the shot.

While this example cannot be generalized, it nevertheless shows that even basic services are not always geared toward working with gender creative kids. Furthermore, when adequate health and social services are available, other challenges emerge with regard to access such as financial need and time constraints, as well as the complexity of the procedures involved. The group discussed, for example, all the procedures involved in undertaking a formal name change which, according to participants who have gone through it, is an expensive, long and complex process.

The Needs of Parents of Gender-Creative Children: Increasing Visibility and Developing Support Network

Over the course of the sessions, the group articulated a number of needs that must be fulfilled in order for their children to enjoy greater health and well-being, and for the parents to more effectively support and protect them. Increasing their visibility and promoting the recognition of gender-creative and transgender youth were central. As discussed in this chapter, these parents identified a number of difficulties, from a lack of services to direct discrimination and oppression. Whether by disseminating knowledge on the topic, making people more aware of their existence, developing new services or working to change the law, participants felt that it was essential to redress the invisibility and stigma faced by these children and their families. As a result of these discussions, participants also became aware that the fundamental rights of their children would need to be secured through legal challenges. According to them, such challenges would allow gender-nonconforming children a greater level of recognition in Canada.

Finding role models was also discussed as a positive way of facilitating a greater level of social recognition for gender-independent children. This was suggested not only as a strategy for bringing greater awareness of gender-creative and transgender youth, but also as a way to provide support and validation to their parents. Indeed, the group discussed the 'domino effect' of positive role models. For example, because Jenna Talackova (the Canadian trans woman who had been disqualified from participating in the Miss Universe pageant in the spring of 2012, but was subsequently allowed to compete) went public with her story, participants felt it may have contributed to increasing the visibility of trans people in Canada. Participants discussed many other role models, including Jazz (a young transwoman who went public in the United States) and Chaz Bono (transman and son of Cher and Sonny Bono).

Participants also identified a need for support, both for themselves and for their children. Specifically, they suggested a need to develop forums wherein parents can share information, support one another and access a safe space in which to freely discuss their parenting experiences and challenges without being judged or discriminated against. The development of similar safe spaces for their (younger) children was also identified as important. Indeed, the group was clear that there exist no specific resources for gender-creative children under the age of 14 years old.

In sum, participants identified that a greater level of recognition of transgender and gender-creative children and people was paramount to bring about many fundamental changes needed to create a more inclusive society. This could be achieved by pursuing legal challenges as well as promoting the emergence of more trans role models and support networks.

OUTCOMES OF THE PROCESS OF THE SOCIAL ACTION RESEARCH (SAR) PROJECT

As discussed at the beginning of this chapter, the research methodology was designed not only to collect data but also to empower participants and support them in the articulation of their own ideas and actions; in our study, Self-Directed Groupwork facilitated this aim. Given our focus on participant empowerment, this section of the chapter evaluates SAR in the development of the group and group discussions during the 14 weeks, including the group's outcomes and outputs. In what follows, we review the aims set by the participants themselves and their own evaluation of the process, placing this in conversation with our own assessment thereof.

As a research methodology, an important feature of Self-Directed Groupwork (SDG) is the facilitator's support of the group members in initially identifying their own goals. Indeed, one of the premises of SDG is that those making up the group should be in control of the knowledge produced about themselves; this is precisely what occurred in this case. The facilitators acted as experts in the process, moving the group from one stage of SDG to the next, while group members generated the content of their discussions by setting objectives and attempting to realize those objectives. Thus, during the first few meetings, parents were invited not only to share information about themselves, their personal histories and experiences of parenting a gender-creative child, but also to begin to identify what they saw as the group's main goal. Although this was no easy task, by the third and the fourth sessions parents described the goals as follows: 1) to inform the community, school and family about gender-creativity in children; and 2) to develop support networks among participants.

During the group's last session, the facilitators were mandated by the researcher to evaluate participants' perceptions of and satisfaction with the process. To do so, the facilitators adapted the 'Bull's Eye' technique (Tayler & Kemp, n.d., as cited in Mullender & Ward, 1991, p. 102), whereby participants decided the extent to which they had achieved their goals on a scale from 1 (completely achieved) to 7 (out of reach). Participants directed the placement of each goal (e.g., to inform the community) in proximity to the center of a flip chart bull's eye diagram, and discussed how they wanted to rate each goal. These discussions were not simply about whether or not to place the objectives over the bull's eye; rather, there were varying opinions. The average scores that participants agreed to for each of their group's goals were:

- To inform the community: 5.5/7
- To inform schools: 5/7
- To inform family: 5/7
- Support among participants: 3/7 to 4/7 (varied)

While participants felt that a good level of peer support had developed in the group, they also felt that this was helped by their access to childcare and to two 'professionals' (i.e., not friends) who could facilitate the discussions. These were identified as principal benefits of the group sessions, an experience defined for them by hope, continuity and stability. We note that this feedback is allied with the fourth objective set by the participants, as the support provided by the facilitators was a means to achieve this particular goal. Nevertheless, this may be because the objectives defined by the group were not measurable or achievable within this span of time and so difficult to evaluate overall by the conclusion of the meetings.

The group seems to have been more successful in creating opportunities for mutual aid (i.e., building supportive relationships among members in the group) than in creating actions, the latter being a key aim of Self-Directed Groupwork. This interpretation came from the participants themselves; when they evaluated the process during the last session they thought that the goal 'support among parents' was better achieved than 'inform the community, school, family' categories. Support happened via their sharing of their lived experiences and strategies for relating within the family, school and community.

It is interesting to note that while the group members did not feel as though they had fully achieved their goals, they nevertheless undertook some actions as part of their participation. These ranged from increasing support among members to accessing information to more easily advocating and mobilizing on a more collective level. In the first instance, the group decided to start a Facebook page for parents of gender-creative children. When the parents realized that one of their challenges was accessing relevant information, they developed the idea of also using Facebook for online resource sharing. They were concerned that information is either overly medicalized or not readily available, and in an attempt to become better informed themselves, they decided to share links to relevant media offerings between meetings. The group also assembled a resource package that was forwarded to the local children's hospital so that other parents who access specialized services could receive relevant information. The resource package was put together by two members and had its content validated by the others.

Additional and more complex actions were also undertaken. One example was writing a letter in support of Bill C-279[3] to be sent to all sitting Quebec senators. However, it was not sent until the bill was sent to the senate. The letter was also circulated by group members on Internet sites in support of trans rights, such as those maintained by Transparents and PFLAG Canada.

Finally, toward the end of the group process, there were discussions about how/if group meetings would continue after the research phase came to an end. One parent noted that, if this were to happen, childcare would be crucial. Another agreed: "I can't talk about my kids in front of my kids." The group has thus far survived and continues to offer support and motivation for parents of gender-creative children. This is attributed to participant recruitment efforts at the National Workshop on Gender Creative Kids that was held in Montreal in October 2012, and Famijeunes's—a partner organization—donation of childcare and the use of their space. The group currently meets on a monthly basis, and a children's group runs parallel to the parents' group in order to facilitate the growth of support networks and the sharing of experiences among youth under the age of 14 who are transgender as well as their siblings. This is an innovative space and there are currently no other 'support' groups for gender-creative children and youth under 14 in the Montreal area. Because their parents are already meeting in a room next door, these young people can easily access the group. This feature is promoted in the group's recruitment materials. The meetings are facilitated by professional gender-sensitive staff who are experienced in working affirmatively with gender-creative children. Both groups are now offered as part of the formal program of the host organization, and are free of charge. At the time of finalizing this chapter, in April 2013, the group was seeking formal recognition as both a Quebec and a Canadian nonprofit corporation and had submitted the relevant paperwork to be registered as Gender Creative Kids / Enfants transgenres Canada. The children who now participate in the young people's group designed the logo and created the slogan "dream big, dream open / voir grand, rêver librement," which was then professionally adapted into many promotional materials such as banners and postcards aimed at promoting their organization in various upcoming LGBTQ Pride days.

Figure 1. Gender Creative Kids / Enfants transgenres logos.

The original logo as designed by the Young People group   The final logo as designed by graphic artist Rosi Georgieva

Taking these above actions into account, we can assert that while some of the objectives set by the group at the beginning were only partially met according to the participants' self-assessment, the use of Social Action Research and Self-Directed Groupwork seems to have been fruitful. Participants were provided with an opportunity not only to contribute to knowledge development, but also to begin collective mobilization in order to develop resources and services to improve their lives and the lives of their children.

CONCLUSION

"Nothing about us without us"—from the disability rights movement to parents of gender-creative children mobilization

Over a period of 14 weeks, the process of Social Action Research was both rich and generative. This was not only the case in terms data elicitation and collection, but also with regard to the possible impact over and beyond the formal group process. Indeed, participation helped researchers and parents alike to understand many aspects related to their experience of negotiating various social environments with their children as well as work together to identify main concerns and pathways for change. In particular, this project has offered better understanding of how parents of gender-creative children understand their children's experiences as well as their own experiences of protecting their children and creating inclusive spaces in which they can thrive.

The group experience illustrated how coming together can become a site of resilience; despite their difficulties, these parents have shown that they are resilient and strong in their affirmative parenting role. That they mobilized themselves and took various actions while participating in the research group illustrates their individual and collective will to make change, protect their children and work toward a better future for them. Participants also began to identify some of the preliminary steps needed to increase recognition of gender-creative children, namely, finding more role models, disseminating more and better information throughout their communities and changing the law so that it protects the rights of gender-independent children and all transgender people.

Taking these conclusions into account, three policy and practice recommendations emerged from this project. These are as follows:

1. Provincial and federal law must to be amended in order to include and protect transgender individuals. Laws such as the *Canadian Charter of Rights and Freedoms* must include the phrase 'gender identity,' transgender people must be protected from hate crimes through changes in the criminal laws, and civil laws, such as civil codes, must be amended to facilitate processes transgender individuals are subjected to when they wish to live according to their true gender identity. Without legal recognition and protection, these children and their families will continue to encounter many basic obstacles in their everyday lives.

2. Knowledge production and dissemination must continue in various areas. In order for parents to feel more confident in their decisions, they must have easier access to information on a variety of services available to their children. This information must also be available to care providers—including school personnel—so that the support and inclusion of children in their community is facilitated for children and parents alike.
3. Parents need access to various forms of support in their local context. The experience of parenting a gender-creative child is a challenging one that may lead parents to feel isolated and anxious. Because recent research suggests better outcomes for children with supportive families, it is crucial that those families are themselves supported by both peers and professionals, regardless of a family's socioeconomic status. We therefore recommend that formal support mechanisms—such as services offered by social workers and psychologists—and informal community support mechanisms—like the parent group formed during this pilot project—be made available free of charge for families in need.

ACKNOWLEDGMENTS

We would like to thank all the parents who participated in this research, as well as the partner organization, Famijeunes, that allowed the group to meet in a safe and friendly space. Thank you also to Andrea Clegg for their work on preliminary data analysis and for writing part of the preliminary report on which this chapter is based.

Finally, we would like to thank Social Sciences and Humanities Research Council for their financial support for this project (grant number 430-2011-0612)

NOTES

1. In this chapter, we will use the term 'gender-creative children' to refer to children and young people whose gender identity does not match their anatomical sex.
2. Hormone blockers are part of what is considered a reversible step toward gender change. It involves taking a prescribed hormone inhibitor that temporary 'blocks' signs of puberty.
3. Bill 279 was put forward to modify the *Charter of Rights and Freedoms* and the Criminal Code by including protection for gender identity. This bill was introduced by Private Member Randall Garrisson (Member of Parliament for the NDP) in April 2012, which went to the Senates in February 2013 after successfully passing through the three readings at the House of Commons.

CHAPTER TWELVE

Supporting Genderqueer Youth in Rural Communities

A Case Study

LYNDSEY HAMPTON

This chapter documents the formation and ongoing facilitation of a peer support group[1] for youth exploring gender identity and expression and their sexual minority peers in a rural Canadian farming community with a population of fewer than 45,000. Considerations for the genderqueer youth in the group will be emphasized; however, because the group was composed of both genderqueer and sexual minority youth, the experiences of these young people cannot be completely separated, nor can these two populations. Many of the youth in the group who were genderqueer were also sexual minority youth and at times members of the group would vacillate between these two populations. Given that the experiences and identities of these youth cannot be completely separated, there will be some overlap between genderqueer youth and sexual minority youth when discussing the formation and ongoing facilitation of the group and experiences of group members.

Genderqueer youth require the creation of safe spaces in which they can explore, experiment with, and express their gender identity, as well as have these identities reflected back to them by affirming peers and adults. These spaces need to be available and easily accessible in all communities, but especially in rural communities where genderqueer youth are at particular risk of isolation and alienation from their peers, schools, families, and the broader community. First, the literature regarding the lack of support and affirmation that genderqueer youth receive, and the risks that this puts these youth at, will be reviewed. Then the concerns and considerations that influenced the formation and facilitation of the group will be discussed as well as consideration given to the location of the group in a small rural city. This chapter then reviews the activities engaged in by the group, as well as the benefits derived by the group participants. It is intended that the process followed in the formation and facilitation of this group is made explicit so that other rural communities may use it as a guideline to develop similar supports.

LITERATURE REVIEW

Lack of Social Support and Risks Faced by Genderqueer Youth

Transgender youth[2] have been found to have lower levels of social support than their cisgender and sexual minority peers (Ryan, Russell, Huebner, Diaz, & Sanchez, 2010), with one study suggesting that some transgender youth cannot identify "even one person they could talk to about LGBTQ matters" (Taylor et al., 2011, p. 18). It is not surprising that, given this lack of support during such a critical time in a young person's life, transgender youth are at a higher risk of academic difficulties, dropping out of school, social isolation, and substance abuse (Grossman & D'Augelli, 2006). Transgender youth are also found to be at significant risk of suicidal ideation, with about 45% of reporting transgender youth seriously contemplating suicide and 26% actually making an attempt (Grossman & D'Augelli, 2007).

Stieglitz (2010) describes how the victimization of transgender youth can lead to these young people facing serious challenges, such as "homelessness, isolation, limited educational opportunities, unemployment, a need to engage in sex work and other illicit means for survival, and substance abuse" (p. 199). Stieglitz discusses how these risks can be mitigated and resilience developed through "peer, family and professional support" (p. 204), yet rarely do transgender youth receive this necessary support. Bird, Kuhns, and Garofalo (2012) state that, for at-risk youth who have fewer resources and support, "role modeling is an important part of adolescent development and a critical factor in reducing risk and increasing protective factors for healthy development" (p. 354).

Accessing support and positive role models is especially important for transgender youth who do not have the support of their family. Ryan et al. (2010) found that young LGBTQ adults who reported low levels of family acceptance were at higher risk for depression and substance abuse as well as suicidal ideation and attempts than were youth who experienced family acceptance. Youth who reported high levels of family acceptance scored higher on measures of positive adjustment and health, self-esteem, social support, and general health. Studies have also found that only 16% of LGBTQ youth identify their parents or other family members as being their role models, with 60% of identified role models being "largely inaccessible in these youths' daily lives" (Bird et al., 2012, pp. 355–356). This is truer for youth between the ages of 16 and 19 years than those ages 20 to 24. Bird et al. suggest that this may be due in part to the younger youth being less likely to be open about their sexual or gender identity and having less access to queer or queer-friendly individuals. The authors discuss how this lack of accessible role models differs in studies of non-LGBTQ youth, who are consistently found to have more role models and role models who are most commonly parents or other adults in close proximity. Ryan et al. (2010) identified factors found to influence the likelihood of family acceptance, including parental occupation status/social class, ethnicity, immigration status, and religiosity. In some rural settings these factors may be more prevalent, thus negatively impacting the levels of family acceptance experienced by transgender youth in these communities. For all transgender youth, but particularly those who don't experience high levels of family acceptance or feel they have social support, it is of critical importance that community supports be put in place to assist these youth in their identity exploration and affirmation.

Genderqueer Youth in School Settings

When family is unwilling or unable to affirm the young person's authentic identity, youth will turn to their school setting to find the acceptance that is missing in their home life. Often school settings and personnel will fill important roles for all youth in the community by providing mentorship and connection, and by offering opportunities that facilitate a sense of belonging. Unfortunately for transgender youth, school settings have routinely been identified as transphobic and even basically unsafe for transgender and gender-nonconforming youth (McGuire, Anderson, Toomey, & Russell, 2010; Taylor et al., 2011). Specifically, participants in the McGuire et al. study "expressed a belief that schools were a place of considerable harassment and victimization for gender-nonconforming and transgender youth" (p. 1182).

Examples of the abuse and mistreatment reported by transgender youth range from hearing negative and hurtful comments (Greytak, Kosciw, & Diaz, 2009; McGuire et al., 2010; Taylor et al., 2011) to reports of physical violence (McGuire et al., 2010, p. 1182). Multiple studies have reported that transgender youth frequently report hearing transphobic or otherwise offensive and hateful comments made by their peers (Greytak et al., 2009; McGuire et al., 2010; Taylor et al., 2011). A shockingly high number of transgender youth (82%) report "sometimes or often" hearing negative comments specific to gender presentation (McGuire et al., 2010, p. 1179). Even more shocking are youth reports of school staff making transphobic remarks; youth are "as likely to hear negative comments by school personnel" as they are to hear school personnel correcting other youth who make negative comments (Greytak et al., 2009, pp. 1179–1180).

These findings speak to transgender youth spending a significant time every day in environments that openly disregard the sacredness and validity of their authentic identities. This is very likely impacting the likelihood of these young people feeling comfortable to explore, experiment with, and express their authentic identities in a school setting. Marksamer (2008) identifies that the opportunity to express one's authentic identity is frequently unavailable in school settings for reasons ranging from the youth's comfort level to schools rejecting the young person's gender expression. This rejection can come in the form of school personnel refusing to honor the preferred name, pronoun, and clothing styles of transgender youth while also failing to make the appropriate facilities available for the safety and comfort of these young people (Feinstein, Greenblatt, Hass, Kohn, & Rana, 2001).

Not having the opportunity to express one's authentic self can further intensify feelings of isolation, as these youth may feel an absence of witnesses to their true self. This isolation and rejection in school settings may be further perpetuated by the fact that many youth activities are sex/gender-segregated (choirs, sports, guides/scouts, etc.), which leaves transgender youth in a difficult position to participate. It's also possible that even if accommodations are put in place so that it becomes possible for transgender youth to participate in their preferred gender role, Kosciw, Greytak, Diaz, and Bartkiewicz (2010) suggest that "students who experience frequent harassment at school may choose not to spend additional time at school and may be less likely to be involved in optional school activities like extracurricular clubs" (p. 55). McGuire et al. (2010) found that even when opportunities for queer-identity-affirming experiences were offered to transgender youth in a school setting, such as a gay-straight alliance (GSA), approximately half of the study participants were not members of these clubs (p. 1186). It is unclear if this is due to the opportunities not being specific to transgender youth—i.e., the name 'gay-straight alliance' suggests a focus on sexual orientation alone—or whether the pervasive transphobic school environment simply makes transgender youth minimize their connections with school altogether. Another theory proposed by Kosciw et al. (2010) suggests that perhaps a barrier to student club participation could be the requirement for parental permission, which may propose a barrier for youth who are not out to their parents or whose parents are not supportive.

Very possibly due to the dangerous and unwelcoming environments described by transgender youth in their school settings, it is not surprising that transgender youth experience multiple school transitions and frequently leave traditional schooling environments for alternative settings (McGuire et al., 2010). Although some alternative school settings can ensure the safety of these youth due to smaller student numbers and the facilitation of a more accepting environment, McGuire et al. highlight concerns that transgender youth may miss out on the social and extracurricular activities offered in more traditional settings, and that these alternative settings may limit a youth's academic options. If school settings feel unsafe or unwelcoming, and school transitions don't work out, these youth may be more likely to consider dropping out of school; this may explain the high rates of early school termination amongst transgender youth (Grossman & D'Augelli, 2006).

The Importance of Support

It is necessary that transgender youth have positive and affirming connections with adults and peers in their communities who celebrate transgender youth, and these connections are all the more important if youth are not receiving this support in their schools or families (Kosciw et al., 2010). Luecke's (2011) case study reviews the experience of an elementary school supporting a transgender youth through gender transition and concludes by highlighting the importance of having a "strong and significant network of support" (p. 149) for transitioning students as well as their peers. It has been suggested that an important way of providing this space is offering a trans-affirmative, community-based youth group, especially where limited support for transgender youth exist, such as in rural communities (Snively, 2004). This is further supported by research indicating the important role of transgender support groups in contributing to the development of a positive identity in trans-identified persons (Hampton, 2007).

Given these negative descriptions of school environments and the immense effect that family rejection has on a young person's well-being, it is unsurprising that transgender youth would benefit from more support from their community, and are in fact requesting it. McGuire et al. (2010) report that study participants expressed a desire for more opportunities to engage in activities with other LGBTQ youth. Not only does this express a need for the creation of safe spaces for the exploration of identity, but it also speaks to the desire to be amongst other LGBTQ youth where their identity can be both explored and deepened; if desirable, in these spaces, gender identity can take a backseat to other aspects of identity that trans youth would like to explore and experiment with.

On the whole, transgender youth perceive there to be few safe environments in which to express their authentic gender identity (Grossman & D'Augelli, 2006) and as reported by the youth in this case study, this is even more likely in rural communities founded on conservative values. In the community to be discussed, there are high levels of religiosity and lower social status, both factors identified by

Ryan et al. (2010) to negatively influence the likelihood of family acceptance. Bird et al. (2012) write that "given the barriers LGBT youth may encounter in finding allies, it is essential that programs be developed to help these youth find caring and supportive adults" (p. 356). The literature clearly indicates the risks posed to genderqueer youth and the lack of supports and affirmation that they receive from their family, school, and community. Next, the findings of this case study will be discussed and how genderqueer youth in a rural community can benefit from the offering of an affirming space in their community in which to explore their gender and build connections with supportive adults and peers.

A CASE STUDY

Identifying a Need

In the spring of 2010 an increasing number of young people exploring gender identity and expression presented to a local mental health counseling clinic in a rural Canadian community. It is unclear if these youth were identifying their gender exploration as a 'mental health problem.' A more likely explanation is that this clinic is based on a self-referral model and provides free services to the public, as opposed to the other counseling centers in the community that have a fee-for-service model which possibly functions as a barrier for young people to access services. As more genderqueer youth were being seen at this clinic, common themes were identified in the types of problems or unique issues they faced. Observed themes included: isolation from other genderqueer youth and adults, lack of information about the possibilities for gender transition or preferred gender expression, lack of familial acceptance, suicidal ideation, school problems, and hopelessness about a future that included authentic gender expression. The counselors conceptualized these problems as a normal response to living in a community in which gender-creativity was discouraged and there were few, if any, opportunities to encounter other genderqueer persons.

There was a lack of opportunity for these young people to explore their gender identity/expression and to connect with other genderqueer people as well as a great deal of concern about the extent of suicidal ideation experienced by these youth. Multiple risk factors were identified, as were a lack of protective factors, such as identified informal or formal supports, hopefulness for the future, and/or having something to be involved and included in. In recognizing the imbalance between the risk and protective factors, and based on the idea that protective factors can be created and risk factors decreased if youth can connect with each other and affirming adults in the community, the idea of this community-based youth group for genderqueer and sexual minority youth was born.

Creating Safe and Welcoming Spaces

One of the most important considerations was the identification of a safe and welcoming space in which the group could meet. Consideration about the location of the group was given high priority as it was likely that some youth would choose not to inform their parents of their participation in the group and would need to find their own transportation to meetings, which in a smaller center with limited public transportation can prove to be quite difficult. Another consideration was privacy, and in particular offering the group in a secluded setting that would afford the youth valuable privacy to explore and express their preferred gender and sexual identities. This was thought to be especially important for genderqueer members who weren't comfortable expressing their preferred gender expression/identity in a public or even semi-public setting. The consideration of privacy was balanced with the consideration of creating a proud space in which to host the group. It was important that the value of privacy was not confused with hiding the group or with other shame-related interpretations. Young LGBTQ people in rural settings—and arguably many urban settings as well—are inundated with both overt and covert messages about hiding their identities (Snivley, 2004). Sometimes these messages are as subtle as the lack of role models and adult LGBTQ persons living openly in their communities. Thus, the facilitators concluded that it was important to create a private yet proud space for these youth to gather in.

As the idea for the group originated in a mental health clinic setting, it was important to consider the messages the host environment conveyed. Given the history of mistreatment of LGBTQ persons by the mental health community, hosting the group at the mental health clinic could promote pathologizing messages about LGBTQ and genderqueer identities and the types of problems encountered by these youth. Similar considerations were taken into account regarding other community counseling settings. And while school settings offered accessible, youth-friendly, and non-pathologizing environments, these also included many barriers. One of these barriers was the rivalry among the few local high schools in the community, thus making the group more accessible to youth attending the hosting school. Another barrier was the possible perception by youth that participation in the group would not be confidential and would somehow be conveyed to school personnel, thus compromising privacy and confidentiality. Lastly, consideration was given to school policy and provincial legislation that limited conversational topics and activities that could be engaged in without parental consent in a school setting. For example, in 2010 the province of Alberta passed Bill 44 which created provincial legislation prohibiting schools from promoting programs, instruction, or materials about sexuality and sexual orientation, amongst other things, without parental permission.

It was decided that securing a youth-friendly partner organization in facilitating and hosting the group would offer the greatest benefits in terms of accessibility, privacy, and allowance for a youth-led agenda. A partnership was created between the local mental health clinic and the Teen Center. However, the Center was undergoing construction and so the space would not be available until a year after the start of the group; therefore, a temporary space was sought. It was determined that the local library would meet the needs of the group and thus space was made available in a private room in one of its corners.

The library was convenient and youth friendly as it was located on Main Street and close to a bus stop. It also had the added advantage that even youth who did not tell their parents of their participation were able to get transportation to the library from them under another pretext. The library staff was informed well in advance of the start of the group and the importance of creating an affirming space was clearly communicated and allies identified, such as the head librarian, who created a resource list of LGBTQ books, videos, and media and made these resources readily available to the group members.

The group was advertised in school and community-counseling offices by known allies only. These allies were identified through the facilitator's historical interactions with each professional in addition to phone calls in which the proposed group was discussed and each professional's reaction and interest in promoting the group in a safe and thoughtful way was gauged. These identified allies were asked to advertise the group in their offices and provide youth who self-identified as genderqueer and/or sexual minority with information about the group. It was a concern that youth who were not 'out' would not be approached with information about the group and would come across this information only if they happened to see it in a counseling office or heard of it by word of mouth.

Although youth participation numbers were initially low, with only three youth attending the first group—two of which were genderqueer—over the course of the first 8 months the number of participants ranged from 1 to 15. To date, over the course of the 2.5 years the group has been meeting, more than 40 different youth have attended various functions, with 9 of them possessing genderqueer identities. At present, the youth range in age from 14 to 20 years, with the average age being 16. Initially all youth recruited were in high school; however, over the course of the 2.5 years that this group has been active, some of the youth have graduated from high school but still continue to come to the group as adult 'youth mentors.' When attendance was low in the first few months of the group's meetings, discussions among the group facilitators and youth occurred about how to advertise the group more effectively. Youth expressed concerns about advertising in public spaces for fear that community members might show up with either the intent to taunt or harm group members or to simply violate the confidentiality of the group. These concerns were taken seriously and it was decided that the group would continue to be advertised only by known allies and by word of mouth, despite the possibility that some youth-in-need may still not hear about the group.

The fact that this group has been well attended can likely be attributed to a combination of factors, the most significant being the commitment and leadership of the youth who regularly attend the group. The importance of having key allies identified in the school and counseling agencies cannot be emphasized enough. These allies identify youth who would benefit from attending the group, as well as often remind the youth in advance when the group meets. Support from an established youth program that proved to have long-term ties to many youth in the community and offered a creative space in which to welcome the youth was also paramount to the group members' attendance. Reported by the youth to be of importance was the lack of need for parental consent. Some of the youth attended the group without their parents' awareness, while others expressed that they would not have come if they needed to be bothered with the process of parental consent, even if their parents knew of their attendance.

Activities and Observations

The group meets once per month, from 6 until 8 p.m. Over the course of the past 2.5 years participants have engaged in many unique activities that were derived from their own brainstorming sessions. Ideas have included meeting with urban LGBTQ youth groups via FaceTime/Skype, watching LGBTQ-themed movies, inviting guests to share their experiences about being LGBTQ, educating schools about LGBTQ issues, planning a drag show, doing crafts, baking, and accessing sexual education. Most activities were actualized, although some suggestions were not as popular with group members or were impractical to implement, and thus they have not yet materialized. For example, the LGBTQ youth group that meets in the nearest urban setting does not do so on the same night as this youth group, making connection more difficult. Most members of the group were not interested in educating schools about LGBTQ issues and thus this has also not occurred, despite a few group members' interest in doing so. The decision regarding what activities to engage in was based on the numbers of youth who were interested. After a group brainstorming session, group members voted on their interest once an activity list was created at the beginning of each group year. Snively (2004) discusses how LGBTQ youth groups that are based in community as opposed to school settings may allow youth to have more influence in the decision making and management of the group, as "participants are not limited by school governance regarding the advisors' role, how and when the group may meet, the group's activities, or what may be discussed in the group setting" (p. 107). As mentioned, this is particularly true for school settings in provinces such as Alberta, where provincial legislation limits important conversation topics in school settings. In a community-based group, youth can discuss such topics and access accurate information from trusted and informed adults without parental consent.

Youth in the case study were routinely asked what activities they would like the group to engage in, allowing for the youth to identify the needs they wanted the group to meet. The youths' requests often spoke to the need for education about sex and sexuality for LGBTQ youth, as they were not receiving this information elsewhere. The genderqueer youth in the group also regularly requested the opportunity to have candid conversations with young adults who were also genderqueer. These conversations were being silenced in school and family settings and the youth were desperate for information about themselves. It is without doubt necessary to offer a safe setting for genderqueer youth to identify their needs and have these needs met, especially in communities that otherwise prohibited these conversations.

The youth in the group were not just hungry for information about themselves, but also were interested in learning about LGBTQ issues on a broader level. One of the first activities that became a ritual to start off the group was the "In the News" segment in which group facilitators would find LGBTQ-themed news stories from around the world and share them with the youth. This gave the youth the opportunity to talk about both positive and negative events that occurred over the course of the month and place their lives in a broader social, cultural, and political context. The group participants got involved and started to bring in their laptops with LGBTQ news segments that they wished to share with the group and then discuss them.

The group also became a place for the youth to share personal stories and join with one another in their experiences. The youth in this group would share incidents of mistreatment that they experienced in their home, community, and school settings. One youth reported that the principal of her public school disallowed her from using the girls' change room due to her genderqueer presentation and identity as a lesbian. This youth in particular did not feel that her parents would or could advocate for her, nor did she want the group facilitators to advocate on her behalf, but she did derive comfort from sharing this experience with her peers and validation from their outrage at this mistreatment. Another genderqueer youth shared how he was made to stand alone among his coworkers and managers while they mocked his feminine gender expression. He was later dismissed from his position. This story was all too common in the group, as other genderqueer youth joined in sharing how they had been dismissed from longer-term employment after experimenting with gender expression in the workplace.

A common story shared was the negative response that youth would receive from their parents or family members when coming out to them about their genderqueer or sexual minority status. These youth would join with one another as they shared the deep hurt and rejection they felt in relation to their families' responses. Other youth in the group would speak of abuse and mistreatment that they endured from strangers, such as having slurs yelled at them from the windows of passing cars as they walked along a street. Frequently the genderqueer youth in this group would share their frustration in response to the questions that they reported being asked by their peers or family members about their gender identity or expression. These stories would evoke tears, outrage, and sometimes even shared laughter among the group members. Although no youth requested formal intervention or advocacy on the part of the facilitators, they joined with each other in these moments and validated their sense of hurt and outrage in the group's unanimous naming of these events as wrong and discriminatory. This collective naming of the abuse and identifying the wrongdoers alleviated doubts about personal responsibility and self-blame for the events. We found that a group setting wherein genderqueer youth can speak to these experiences helps solidify their right to experiment with gender expression in both private and public settings and to be treated with dignity while doing so.

The group was also a place in which positive stories of success were shared. The stories unique to genderqueer youth included youth reporting that they 'passed' or had secured a relationship in which their authentic gender was recognized. Other stories included parents becoming more affirming of a youth's preferred gender identity and/or expression. These young people discussed boycotts of certain businesses that discriminated against genderqueer people, resulting in the strengthening of their personal agency. They also shared those places where they had been successful in finding employment as genderqueer youth, often encouraging other gender youth in the group to apply to these organizations, thus creating pockets of affirming space throughout the community. One genderqueer youth shared how his experience of attending a national LGBTQ summer camp was one of the best experiences of his life thus far, inspiring other youth to ask about how they themselves might attend such camps in coming years.

One positive story revolved around community activism. Two group members—a same-gender couple—had been dating for some time and shared how they had entered their names into the competition for what is essentially known as Prom King and Queen. This was not without controversy in the school setting and the group shared how the reactions of their peers ranged from support to disgust. One student had written a hateful message on the bathroom stall about these youth and the two teens struggled with how to address this. The group rallied around them, offered their support, and generated the idea of taking a photo of the message and writing a caption—"This Is Hate"—and posting this publicly all over the school. The process of taking a hateful anonymous message and making it public and shameful to the person who had written it once again strengthened personal agency and had an empowering effect on the group and especially the couple.

Community activism was also encouraged through the youth group during craft nights that focused on preparation for Spirit Day and Pink Shirt Day, both of which focus on taking a stand against bullying, specifically the bullying of LGBTQ youth. Whether youth chose to display their crafts publicly on these days or thereafter was secondary to the benefit they derived from surrounding themselves with a community of people who opposed the mistreatment of LGBTQ persons and passionately discussed this opposition at length.

Watching LGBTQ-themed movies, documentaries, and television shows became a much requested activity, partly due to the fact that many of the group participants reported that they did not feel comfortable viewing this material at home. Others noted that watching shows with LGBTQ characters in the youth group setting was more affirming than it was with other peers or at home because of the frequency of homophobic and transphobic comments. It was clearly important to the youth that they had the opportunity to witness LGBTQ people living their everyday lives and the opportunity to do so in a safe space.

The most frequently requested activity involved inviting LGBTQ young adults to come to the youth group to talk about their experiences in being a member of this population. To ensure that the genderqueer members of the group had contact with accessible role models, a panel of transgender people and parents of transgender youth were invited to speak with our group. This was important as it allowed for the witnessing of transgender persons and the opportunity to access accurate information about gender expression and transitioning, if so desired. Having access to loving and affirming parents of transgender youth was instrumental to many of the young people's understanding of the process that their parents were at present going through or might go through in the future if disclosure occurred. Many of the genderqueer youth in the group exchanged contact information with guest speakers, thus expanding their support network. Similarly, Snively (2004) emphasizes the importance of creating opportunities for LGBTQ youth to meet adult allies who can act as mentors. Snively highlights how opportunities such as these allow group members to meet other LGBTQ persons in a safe environment, providing an alternative to bars and other high-risk environments. It is also an alternative to young people seeking out anonymous mentors and support online, which poses its own risks. Many of the genderqueer youth in the group would discuss how they accessed most of their information about diverse gender expression and identities on the Internet and how most of their support existed online. The Internet is often highlighted (Hampton, 2007) as a means for transgender persons to connect with each other and access necessary information. However, in-person connections may be more important in alleviating isolation and feelings of alienation in small rural communities where youth often feel completely alone, even when connected to online communities. As previously highlighted, Bird et al. (2012) suggest that role models can be important in reducing risk, a concern identified both in the research and in precipitating the development of the youth group. Also worth considering is that information about transitioning and local supports may be more accurate if gathered by other transgender people living in the same geographical area rather than in international online communities.

More obvious, but not less important, is the role that a community-based LGBTQ youth group can play in providing young people an opportunity to meet youth from other schools or in their broader community. Snively (2004) states that "this is particularly important in rural areas, where the numbers of persons willing to participate in school-based GSAs may be very small and the climate may be more harsh than in urban areas" (p. 107). Observations from the present case study support Snively's findings, particularly regarding how these youth broadened their support networks by meeting other genderqueer and sexual minority youth in their community. This is particularly true for the genderqueer members, as initially the youth would voice perceptions of being "the only one" in the community or not knowing of any other genderqueer youth.

Another activity that served to expand the support networks of the group participants was a family dinner night. Youth who felt comfortable bringing their family members to a dinner hosted by the group were invited to do so. There was an emphasis on inclusion for those youth who did not feel comfortable bringing any family members and they were included at another family's dinner table. The parents who attended this evening also benefited from being connected with other parents of genderqueer and sexual minority youth and in seeing their child as one of many genderqueer and sexual minority youth in the community, possibly reducing parental fears about their child experiencing isolation and loneliness. The nearest urban PFLAG chapter was present that evening to offer support to families and to be available to answer questions.

One of the best-attended evenings has been the group's annual Pride Prom. This idea originated within the group in response to a group participant who was unable to attend school graduation in the role of their preferred gender. Instead, they reported feeling highly pressured by parents to adhere to very heteronormative and gender-normative expectations. The group participants requested that the group host a Pride Prom for the youth group members to attend as their preferred gender and with their preferred partners. This night is attended by many youth in the community who do not attend group regularly or have never attended group, and offers an opportunity for all youth to participate in an environment in which genderqueer and sexual minority identities are celebrated.

Once a year the youth are invited to attend the closest urban center's Pride Parade. Youth in the group often have misperceptions and fears about the Pride Parade and this allows them to attend the event with the support and safety of the group. By being included in this larger urban celebration they are able to witness the outpouring of affirmation toward gender and sexual diversity that is not made available to them in the smaller rural community in which they live.

DISCUSSION

Since the inception of the group in September 2010, several genderqueer youth have made comments about the importance of the group in their lives, yet to date they have been observed to attend fairly infrequently. Barriers to attendance should be considered, such as a lack of parental support, other extracurricular activities that were more supported by parents that competed with the time the group was offered, and lack of transportation. However, it is also important to consider the possibility that simply having the group available and meeting in the community, even if the youth rarely or never attended it, met a need for these youth. Toomey, Ryan, Diaz, and Russell (2011) support this consideration in school settings: "Consistent with previous research, we find that the presence of a GSA seems to be a more salient predictor of well-being than GSA membership" (p. 182). Perhaps simply the presence of these groups communicates to genderqueer youth that they have peers and community members who affirm their authentic identity and their right to explore and experiment with gender, thus offering as much support as needed. This should be a subject of further research in community and school settings.

When the group in the case study was initiated, no GSAs existed in either the junior or the senior high schools in the community. Within months of the initiation of the group, the youth in the group from one local high school had started a school GSA, furthering the support networks in the community. Two years later, youth from the group started a second GSA in another local high school. It is worthwhile to consider the role that having a community-based peer support group for these youth has played in the development of these two GSAs. These observations have been made previously: "As communities with local supports are more likely to have GSAs in their schools, these findings also highlight the important role local community advocates may play in supporting GSAs" (Kosciw et al., 2010, p. 57).

There may be benefits to community-based groups that school-based programs cannot share, even in communities with schools that have established GSAs. Snively (2004) discusses the importance of the youth having greater anonymity and control over what information about their gender and sexual identity is shared and with whom in a community setting as opposed to a school-based GSA. In particular, Snively goes on to state that "teachers and fellow students are less likely to know of a person's participation in a community-based queer youth group unless he or she wants them to know" (p. 107). Interestingly, in the case study all youth in the group who had a GSA at their school did report attending the GSA; it is therefore unclear whether these youth valued anonymity and control over disclosure as Snively suggests. It is unknown the degree to which the genderqueer youth who attended their school's GSA disclosed in the school-based group about their preferred gender identities; it is similarly unclear the extent to which gender identity and expression are discussed or explored in GSAs, particularly those in rural communities. Often GSAs will be held on lunch breaks or after school; genderqueer youth who are not comfortable expressing their gender or exploring their gender expression in a school setting would face a barrier in doing so in these meetings. In a community setting, however, genderqueer youth may have more of an opportunity to experiment with different gender markers, such as styles of clothing, accessories, makeup, hairstyles, names, and pronouns, without fellow students or teachers witnessing or hearing about this experimentation. We need further research on the question of whether a community-based group for genderqueer youth provides a setting in which they are more comfortable exploring gender in a safe environment away from both home *and* school.

The role that a community-based LGBTQ youth group can play in providing young people an opportunity to meet youth from other schools or in their broader community is of great importance. Snively (2004) states that "this is particularly important in rural areas, where the numbers of persons willing to participate in school-based GSAs may be very small and the climate may be more harsh than in urban areas" (p. 107). Observations from the present case study support Snively's findings, particularly regarding how these young people broadened their support networks by meeting other genderqueer and sexual minority youth in their community. This is particularly true for the genderqueer members, as initially the youth would voice perceptions of being "the only one" in the community or not knowing of any other genderqueer youth.

CONCLUSION

Many of the benefits identified by Snively (2004) regarding the importance of community-based LGBTQ youth groups were observed over the course of facilitating the group discussed in this case study, with a particular emphasis on the benefits derived from participation by the genderqueer youth members. Overall, all activities were focused on allowing the youth the opportunity to explore aspects of their gender and sexual identities that they would otherwise not have been able to, and moreover in a public setting surrounded by affirming peers and adults. These youth benefited from witnessing each other's exploration and identity growth, as well as expanding their connections with other youth and adults who may function as accessible role models or sources of support. Otherwise inaccessible information was also made accessible through group activities. Further research is needed about the benefits of community-based youth groups for LGBTQ youth in rural communities, particularly so for genderqueer youth; however, it is certainly clear from current research and this case study that genderqueer youth are in need of increased support and that this support can and should be offered in community settings.

NOTES

1. The youth in this group were in various stages of exploring their gender *and* sexual identities. Not all of the youth exploring gender identity and/or expression identified with the term 'transgender,' nor is it assumed that all youth in this case study will go on to identify with the term 'transgender' or to transition genders. To honor the process of each young person's gender development, the term *genderqueer* will be used in this chapter to capture the youth in this group experimenting with gender identity and/or expression. *Sexual minority* youth refers to lesbian, gay, bisexual, and all other youth exploring diverse expressions of affectional/emotional attraction. I will refer to the peer support group for genderqueer youth and their sexual minority peers as *the group* throughout this chapter. The acronym *LGBTQ* (lesbian, gay, bisexual, transgender, and queer) will be used when referring to a broader population of gender and sexually diverse persons.
2. In this section, when the language varies from the terms outlined in the introduction, I am using the language used by the particular study's authors.

CHAPTER THIRTEEN

"Expanding the Circle"

Serving Children, Youth, and Families by Integrating Gender Diversity and Affirming Gender-Independent Children

LORRAINE GALE AND HALEY SYRJA-MCNALLY

Dedicated to the memory of Kyle Smith Scanlon (1971–2012), Trans Leader, Educator, and Advocate

PROLOGUE

Take a moment, sit back, and imagine …

> … a bright, energetic 6-year-old child bursts into the room, dancing around in a spar-kly, swirly pink dress … a child whose eyes shine even more than the dress. … You revel in watching this child dance about, satisfied that this is a happy, healthy child developing well. You remark with a smile, "Sign that girl up for dance classes!" But then the realization hits home … it's not a girl, it's a BOY!

Or at least, the child has a male body and, consequently, people made an automatic decision to raise the child in ways we think boys need to be guided—with trucks instead of dolls, with action figures instead of princesses, with hockey instead of ballet, to be like "Daddy" instead of "Mommy." Now imagine you provide some kind of human service to this child or the family. Perhaps you are the child's teach-er, or a parent-child drop-in coordinator. Or perhaps you provide support services to the family, or you are a child welfare worker, mandated to protect children from physical, sexual, and psychological harm. What do you do? Some options may include:

1. Leave him alone and hope he grows out of it?
2. Express your concerns to his parents about his troubling gender confusion and advise them to reinforce his correct gender role identity?
3. Recommend a psychiatrist to unearth the family dysfunction that must have caused this abnormality?
4. Or ... something else?

This chapter will introduce a paradigm shift in how human service organizations and professionals view and communicate ideas about gender with the children, youth, and families we serve. The Children's Aid Society of Toronto (CAS-Toronto) has developed an anti-oppressive practice model to integrate an affirming approach on gender and sexual diversity into service provision for our own use as a child welfare agency, as well as for other human service organizations and professions. The model, the *Out and Proud Affirmation Guidelines: Practice Guidelines for Equity in Gender and Sexual Diversity,* includes a framework, "Expanding the Circle," that encourages listening, affirmation, a person-centred approach, and a focus on equity. In this chapter, we will apply this framework to our work with gender-independent children and their families.

CROSSING THE LINES

How Human Service Professionals Respond to Kids Who Cross Gender Lines

Let's call this child "Leslie." For now, we will refer to Leslie as a boy and use male pronouns—"he," "him," "his." Leslie crosses gender lines—as a child with a male body, he likes to do things many of us think of as only for girls. This kind of scenario will often elicit strong feelings. Opinions abound, wanted or not, from a myriad of sources ... the child's family, teachers, other parents, people in the community, and human service professionals. Responses by human service professionals tend to fall into three camps in terms of how the behavior is understood and what intervention, if any, is recommended. First, is the *Pathology Response* which views cross-gender expression and feelings as indicators that something is wrong with the child; the child is failing to learn an "appropriate" gender role and may grow up to be gay and/or transgender, which are viewed negatively. Immediate intervention is recommended by reinforcing "appropriate" gender behaviors and decreasing "inappropriate" ones (Zucker & Bradley, 1995). Typical responses from providers in this camp may include:

No more dressing up in Mom's skirts and heels. Don't let him dance anymore. ... It's time he started acting like a boy so he doesn't turn funny or queer!

Don't let him be a sissy! ... Mom is mollycoddling him too much and he lacks a good male role model. Match him up with a tough, masculine Big Brother who can show him how to be a real man.

Second, there is the *Wait-and-See(-and-Hope) Response*. This response also views cross-gender expression as undesirable and concerning in children; however, it is believed to be temporary and will dissipate over time. Direct intervention is not required ... yet. Common statements reflecting this viewpoint include: "Don't worry, he'll grow out of it. It's a phase. Give him time, but watch him closely. Praise him for anything masculine he shows interest in."

Finally, there is the *Protective Response*. In this perspective, cross-gender expression is not viewed as directly problematic in and of itself, but is viewed as a cause of bullying. This can amount to "blaming the victim." Cross-gender expression is discouraged to ensure he "fits in" and to protect against harassment from others, and may include statements including: "He'll get bullied ... better toughen him up right away. Enrol him in wrestling, hockey, and football fast!" or, "If he would just try to 'fit in' more, he wouldn't get picked on so much."

Actually, all of these responses are variations on the same "pathology-based" theme. They all presume that gender fits neatly into socially prescribed boxes—the "girl box" and the "boy box"—and that any digression is problematic. Cross-gender expression, especially in boys, is viewed as abnormal or undesirable and should be changed to make it more stereotypically masculine. When girls cross gender lines, there may be more tolerance for a while, but eventually there will typically be pressures to eliminate "masculine" behaviors and follow socially constructed notions of femininity.

Gender-independent children who cross gender lines are the ones seen as "sissy boys" and "tomboys." Some will grow up to adopt an LGBTQ identity on the sexual orientation spectrum and/or the gender identity spectrum. Others will grow up to identify as heterosexual and may still have "cross-gender" interests without identifying on the trans spectrum. Others will identify as heterosexual and will become more gender conforming over time. The key is that we don't know how children will later identify; we can't know, nor can we "make" them be one way or another. It is a personal journey of exploration and self-discovery for each individual.

We do know that many of these children will experience harassment and possibly violence based on how they express their sense of gender, fueled by homophobic and transphobic assumptions and judgments. Much of this will occur among peers (GLSEN, 2012; Taylor et al., 2011). Some will experience it from family members (Roberts, Rosario, Corliss, Koenen & Austin, 2012). They will need our support to build resiliency against the negative messages and to make their environments safe and equitable.

Since 1960, many mental health professionals and gender identity clinics serving children have used a "pathology" model with gender-independent children, in which diverse gender identity and expression are viewed as abnormal. "Reparative" behavior modification treatments are designed to prevent transsexualism (and sometimes homosexuality) by reinforcing "gender-normative" behaviors (Lev, 2004; Pyne, 2012; Zucker & Bradley, 1995). Families are expected to implement these treatments at home. Other professionals, organizations, and human service systems serving children, youth, and families, such as the child welfare system, are a microcosm of the broader society. Just as social trends ostracize anyone stepping outside gender or sexual norms, so too have human services tended to adopt the "pathology" approach toward trans and gender-independent children and youth, viewing transsexualism and homosexuality as negative and undesirable. (Brill & Pepper, 2008; Goodbaum, Huot, & Patterson, 2012; Mallon, 1999a; J. McCullagh, personal communication, January 2, 2013; Namaste, 2000; Pyne, 2012; Wilber, Ryan, & Marksamer, 2006; Woronoff, Estrada, & Sommer, 2006).

Child welfare services have participated in discrimination, alienation, inequity, and sometimes abuse against gender-independent and LGBTQ children and youth, whom they were mandated to protect (Woronoff et al., 2006). This is not a proud legacy. As John McCullagh, a longtime Canadian child welfare worker, administrator, and evaluator, noted, "it was just the way things were done. Gender and sexual diversity were seen as bad; it was to be stamped out." (J. McCullagh, personal communication, January 2, 2013).

"No Longer Considered Ethical"—Critiques of the Pathology Model

Various critiques challenge the theoretical premises and treatment protocols of the traditional pathology model. Critics cite negative impacts and outcomes for gender-independent and LGBTQ children and youth subjected to these approaches, as well as gender-biased assumptions and ethical concerns (Brill & Pepper, 2008; Ehrensaft, 2011; Lev, 2004; Mallon, 1999a; Pyne, 2012). Groundbreaking outcome studies by the Family Acceptance Project (FAP) and Trans PULSE indicate that mental health, risks, and outcomes are dramatically worse for LGBTQ youth whose parents reject their identity and gender expression. Trans youth were found to be 14 times more likely to attempt suicide in the past year if their parents were not very supportive, compared to trans youth with very supportive parents

(Travers et al., 2012). Conversely, navigation through adolescence into adulthood is much more successful when parents accept and support their LGBTQ children, including their diverse gender identities and expressions (Ryan, 2009a, 2009b; C. Ryan, personal communication, November 13, 2011; Ryan, Russell, Huebner, Diaz, & Sanchez, 2012; Travers et al., 2012).

Caitlin Ryan, lead researcher for the FAP, indicates that "supporting an adolescent's gender expression is among the most important family responses in reducing risk and promoting well-being in adulthood. ... High levels of family/parental pressure to enforce gender conformity in LGBT youth is related to very high levels of depression, attempted suicide, illegal drug use and risk for HIV in young adulthood" (C. Ryan, personal communication, November 13, 2011). Moreover, the World Professional Association for Transgender Health (WPATH) has declared that, for both adults and children, "treatment aimed at trying to change a person's gender identity and expression to become more congruent with sex assigned at birth has been attempted ... without success. ... Such treatment is no longer considered ethical" (WPATH, 2011, p. 16).

The Voice of Children—A Paradigm Shift

New research findings and equity-based professional values are converging with changing social attitudes, evolving community-based services, LGBTQ activism, and some expansion of human rights legislation to include diverse gender identity and expression (Ontario Human Rights Commission, 2012). This convergence points to a new lens on gender, suggesting that a paradigm shift is warranted, even essential, in relation to how we understand gender. The shift is toward greater acceptance of diverse gender identities as natural variations on a spectrum of possibilities, and away from the notion of two restrictive gender categories. (Brill & Pepper, 2008; CAS-Toronto, 2012; Children's National Medical Center, 2005; Ehrensaft, 2011; Lev, 2004; Mallon, 1999a, 1999c; Pyne, 2012; WPATH, 2011). Within this context, there is another important factor in the evolution of this new paradigm, involving a grassroots process of community engagement and activism. In astonishing contrast to traditional academic and medical models, it is actually *children* who have ushered in a new era by simply and courageously being who they are in the face of pressure to be otherwise. Furthermore, it is their parents who have enabled children to take the lead by listening to and affirming their own children, and by having the courage to challenge echelons of power holders. Finally, it is LGBTQ communities, particularly trans activists and allies, who have advocated and struggled for the space to hear and respond to these children and their parents with respect (Brill & Pepper, 2008; Children's National Medical

Center, 2005; Ehrensaft, 2011; Lev, 2004; Pyne, 2012). Human services are moving toward a future where we listen to the people we serve, affirm who they are, support self-determination and self-expression, and keep our eye on the prize ... greater equity for people with the courage to be their own unique individual selves.

Rooted in a commitment to anti-oppression, this paradigm shift may be described as a "diversity" or "affirmation" model which views gender and sexual diversity as healthy for individuals at all ages, and an asset to communities. It establishes the goal as justice and equity, rather than gender conformity and heteronormativity. The "problem" is identified as societal bias against diverse gender identities and expressions; corresponding messages of pathology and discriminatory behaviors are identified as aspects of oppression. The solution is to be an ally to gender-independent children, affirming who they are, and working to eliminate oppression through education, advocacy, and support for families. So it is society that is mistaken and unjust and so must change, not the child.

This is a radical departure from viewing the gender-independent child as the problem, expecting that child to hide or change, and reinforcing notions that gender diversity, homosexuality, and transsexualism are abnormal or inferior. Human service sectors are at a crossroads in terms of how they understand gender, especially in children. Some human service organizations are at the crest of the wave of this paradigm shift, transforming their agency cultures and practices toward greater gender and sexual equity. The CAS-Toronto is one such organization at the forefront in the Canadian child welfare field in developing services that affirm gender and sexual diversity and strive for equity. In response to requests for practical strategies from staff and foster parents, we at the CAS-Toronto began by listening to LGBTQ and gender-independent young people and communities, as well as staff and foster parents. We have developed policies and the *Guidelines* identified above, within the context of an anti-oppression/anti-racism organizational transformation process.

ABOUT THE OUT AND PROUD AFFIRMATION GUIDELINES

The *Guidelines* were developed with the generous support of Advisory Committees, including internal staff and several trans community members. In particular, we remember one community Advisory member, Kyle Scanlon (1971–2012), a spectacular trans activist and educator from the 519 Church St. Community Centre in Toronto, whose voice resonates on every page of the *Guidelines*. In the *Guidelines*, the "Expanding the Circle" framework rests on four pillars: (1) listening; (2) affirmation; (3) a person-centred approach; and (4) equity. This is reinforced by a series of 20 practice guidelines based on principles already held in social work and other human service professions. The *Guidelines* indicate strategies to create safer spaces, provide competent services, and solidify organizational transformation in how we approach gender and sexual diversity and equity with everyone we serve, toward the best interests and outcomes for the child. Although they are developed for the child welfare field, the *Guidelines* are written in clear language and are easily applicable to a wide range of human service sectors that serve children, youth, or families. They address young children up to young adults, and integrate broad aspects of gender and sexuality that are not often addressed together in existing resources.

THE FRAMEWORK: "EXPANDING THE CIRCLE"

Why "Expand the Circle"?

Human services workers who work with children like Leslie, the 6-year-old boy who loves sparkly pink dresses, may feel conflicted. It may jar us to see a boy dressed in what are considered "girls' clothes" and doing "girly" things. It's uncomfortable. This is not the way things are "supposed" to be. We may ask questions that suggest there is something seriously wrong with the child, the parents, and/ or their parenting practices. We wonder what to do. We feel a responsibility to do the "right" thing, but there may be few organizational or professional guidelines to tell us what to do. We may look to the DSM-IV-TR (American Psychiatric Association, 2000) and find that "gender dysphoria in children" is a diagnosable mental illness. We may conclude that something is indeed wrong, we fear (rightly so) that Leslie is likely to be bullied, and we want to find a way to help him become more "normal" and "fit in," so he will be happy. We are faced with a dilemma, figuratively speaking: "How do we fit a square peg into a round hole?"

What do we imagine needs to happen to get that square peg to fit into that round hole? So often we try to chip off the squared edges, and then we push and shove and wedge, trying to jam that re-shaped peg into the hole until, at long last, battered and bruised, it finally, more or less, fits. The problem is that identity is not pathology. Jeremy Vincent (2011), a Toronto teacher who grew up gender-independent, said, "As a child I thought, 'How do I fit into this little space when I am really THIS BIG!?' This is where the paradigm shift comes in. Instead of trying to re-shape and ram that square peg into that round hole, can we not think outside the box and simply adjust the space surrounding the peg? Does that space really need to be static, rigid, and unchanging? Or can it be adaptive, flexible, nurturing? Can we create a space that moulds itself to the shape of the peg? Appreciate the special qualities of that peg?

Traditional Aboriginal teachings tell us there is "room for everyone" in the circle as they are. Indeed, many First Nations from North America ("Turtle Island") and elsewhere traditionally held Two-Spirit people (Aboriginal people whom Western people might today think of as LGBTQ) in high esteem. Before colonization, Two-Spirits traditionally were valued as special gifts in many communities, holding "two spirits," that is, both male and female qualities. They held places of honor, such as teachers, healers, visionaries, and spiritual leaders (2-Spirited People of the First Nations, 2008). We give appreciation to First Nations communities for sharing the circle image and the wisdom inherent in the traditional Aboriginal principle that "we are all part of the circle."

The theme of the *Affirmation Guidelines* is "Expanding the Circle." This involves stretching our communities, our ideas, and our hearts to embrace every kind of child or youth, in the spirit of these Aboriginal teachings. "The circle is elastic. It stretches to welcome and include all diverse gender and sexual identities" (CAS-Toronto, 2012, p. 66). We can "expand the circle" to make room for everyone as they are, so that children and youth have space to explore who they are, be themselves, and receive affirmation and appreciation. If we imagine that the peg is the unique child and the hole is the world we live in, we know neither is static or unchanging. Children need a strong place in the circle, where they are accepted and loved by their families and communities. However, when the child is expected to change the essence of their being in order to access that acceptance and love, it is too great a burden. It is the community circle that must be flexible enough to welcome every child, valuing all the ways that a child is unique, offering special gifts to the community.

THE FOUR PILLARS OF THE "EXPANDING THE CIRCLE" FRAMEWORK

LGBTQ and gender-independent children and youth have told us how we at CAS-Toronto need to serve them, in four fundamental learnings that have been adapted into four key "pillars." These pillars form the foundation of the "Expanding the Circle" framework in the *Guidelines*. Each pillar in turn offers a key message for service providers to give to young people.

Pillar 1—Listening

In the early 1990s CAS-Toronto was faced with a stark reality—many LGBTQ youth felt safer living on the dangerous streets of Toronto than they did living in our care (CASMT, 1995). We were forced to ask ourselves why we were failing our youth. One of the first and most critical things we had to learn was, in fact, to actually listen to young people. A foster parent tells this story about a 10-year-old child in care.

The agency sent a child to my foster home who was technically a girl, but hated all things we think girls should wear or do. She was a "tomboy" in the fullest sense of the word. In her previous foster home, she was forced to wear pink frilly dresses and do her hair up with barrettes. They tried to make her like 'girly-girl' kinds of play. She was miserable, angry, and labelled a 'behavior problem.' So the foster parents gave up on her and she was sent to me.

When she peed on all her dresses in her closet on the very first day, we talked about it. She was clear she didn't want to wear them, ever. I said, "Ok, you can wear what you want." She revelled in wearing boys' clothes and rough-and-tumble play … no dolls or games of 'house' for her! She even taught herself to pee standing up … with better aim than the boys! It was amazing to see how quickly she settled down. She began to trust me, and all the behavior problems vanished. She just needed someone to see her for who she really was and trust her to know what was right for herself. Why is it so hard to trust children? (CAS-Toronto, 2012, p. 139)

When CAS-Toronto talked to trans youth who had been in care, the resounding chorus was "admit that we exist" (CAS-Toronto, 2012, p. 32). This is a profound statement about the importance of visibility and seeing our young people for who they are. We deny their existence when we insist that they express their gender in a way that is contrary to how they feel, or when we doubt their identity or say they are just "going through a phase." We send a message that we do not really believe they can know who they are. Young people tell us that when we judge and stifle their core gender identity and expression, they become distressed, alienated, and psychologically harmed (Brill & Pepper 2008; Ehrensaft, 2012; Lev, 2004; Marksamer, 2011; Pyne, 2012; Wilber et al., 2006; Woronoff et al., 2006).

Active Listening

Real listening is not a passive activity, waiting patiently for children and youth to "come out" to us as service providers. Too many will assume we are not safe and will never divulge their gender or sexual identity or any related struggles to us. In so doing, we deny them important opportunities to explore who they are, share their musings and dilemmas with us, and experience our support. To listen effectively in a way that most benefits the young person, we need to use "active listening" skills.

1. Listen with open curiosity: Approach the child or youth with open curiosity and nonjudgment. Let them know we make no assumptions about who they may grow up to be attracted to, how they may experience their gender, or how they might like to express it. Listen to what they say, what they

don't say, and what they convey with actions. Express genuine pleasure at their delight in their gender play, as in, "Wow! You look so happy dancing in that sparkly dress! How does it feel for you?"

2. Create a safe space: Open up a positive and safe environment that encourages children to share their feelings. We, the adults in their lives, must be proactive and take initiative to open the conversation and communicate acceptance. Why would young people trust us to talk about taboo topics like gender and sexual identity, when any judgment or rejection could be devastating for them? Instead, the onus is on us as adults to first send a message that we accept and support them for who they are, no matter what. We can be frank that some people may not understand, and indicate that we support them and really want to hear what it feels like for them.

3. Encourage young people to explore who they are: Identity must emerge from within over time. When we consistently create a safe, nonjudgmental environment that communicates acceptance and open curiosity, children and youth may be able to allow their true feelings to emerge. They can "try on" different possibilities and learn to understand and express their feelings. This is a crucial part of identity formation. It can be a powerful act to give young people the message that it is just fine to "explore who you are," and engage with them to talk about their feelings, their experiences, their yearnings, who they are inside, how they like to present themselves, and how they like to play. We can let Leslie know there are lots of kids who like to express their gender differently from others, and that, by listening to his own feelings, over time he will understand who he is ... "It's what's inside that counts."

Pillar 2—Affirmation

Another lesson that the CAS-Toronto learned from LGBTQ youth was that "we are your children too" (CASMT, 1995). All children and youth need affirmation for who they are, as they are—to be accepted, valued, respected, and loved as their authentic self with positive support and encouragement. This is especially true for LGBTQ and gender-independent children and youth, who typically receive ongoing negative messages, disapproval, and harassment. They need us to proactively appreciate them and let them know they are wonderful, not just *in spite* of their unique variations, but also *because* of these variations. And they need us to help them learn to affirm themselves.

Unfortunately, the youth told us "the system has failed us in a fundamental way, in not providing a sense of family, belonging and support to help us get through" (CASMT, 1995, p. 10). As a Canadian child welfare organization, we at

CAS-Toronto are "in the family business." We are sometimes the legal "parent" of a young person or we support families to care for their children, or we create new families through adoption and permanency planning. We learned that we need to love and affirm our LGBTQ youth and our gender-independent children for who they are, unconditionally, and that we need to support their families to do the same.

As service providers, we can give clear, positive messages that who LGBTQ and gender-independent young people are is wonderful, even if some people don't understand. Young people need to know we recognize and value their courage to be who they are and their uniqueness as the gift and strength it is. They need messages that affirm who they are—"I am so proud of you!" Even at age 6, Leslie can be told that there have been many people like him who cross gender lines all through history and all over the world, who are gifts to their communities. We can tell him that if other people respond negatively, "the 'problem' is not with you, but with others who don't or won't understand unique kids like you." So often young people who are "different" from the majority internalize the discomfort, disapproval, and hostility they experience from others. They turn it inward and conclude that "something is fundamentally wrong with me." Instead, this young person needs an ally who can be affirming and reinforce that they are not the problem. Addressing this core internal belief in a young person is the foundation for any other support or intervention.

Pillar 3—A Person-Centred Approach

Identity is as personal as a fingerprint. Gender and sexual identity are valuable parts of a whole self that emerge from within. They can only be discovered and defined by the individual. Identity is not pathology; it cannot be effectively or ethically manipulated into something that is not authentic to that individual (WPATH, 2011). Services and care for LGBTQ and gender-independent children and youth are more effective when used with a "person-centred approach" that supports each person's authentic self. This approach includes a commitment to support self-exploration, self-identification, and self-determination.

In adopting a person-centred approach, we trust young people to lead their own process, and to be able to sort out, over time, who they are and how they identify, with support. In a process of self-identification, young people need accurate and affirming information, a sense of community, support, and strategies for safety. The emergence of identity can take time and many children and youth need to explore several possibilities. For example, on one day, Leslie may relish pink from head to toe including jewellery, nail polish, and high heels; on another day, he may be covered in mud after playing football for the first time. These seemingly contrary play explorations are not actually in conflict. Rather, they reflect a child who is free to play in ways that feel natural in that moment, and this supports self-actualization.

As service providers, we can use our knowledge of community supports and services to assist a young person to explore options and to find resources to be safe and feel valued. For example, let us imagine that Leslie feels intense distress in early puberty, especially about the *direction* puberty is taking. Perhaps Leslie is specifically upset that his body is becoming more masculine, when "she" clearly states she is a girl inside and wishes she had a girl body. Or perhaps Leslie is unclear about his identity and is trying to understand if, deep inside, he might be a girl, or a boy who likes "girly" clothes, or neither a "boy" nor a "girl," or some combination.

Depending on the situation, service providers can encourage opportunities for Leslie to explore and discuss his gender feelings, and experiment with diverse gendered interests and expressions in a supportive environment. We can encourage the family to support Leslie to dress freely at home, as desired, in masculine, feminine, or gender-neutral clothing. We can support the family to listen to her verbal and nonverbal cues about gender, to ask questions with open curiosity, and to engage her in self-reflection. We can encourage the family to accept Leslie as he is, affirm the ways he is unique, encourage him to explore, and allow him to eventually self-identify.

It is important to build a supportive community for the gender-independent child. We can help the child to find a range of other kids who also cross gender lines, such as the "Gender-Independent Group" for such children currently offered by the Toronto District School Board. We can also help the child to find other adult role models who were once gender-independent children like them, even if only by viewing carefully selected websites. As gender-independent children explore and grow, they need information about positive futures. If they only see two rigid gender boxes that don't fit how they feel, the future can be a source of despair. We can give children information about various identities they could explore. We can explain to Leslie the different ways his identity may emerge over time and corresponding options that he may wish to consider as he gets older, including:

- Being a boy who likes to do things people think are just for girls
- Growing up to fall in love with just boys or any gender and identifying as gay, bisexual, queer, etc.
- Becoming more interested in stereotypically "boyish" things over time
- "Socially transitioning" to start living life as a girl rather than as a boy
- Medically delaying puberty to allow time to sort out feelings and plans
- Identifying as "genderqueer" or "genderfluid," wherein gender is not easily contained as just male or female
- Identifying as female and transgender/transsexual, and seeking medically prescribed "cross-sex" hormones at age 16+ to make her body become more feminine

- Identifying as female and transgender/transsexual and seeking sex reassignment surgery at age 18+ to surgically change her chest and/or genitals into a woman's body

As adults, we often think children cannot understand such concepts. But children's imaginations are more flexible in visioning diverse possibilities than we give them credit for. A 6-year-old gender-independent child in care at CAS-Toronto asked, unprompted, "Is it true that a boy can get an operation to change into a girl?" (CAS-Toronto, 2012, p. 152).

Safety is an important concern for gender-independent and LGBTQ children and youth. Although each context and situation is different, finding the right balance between self-expression and safety is critical. Some children may feel fulfilled to express their gender just at home, in a supportive environment. For others, only being able to express their gender at home may feel stifling— they may increasingly need to express their authentic gender at all times. In this case, it will be important to establish support for the child and family, and to plan carefully with the school to ensure the child will be supported and protected. Part of safety planning involves building resiliency skills in young people to trust themselves, to be able to listen to their instinctive feelings about safety and risk, to develop safety plans, and to learn strategies to protect themselves.

Pillar 4—Equity

Finally, LGBTQ and gender-independent young people asked us, "Who's in MY court?" They need to know whom they can count on, who will stand up for them, who will make change in the spaces and systems they move in. They want to know what we are prepared to do about the world they live in to make it fair and safe and positive for them. Many are not prepared to accept second-class status, in which their very right to be is continually called into question. They want, and deserve, equity—our fourth pillar in the "Expanding the Circle" framework.

As noted above, the "problem" is not the gender-independent child, but a social environment that fails to accept or value diverse ways of being. The solution therefore lies in shifting the world we live in to create equitable and accepting environments that value a spectrum of gender possibilities. This requires both a paradigm shift in how we think about gender and sexual diversity, as well as systemic change in practice. As service providers we can be change agents. We can contribute to creating supportive, affirming, and safe environments at all levels of the organizations we work in. When we do this, we deliver the message that our young people deserve equity and no less.

One of the first steps in working toward equity is to listen to the voice of the young person about the day-to-day experiences they have where they live, learn, work, and play, at home, school, and in the community. Equipped with information from the young person and working with them, we as service providers can advocate in all areas of the child's life to ensure safety, acceptance, full inclusion, appreciation for their uniqueness, and we can work to eliminate negative attitudes, harassment, and discriminatory practices.

When an organization says, "We don't have a problem here. ... We serve everyone equally," this is the first clue that there is a lot of work to do. It is not sufficient only to say, "We don't exclude." Organizations must actively plan to be inclusive, dig deep in critical self-reflection, and carefully build positive, affirming, and safer spaces in order to achieve equity. Especially in systems that affect children and youth so greatly, like schools, residential care, and foster homes, service providers can proactively examine and work to eliminate gender bias, homophobia, and transphobia to secure safety for everyone.

For example, we can advocate for gender-inclusive washroom and change room facilities in schools and public spaces. We can teach young children that there are all kinds of families—some with two dads, or two moms, or mom and grandma. We can interrupt bullying and unearth the beliefs and ideas about power, difference, and gender that underlie this aggression. We can advocate with schools to be safe spaces, to provide equity education about gender and sexual diversity, to support GSAs (gay-straight alliances), and to address bullying. We can foster multi-gendered play for all children, with boys sometimes wearing an apron and playing with dolls, and girls sometimes wearing a firefighter hat and playing with trucks. We can encourage all young people we serve to question gender stereotypes, and to challenge homophobia and transphobia.

Be the ally. Let 6-year-old Leslie know that, regardless of how he later identifies, he deserves to feel safe, respected, and accepted for who he is, and that you will work hard to make that happen in all areas of his life. As Desmond Tutu declared, "A rainbow is a rainbow precisely because the colors are different. The different colors come together—and then you have—a rainbow!" (Egge, n.d.).

BEST PRACTICES—20 GUIDELINES, A SUMMARY

In addition to the "Expanding the Circle" framework to approach our work with gender-independent and LGBTQ children and youth, there are 20 specific guidelines to assist us in creating safe, affirming spaces for young people. The guidelines are divided into three sections targeting, respectively: (1) everyone within an organization; (2) direct service and care providers; and (3) management and organization-wide concerns, from the top down. While it is beyond the scope of this chapter to review each of the 20 guidelines in depth, we present them here in summary form as an opportunity for reflection and as a roadmap indicating how to implement the framework into day-to-day practice.

Guidelines for everyone within an organization

1. **Educate yourself and reflect.** Eliminate harmful biases, beliefs, attitudes, prejudices, and behaviors about gender and sexual diversity.
2. **Be an ally.** Seize opportunities to be an LGBTQ ally. Eliminate systemic biases and barriers.
3. **Create positive spaces.** Create positive spaces that are safe, affirming, positive, and inclusive about gender and sexual diversity for all children, youth, and families. Normalize diversity.

Guidelines for direct service and care providers

4. **Affirm diversity.** Affirm diversity along many spectrums, including gender identity, gender expression, physical sex, and sexual orientation. Normalize diversity as positive and valuable.
5. **Promote dignity, respect, and human rights.** Promote respect for the inherent dignity, worth, and human rights of children, youth, and families of all gender and sexual identities.
6. **Foster self-actualization and self-expression.** Foster self-actualization and self-expression in all children and youth, especially those who may be gender-independent or LGBTQ.
7. **Support empowerment and self-determination.** Support children and youth to become authentic and fulfilled individuals. Support them to develop autonomy and self-determination in relation to their sexual orientation, sex, gender identity, and gender expression.
8. **Ensure safety.** Ensure LGBTQ and gender-independent children and youth are safe in all areas of their lives.
9. **Build resilience.** Build resiliency skills in children and youth who may be LGBTQ or gender-independent.
10. **Connect to resources—affirming information, services, and health care.** Ensure all children and youth who may be gender-independent or LGBTQ have access to affirming information, services, resources, and health care that address their unique experiences and needs.
11. **Build community.** Support children, youth, and families who may be LGBTQ or gender-independent to find supportive, interdependent, and affirming communities.

12. **Protect confidentiality.** Protect the right to confidentiality for children, youth, and families in relation to gender and sexual diversity. Manage any internal disclosure respectfully.
13. **Support families to affirm their children.** Support families to accept and affirm their children for who they are.

Guidelines for management and organization-wide concerns

14. **Promote a positive organizational environment.** Promote a positive environment in the entire organization that is free from bias, discrimination, and systemic barriers related to gender and sexual diversity.
15. **Develop policies.** Develop organizational policies that establish a vision and a commitment to value gender and sexual diversity, and that promote equity for gender-independent and LGBTQ people.
16. **Develop best practices.** Develop best practices, procedures, and guidelines to embody equity-based policies, and strive toward equity related to gender and sexual diversity.
17. **Implement an effective process.** Implement an effective process to achieve equity related to gender and sexual diversity. Transform equity-based policies and practices into day-to-day reality.
18. **Ensure education and professional development.** Ensure that equity-based education and professional development about gender and sexual diversity are accessed by everyone in the organization.
19. **Monitor and evaluate.** Monitor and evaluate the effectiveness of equity strategies related to gender and sexual diversity, at both individual and organizational levels.
20. **Advocate systemically.** Advocate for systemic change to ensure LGBTQ human rights, equity, and positive spaces.

CONCLUSION

CAS-Toronto is one of the largest independent, board-operated child welfare organizations in North America. We are proud of the work we have done regarding LGBTQ and gender-creative children, youth, and families. We are aware of the power we have to create positive transformation within our communities. We have established the Out and Proud Program to develop responsive policies and practices, including the *Guidelines*. We deliver gender and sexual-diversity training, required for all staff and foster parents. We provide consultation and advocacy, and continue to develop resources. Despite the hard work that has gone into creating a more positive, inclusive, affirming, and equitable environment, we recognize there is still a long way to go. Finally, we celebrate our achievements and the diversity within our community … especially among the young people who have taught us so much, and to whom we continue to look with humility for new learning along our journey.

Let us cast our imaginations to the annual CAS-Toronto Pride Barbeque in June. There are 300 people in attendance and everything is festooned in vivid rainbow Pride colors and amazing decorations created by youth, staff, and volunteers. There are little kids in foster care or who are newly adopted, gaping open-mouthed at a balloon artist magically twisting an animal out of nothing. Older youth play foozeball or get henna art applied to their hands, and somehow down three hamburgers in about as many seconds. There are lively performances by trans and queer youth. Youth who courageously raised awareness of LGBTQ issues or challenged transphobia, homophobia, or rigid gender boxes receive youth recognition awards.

At one such Pride event, an agency group home brought all their kids to the event, and they all enjoyed it—the burgers, the games, the music! But there was one kid who particularly loved it, a boy who might have been "Leslie"—a boy who absolutely delighted in dressing up in sparkly, swirly "girls' clothes" and dancing around the house. Leslie spied a rainbow feather boa from our dress-up corner that became figuratively glued to him. He was mesmerized by the trans performers, perhaps the first openly transgender people he had ever seen. As he danced to the beat of the music, he was in his glory! Finally it was time for that group home to leave the BBQ. As they were heading back to their van, one of the other kids said ruefully to Leslie, "Okay, man, you can take off those feathers now." Without skipping a beat, a staff person replied, "But that's the whole point of the BBQ we were just at. CAS-Toronto is a safe space where you can just be yourself. And whenever YOU want to wear a feather boa, you can." And with that, Leslie beamed, flung that feather boa proudly over his shoulder, and pranced his way into the van like he was on top of the world!

That's when we know we have, at least a little bit, "expanded the circle."

For more information about the Out and Proud Affirmation Guidelines, *contact the Out and Proud Program at the Children's Aid Society of Toronto at 30 Isabella St., Toronto, Ontario, Canada M4Y 1N1. Phone (416) 924–4640 x2987 Email:outandproud@torontocas.ca*

Conclusion

Looking Back, Looking Forward

ANNIE PULLEN SANSFAÇON, ELIZABETH J. MEYER, KIMBERLEY
ENS MANNING, AND MARIE-JOËLLE ROBICHAUD

This book sought to bring together knowledge and experiences from various perspectives: professionals from within social institutions, activists in queer and trans communities, and family members who all are invested in creating environments that are supportive and affirming of transgender and gender-creative youth. The contributors in this anthology represent trailblazers who have successfully challenged institutional norms that contributed to the oppression of transgender youth in Canadian medical, educational, familial, and community life. In this conclusion, the authors, three of whom were among the organizers of the conference that led to this volume, reflect on key points raised by the contributors as well as present the outcomes of the first National Workshop on Gender Creative Kids (GCK Workshop). As each of the authors in this volume presented an initial version of their chapter at this conference, it is possible to see how the themes presented throughout this volume were echoed and built upon in the closing session that provided the rich data for discussion and analysis.

This book opened with a section on clinical and theoretical perspectives in which the authors all presented a strong critique of the historical issues that have caused deep trauma to many transgender adults who survived reparative therapies, improper diagnoses, and deep hostility and discrimination from the clinical professionals they came into contact with. Ehrensaft's call to understand and respect a child's "true gender self" and the need to build a gender-creative world is revisited throughout this volume. Pyne's comprehensive summary of the research provides an overview of harmful practices as well as more ethical and supportive practices for clinicians working with GCK and trans* youth. Finally, Tosh's critique is essential to keep in mind: that while the *Diagnostic and Statistical Manual of Mental Disorders* (DSM) produced by the American Psychiatric Association is increasingly subjected to various critiques, it remains a dynamic document that has an enormous impact on the lives of many individuals based on the inclusion of certain "mental disorders" and the accompanying diagnostic criteria. This section concluded with Ann Travers's chapter, which advances a theory of gender justice that can inform community, educational, and professional approaches to create more inclusive and positive spaces for any person experiencing gender oppression.

In the second section on education, the authors address the challenges and opportunities of working with teachers and K–12 classroom settings. Meyer's chapter on professional and legal issues frames the issue for educators in a language that is familiar and foundational to most educators' practices. In the chapter by Pendleton Jiménez, the author provides rich examples of ways that classroom teachers can present productive lessons about gender that align with existing curricula and priority areas for schools around bullying, respect for diversity, and school safety. The third chapter in this section proposes several different approaches that offer teacher education programs ways to consider preparing future teachers to be more informed and competent in working with students who may be transgender. Ingrey's examples provide a window into practice that offers frameworks and insights that are applicable in teacher education programs around the world that would help create more gender-inclusive classrooms.

Finally, the third section gives us much to learn from the voices and experiences of parents. Many parents are struggling to do their very best to provide warm and loving environments that allow their children's unique identities to develop and thrive. This is a struggle simply because of the narrow limits that Western culture places on gender expression and the related homophobia and transphobia that police any behavior that transcends "acceptable" limits of expression. Françoise Susset describes her work with parents of gender-nonconforming boys and summarizes some of the key challenges and common themes these families experience. Daemyir's presents a theory of Gender-Diverse Parenting (GDP) to promote more inclusive and less harmful family environments for all children. Walks's chapter contributes to the concept of gender-diverse parenting and the idea of queer parents who raise children with queer sensibilities, or "queerlings." The section on families and parenting concludes with three chapters outlining various projects working to support families and youth. Pullen Sansfaçon, Dumais-Michaud, and Robichaud provide an overview of a project working with parents of gender creative kids. Their recommendations, based on their work with a group of parents in Montreal, map well onto the recommendations that emerged from the GCK Workshop presented below. Hampton's case study of a youth support group in rural Alberta offers helpful lessons for others interested in doing similar work. Finally, Gale and Syrja-McNally offer an inclusive framework currently being used by Rainbow Health Ontario to ensure that their services were supportive of all families.

So where do we go from here?

WORKING WITH GENDER-CREATIVE CHILDREN AND TRANS YOUTH: SOME WAYS FORWARD

In addition to the various recommendations that emerge in this book, we would like to highlight key issues and recommendations for ways forward identified by a number of the participants at the GCK Workshop. Given the wide range of backgrounds of participants, including parents, activists, teachers, civil servants, academics, members of the trans community, and medical and psychosocial providers, the workshop proved a rich place to discuss experience and research, and to frame solutions to improve the lives of young people from various perspectives. After two and half days of intensive work, the closing session of the workshop offered a great opportunity to summarize key discussions and pursue emerging ideas to continue the work above and beyond the conference. In the spirit of Social Action Research,[1] a key methodology used throughout the research project behind the development of the GCK Workshop, we, the conference organizers, decided to facilitate a final brainstorming activity during the last session to help build a broader and more inclusive vision of the various needs and possibilities for future work. Consent forms, available in French and English, were signed by participants before they engaged in the activity in order to be able to disseminate the outcomes of the group work and use the material for analysis and dissemination after the GCK Workshop.

Inspired by the Statement Card activity framework proposed by Mullender and Ward (1991), the participants[2] were first split into table groups based on where people were sitting in the room to allow a good mix of parents, researchers, practitioners, and activists in each group and to ensure all participants could engage in their preferred language (French or English). Each group was invited to define and prioritize problems to tackle, answering the questions 'What?' and 'Why?,' two key questions central to the Social Action process (Fleming & Ward, 2004; Mullender & Ward, 1991; Mullender, Ward, & Fleming, 2013; Pullen Sansfaçon, Ward, Robichaud, Dumais-Michaud, & Clegg, in press). Specifically, participants we re asked to write down statements about what they saw as the chief problem/issue/

the most important thing that needed to be pursued after the GCK Workshop. Each participant was given five blank cards and asked to write one idea per card, up to a maximum of five statements. Participants were then asked to explore all of the cards produced by their group and select three new cards that resonated with them. With these three cards in hand, the group worked to find themes from the selected cards to summarize the most pressing concerns emerging from the content. The various themes from each table group were then shared with the large group. In total 219 cards were collected from the closing workshop. The main themes, identified as the 'What?' or 'Problems to Tackle' from a group perspective, are as follows:

1. GCK/Trans* Youth voices: The need to increase "kids' participation and representation" in various services and research, to "give kids a voice," and to "listen to their expertise" as a means of addressing the frequent absence of those concerned

2. Family: Lack of support for gender-creative children and their parents and extended family; a clear need for creating supportive spaces and networks

3. Institutions:

   a. The overly medicalized relationships between families and service providers and pathologization of gender-creativity in children; a need to develop "alternative," "ethical," "accessible" approaches and understanding care and, when necessary, to move away from unnecessary medicalization (or, in the words of one participant, "no pathology for access")

   b. Youth agencies & schools: The lack of preparation of many professionals, in schools and in other organizations serving children, to address the specific needs of gender-creative children and transgender youth. There is thus a need to train the various professionals who work with gender creative kids and trans youth to be more sensitive and aware of gender issues, or as one participant wrote, to be "mindful of their practice."

   c. Legal protections: The lack of gender justice and recognition of gender-creative children and trans youth, an absence of specific legal rights and protections

   d. Research practices and knowledge transfer: The continuation of oppressive research practices, including a lack of consideration of gender-creative children and the larger trans community's perspective on knowledge building and research; barriers to knowledge dissemination. Knowledge is not accessible to all, and resources are not shared widely.

4. Cis-normativity, transphobia, and the need for "gender justice": Lack of social acceptance, and a lack of positive / success stories about gender creative kids; oppressive society to gender creative kids and trans youth built on cis-normative / binary view of gender

After identifying the main themes from the cards as a group, participants were asked to split into 'interest groups,' for example: research, practice, education, activism, medicine, or parenting. The various interest groups were then asked to think about plans for action ('how'—see Mullender & Ward, 1991; Mullender et al., 2013; Ward & Fleming, 2004) to tackle the various problems identified in the first stage (themes—issues) of the activity. At the end of the activity, each 'interest group' had to present its plans of action. A total of 53 propositions were discussed in the various groups and written onto posters.

Overall, we identified four general themes that were highlighted through this exercise. Those themes encompassed core areas that affect the lives of gender-creative children and trans youth. Figure 1 illustrates the interconnections of the themes. Gender-creative children and trans youth were the center of attention of all priorities as every topic focused on a specific aspect of their well-being. Regarding themselves more directly, participants mentioned the need to improve the support systems of gender-creative children and trans youth, and were keen to see a better consideration of their point of view in research and actions. The creation of support systems for families was repeatedly mentioned. This theme is coherent with the knowledge we have regarding GCKs, whose families currently struggle to get help and face considerable social stigma (see Pullen Sansfaçon, 2012). It is clear that increasing the support and capacities of the parents and families of gender-creative children would benefit gender-creative children and trans youth as their primary environment of socialization is better equipped to support them.

Many recommendations prioritized actions that challenged the main institutions working with gender-creative children and trans youth: educational and medical institutions. Many expressed concern about the ways in which current educational and medical systems impose normativity through a binary understanding of gender and thus oppress gender-creative children and trans youth. Participants suggested that more training on critical perspectives of gender and trans issues is one important step to revolutionize these institutions, which are powerful vectors of socialization that have a considerable influence on the well-being of gender-creative children. Research was also an important theme, as participants voiced the strong desire to ensure that future scholarship takes a more child-centered and affirming view of gender-creative children and trans youth.

Figure 1. GCK Workshop themes.

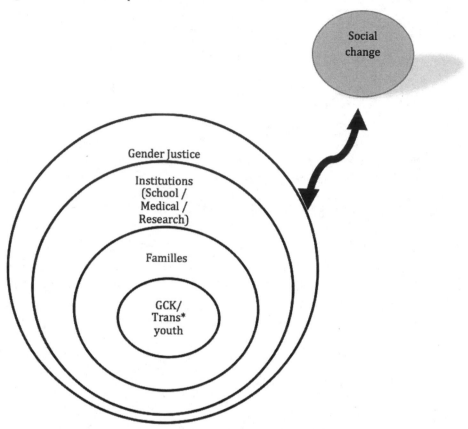

The concept of justice emerged as the paramount theme of the exercise. Behind each card and poster was a claim for the recognition of the identity and equal value, rights, freedom, and life of gender-creative children and trans youth. Justice was also at stake in the desire to achieve fair treatment in communities, schools, and medical and scientific environments. Some participants explicitly mentioned the need for "gender justice" as introduced in Ann Travers's presentation (see Travers, this volume), a vision of a society free of gender barriers and prejudice. Finally, participants articulated that major social change needs to be brought about to encompass all of the priorities mentioned above and build the world envisioned by the participants. Many participants advocated forms of activism that would render the gender binary void and that could bring about a less oppressive and more humane society in which children can grow freely and without fear.

Specific Recommendations for Future Research

In closing, we would like to build on the themes that have emerged in this volume as well as in the Social Action Research exercise that concluded the National Workshop on Gender Creative Kids to identify future areas of research that might begin to achieve the objectives identified. Specifically, we identify ways in which children and youth might play a more prominent role in research going forward, and ways in which new communities and coalitions might build around creating gender justice for all children. Moving forward, the need to better understand the lived experiences of children and youth growing up as "gender-creative" must be a top priority. In our view, this means incorporating a much more textured understanding of how childhood gender-nonconformity takes on different forms of social meaning in different contexts.

As was noted in the Introduction and in various chapters, families who are racialized, queered, and classed by educational, state, and medical institutions already encounter forms of oppression not experienced by families with two white, middle-class parents in a heterosexual relationship. The risk of child apprehension (or at the very least increased surveillance) by social service authorities may not be as high in Canada as it is in other countries, but it nonetheless remains a real threat for "non-normative" families.[3] Undertaking research that focuses on the needs of children across a diversity of families will aid attempts to reform systems that unfairly target and marginalize certain populations while exempting others.

Language, culture, and disability are also coded within and outside of families in such a way that children grow into their gendered selves on very different terms, depending upon a variety of interacting factors. As researchers working in the bilingual and multicultural environment of Montreal, we are keenly aware of how meaning and priorities can shift depending upon the cultural location of children and their caregivers. Much more scholarship is needed on how social reception of gender diversity shifts within different contexts, and how families and their providers can move forward with an integrated understanding of a family and child's uniqueness, to avoid the perils of a "one size fits all" approach to advocacy and change. Indeed, Pride parades, LGBT camps, and affirming support groups may be a great source of vitality and hope for some families and children, but not for others. We thus need to continually ask ourselves hard questions about visibility and recognition in our projects of community research and action, and create spaces and opportunities for new identities, coalitions, and practices to emerge.

One potential source of community transformation not featured in this volume, for example, is that of faith communities.[4] While it is certainly the case that many fundamentalist religious institutions do not make space, and, indeed, condemn non-normative modes of gender expression, this is not true for all religious denominations. In fact, affirming gender diversity has increasingly become an urgent point of concern of some religious institutions, as well as a way of rethinking and deepening faith.[5] For children, youth, and families deeply attached to a particular faith tradition, new meaning and expression might be found in adapting particular rituals to their own circumstances. How might a Bar Mitzvah or Bat Mitzvah honor the gender-creativity of a youth? How might a baptism affirm a child or youth who is socially transitioning? How might a Buddhist family incorporate particular meditation practices into generating strength individually and as a collective? There is a great deal of need for research, writing, and experiment at the intersection of faith, family, and gender diversity.

We must also find ways to incorporate into research and community strategies the children and youth whose gender-nonconformity is not affirmed by their caregivers. American statistics suggest that 40% of street youth are LGBT, in no small part because of parents who have rejected the sexual and/or gender identity of their children (Durso & Gates, 2012). At present, we know even less about gender-nonconforming youth who end up on the streets than we know about those who grow up in households where they receive some kind of support. The graphic representing the GCK Workshop themes (Figure 1) looks very different for those who are without the buffer of an affirming family. On the one hand, encounters with educational, medical, and research institutions may transform or disappear altogether. On the other hand, the state may emerge even more prominently as law enforcement, social services, and the youth correctional system are called in to regulate, monitor, and manage gender-independent youth. Achieving justice will require a multi-pronged effort by scholars, community advocates, state officials, and, most important, the participation of youth themselves.

So how can children and youth be fuller participants in research and advocacy being conducted on their behalf? As is evident from some of the comments from the closing session, there are ongoing concerns that children and their families will be disempowered and even revictimized, much in the same way that trans* individuals have been pathologized in research for decades. This is a huge issue, one that deserves another book in its own right. From our own perspective as scholars working at the intersection of advocacy and research, we see Social Action Research as one inclusive and empowering strategy in which youth and their caregivers can engage. Although not applicable in all contexts, it disrupts some of the preexisting hierarchies and offers a hopeful tool for change. Moving forward, we look to learning from the research and community experience of others as we all continue to wrestle with how to dislodge the harmful vestiges of traditional modes of inquiry when it comes to transforming the social worlds of the gender-creative child.

By working with a Social Action Research methodology in this project, we are engaged in an ongoing process of learning from and applying many of the recommendations presented at the workshop. Our research team started with a small Social Sciences and Humanities Research Council (SSHRC) grant that led to a second SSHRC grant that funded the workshop and in turn helped with the creation of this volume. Two other outcomes of this project include the development of a new Canadian networking and advocacy group: Gender Creative Kids—Enfants transgenres and a website that includes additional resources and updates on this and related projects at www.gendercreativekids.ca. The creation of this website is the reason we have not included a list of resources at the end of this volume—we wanted to produce something more dynamic and accessible for readers and for those who might not have access to this book. Ultimately, we hope that both book and website will offer new ideas for research and action and help spark new forms of creative inspiration in the quest to transform the social worlds of present and future gender creative kids.

Glossary of Terms

LEE AIRTON and ELIZABETH J. MEYER

This glossary is intended to help readers navigate this volume and contemporary resources or conversations about trans/gender diversity. Please note that definitions refer to common usage at the time of publication.

Ally Someone who, while not necessarily identifying as a member of an oppressed group or experiencing a particular oppression, commits to lessening the effects of that oppression on group members through interpersonal or structural change.

assigned sex or assigned gender The designation, usually male or female, given to infants at the time of their birth and based in most cases on a cursory visual inspection of primary sex characteristics. See also intersex.

bisexual A person who is attracted to some members of both sexes to varying degrees. The prefix "bi" references the idea that there are only two sexes. Other related terms that are distanced from the two-sex model are omnisexual and pansexual.

cisgender (adj.) A term characterizing people who are not transgender or transsexual or whose gender aligns with the sex they were assigned at birth.

cis-heteronormativity (n.), cis-heternormative (adj.) An adaptation of the term 'heteronormative' which explicitly references the cissexist (see below) implications and assumptions of heteronormative beliefs and social structures (see Daemyir, this volume).

cis-sexism (n.), cissexist (adj.) A term popularized by Julia Serano (2007) that refers to the systemic privileging of non-trans people's genders and gender identities as well as the assumption that all people are cisgender (see above).

compulsory heterosexuality The theory advanced by poet and lesbian feminist Adrienne Rich that asserts that women are coerced by social structures to engage in heterosexual relationships with men. She argues that heterosexuality is a political institution, not just a naturally occurring phenomenon, and is a central feature of patriarchy (Rich, 1978/1993).

cross-dressing The practice of dressing in the clothing of a sex that is not one's own or that is typically referred to as the 'opposite' sex within the sex/gender binary. The noun form—'cross-dresser'—has generally fallen out of favour and so ought to be avoided unless one is given explicit authorization in a particular encounter or relationship.

DSM (DSM-IV, DSM-5) The acronym of the *Diagnostic and Statistical Manual of Mental Disorders* of the American Psychiatric Association (APA), in its fifth printing at the time of publication. See Tosh's chapter in this volume for the role of the DSM and the APA in the history of gender identity and expression regulation up to the present.

effeminacy (n.), effeminate (adj.) A term denoting the presence of feminine or female-associated behaviors, grooming styles, or mannerisms in a person who is male or masculine presenting (whether trans or cis).

Essentialism An 'essentialist' position on gender would hold that, for example, men and women have innate, immutable masculine and feminine characteristics, respectively, that define and set them apart. The existence of gender-creative (etc.) and trans people has been variably deployed to both refute and affirm gender essentialism.

GLBT Abbreviation of gay, lesbian, bisexual, transsexual, and transgender people wherein the latter two are generally thought to share the same 'T.' Other letter orders are also common, such as LGBT, as well as other acronyms incorporating more of the gender and sexual diversity spectrum. For example, 'LGBTTSIQQ' also includes two-spirit (see entry below), intersex (see entry below), queer and questioning (of one's gender and/or sexuality) people. The term 'queer' is often used as an umbrella term in place of such acronyms, although this is contested.

gay The most common term for a person who engages in same-sex relationships and identifies as a member of this community. It is preferred above the term 'homosexual' as homosexual has medical-psychological meanings that apply specifically to same-sex behavior and does not consider a person's identities and relationships. 'Gay' can refer to both men and women, although many women prefer the term 'lesbian.' Many but not all people use the terms 'gay' and 'lesbian' interchangeably with the term 'queer' (see below; see also GLBT).

gender A term generally used to describe those characteristics of people that are socially constructed, in contrast to those that are legally and biologically determined (sex). People are assigned a sex at birth, but learn to act like girls and boys who grow into women and men, in most cases. We are taught the appropriate behaviors, attitudes, roles, and activities for people of our assigned sex, and how we should relate to others. These learned attributes are part of what make up gender identity and expression as well as determine gender roles.

genderism (n.), genderist (adj.) The systemic privileging of gender normativity (see below) as normal, natural, and superior (Airton, 2009).

genderqueer Refers to people whose gender identity and/or expression explicitly challenges the gender binary, but is *not necessarily* fluid or indeterminate (see gender fluidity).

gender binary The culturally normative construction of gender in which people, things, habits, affinities, etc., are thought or experienced as *either* male or female, masculine or feminine. The gender binary supports and is supported by the heterosexual matrix (see below).

gender creativity (n.), gender-creative (adj.) A recently developed phrase describing (most often) a child "who does not abide by the binary gender norms, prescriptions, or proscriptions that might exist in the child's culture, but transcends and transgresses those norms to independently, uniquely, and with artistry evolve into the gender that is 'me'" (Ehrensaft, 2011). This term is often preferred for its celebratory connotation.

Gender Dysphoria The medical and psychological diagnosis in the DSM-5 (see DSM above) often ascribed to gender-creative children who come into contact with the medical and/or psychiatric systems. Although medicalization is controversial among many trans people and allies, diagnosis can often facilitate access to medical transition under government and other health insurance plans. See Tosh's chapter in this volume.

gender expression How one chooses (whether consciously or unconsciously) to dress, walk, talk, accessorize, etc., in ways that express one's gender identity. Related terms include 'gender role performance' and 'gender presentation.'

gender fluidity(n.), gender-fluid (adj.) Wherein one weaves together many possibilities of gender in one's identity or expression, whether at one point in time or across the life course.

gender independence (n.), gender-independent (adj.) A term with similar meaning, usage, and connotation to gender-creative (see above). Applied in the case of children who are understood to be developing and living their gender 'independently' of local gender norms.

gendered harassment Any unwanted behavior that polices and reinforces the traditional norms of heterosexual masculinity and heterosexual femininity and includes: (hetero)sexual harassment, homophobic harassment, and harassment for gender-nonconformity (Meyer, 2006). It is important to note that all communities, including non-heterosexual ones, have gender norms that are enforced to varying degrees.

gender identity Refers to an individual's sense of self as a man, woman, transgender, genderqueer, etc. This is often shaped by one's assigned sex (see above) and the gender in which one is raised. Gender identity may change over time.

gender markers Outwardly apparent elements of behavior, dress, grooming, etc., that are generally thought to indicate someone's gender identity. See also gender expression.

gender-nonconformity (n.), gender-nonconforming (adj.) When a person's gender expression varies from that which is traditionally expected of a person of their assigned sex.

gender non-normativity (n.), gender-non-normative (adj.) The opposite of gendernormativity (see below).

gender normativity (n.), gender-normative (adj.) When a person's gender (expression, behavior, attitudes, affinities, etc.) is in line with what is locally determined to be 'normal' for persons of their assigned sex, that person can be said to be *gendernormative* on the level of gender expression (Airton, 2009). Activities, preferences, affinities, styles, and behaviors can also be described as gender-normative (or non-normative) for people of a particular gender.

gender variance (n.), gender-variant (adj.) A term synonymous with gender-creative, gender-independent, gender-nonconforming, gender-non-normative, etc.; denotes someone whose gender varies from local norms of behavior, grooming, and affinity for persons of their assigned sex.

harassment Biased behavior that has a negative impact on the target or the environment (Land, 2003), and may be intentional or unintentional.

harassment for gender-nonconformity Any unwanted behavior that targets a person's perceived lack of fit with gender norms. Also referred to as transphobic harassment.

hegemonic masculinity Developed by gender theorist Raewyn Connell (1995), 'hegemonic masculinity' is the form of masculinity that occupies a dominant and privileged position in a given gendered context. In Western cultures this is often defined by: claims to authority (often through aggression, physical strength, dominance, institutional power), and heterosexuality, but is subject to change if social relations shift.

heterosexuality (n.), heterosexual (adj.) The phenomenon of being sexually and affectionally drawn to people of a sex other than one's own for the purpose of non-platonic relations or partnership.

hir See pronouns.

homonormativity (n.), homonormative (adj.) A term used to critique non-heterosexual peoples' real or perceived conformity with hegemonic (and heterocentric) norms of sexuality and kinship (e.g., government-sanctioned marriage, the nuclear family, lifelong monogamy). See Travers, this volume.

homophobia Fear or hatred of those assumed to be GLBTQ and of anything connected to GLBTQ culture; when a person fears homosexuality, either in other people or within themselves (internalized homophobia). Homophobia can be expressed in attitudes or behaviors that range from mild discomfort to verbally abusive or physically violent acts.

homophobic harassment See sexual orientation harassment.

homosexuality (n.), homosexual (adj.) The phenomenon of being sexually and affectionally drawn to people of one's own sex for the purpose of non-platonic relations or partnership.

heteronormativity (n.), heteronormative (adj.) A term coined in 1991 by Michael Warner to describe a system of behaviors and social expectations that are built around the belief that everyone is or should be heterosexual and that all relationships and families follow this model (Warner, 1991). See also cis-heteronormativity, compulsory heterosexuality, heterosexism, heterosexuality, and heterosexual matrix.

heterosexism (n.), heterosexist (adj.) The systemic privileging of heterosexuality and heterosexuals as normal, natural, and superior to non-heterosexuality and non-heterosexual people. 'Heterosexist' behaviors, utterances, and beliefs are those expressing heterosexism. Heterosexism is often conceived as being less overt or apparent than homophobia, and more likely to be implicit within institutions and social structures.

(hetero)sexual harassment Any unwanted interpersonal behavior that has a sexual or gender component and is enacted within the matrix of heterosexual relations. This includes two main types of harassment: *quid pro quo* and hostile environment.

heterosexual matrix A concept advanced by gender theorist Judith Butler that builds on Adrienne Rich's (1978/1993) notion of compulsory heterosexuality. Butler states that all gender relations are built within the boundaries of the "oppositionally and hierarchically defined . . . compulsory practice of heterosexuality" (Butler, 1990, p. 194).

intersex "Technically, intersex is defined as [a] 'congenital anomaly of the reproductive and sexual system.' Intersex people are born with external genitalia, internal reproductive organs, and/or endocrine system that are different from most other people. There is no single 'intersex body;' it encompasses a wide variety of conditions that do not have anything in common except that they are deemed 'abnormal' by the society. What makes intersex people similar is their experiences of medicalization, not biology. Intersex is not an identity. While some intersex people do reclaim it as part of their identity, it is not a freely chosen category of gender—it can only be reclaimed. Most intersex people identify as men or women, just like everybody else" (Intersex Initiative Portland, 2003, p. 3).

lesbian The preferred term (over 'homosexual'—see gay, above) for a woman who engages in same-sex relationships and identifies as a member of this community. Many non-heterosexual women prefer the adjectival term 'queer' (e.g., 'I am queer') or the phrase 'queer woman.'

misogyny Fear, hatred, disgust, or devaluation of (trans or cis) women, girls, femininity, and femaleness. See also sexism, transmisogyny.

patriarchy The basic definition of a patriarchy is a society that is governed and controlled by men. Feminist theorists have used this term to explain the current gender system that gives males access to power and social privileges and in turn marginalizes and oppresses people of all other genders. See also heterosexism, sexism.

pronouns Gender-neutral pronouns are used by non cisgender people (e.g., trans people, genderqueers) in order to allow the everyday recognition of their gender in language. Although ze/zie (in place of she and he) and hir (in place of his and her) have been the most common, the grammatically correct use of singular 'they' (their/they're/theirs) is growing in popularity.

queer A widely variable term used by people whose identities and lived experiences fall outside of heterosexuality and heteronormative structures of kinship and/or sexuality. Also a frequent umbrella term used in place of acronyms like GLBT (see above).

sex A primarily medico-legal category that is assigned at birth based on certain biological characteristics whose significance in influencing categorization varies by region. Such characteristics may include a child's chromosomes, gonadal tissue, hormone levels, and/or external genitalia. This is different from gender, as noted above.

sexism The systemic belief that men/masculinity are/is superior to women/femininity, resulting in oppression and discrimination against women in patriarchal societies. See also misogyny.

sexual harassment Any unwanted interpersonal behavior that has a sexual or gender component (see [hetero]sexual harassment for a more detailed definition).

sexual orientation This term describes the genders and sexes toward which a person is emotionally, physically, romantically, and erotically attracted; one's sexual orientation can be homosexual, bisexual, omnisexual, heterosexual, or asexual, and is informed by innate and socially cultivated desire. In all instances, use this term instead of 'sexual preference' or other misleading terminology. Trans and gender-variant people may identify with any sexual orientation, and their sexual orientation may or may not change before, during, or after transition.

sexual orientation harassment Any unwanted behavior that insults or harms non-heterosexual people, or uses anti-GLBQ slurs to insult or harm another person. May be targeted at GLBQ people or non-GLBQ people. See also homophobic harassment

social construct This concept emerged from sociology and psychology to describe concepts and terms that exist because a society or culture has collectively decided to agree and behave as though they exist. Some examples include money, citizenship, race, and gender.

Tomboy A colloquial term most commonly applied to female-assigned children with masculine gender expressions.

trans*/transgender Umbrella terms for individuals who blur the lines of traditional gender expression; usually include transsexuals and sometimes also 'cross-dressers.' Trans- or transgender-identified individuals may or may not choose to change physical characteristics of their bodies or legally change their sex. Transgender *children* are those who generally affirm their gender identity as the 'opposite' of that written on their birth certificate. Many people also use trans and/or transgender as an identity term.

transgendered An adjectival form of 'transgender' thought by some to be outdated, while others choose to use it to emphasize the way gender is always actively produced. 'Transgender' is the more widely accepted term.

transition (n./vb.), transitioning (adj.) "The process of attaining congruence and affirmation of the gender identity and presentation with which one feels most comfortable. 'Transition' most often refers to a medical process of hormone replacement therapy (HRT) and/or surgeries, in order to induce sex characteristics which society largely constructs as 'opposite' to the gender assigned to a person at birth. Distinctions have been made between 'social' and 'medical' transition, but each trans person determines for themselves what a transition looks like. Changes aligned with 'social' transition can involve choice of dress, physical embodiment, gender role, social perception, pronoun use and name change, for example" (X. Sly Sarkisova, personal communication, June 13, 2013).

transman, transwoman Terms used by some transgender or transsexual men and women to express their trans *and* male or female identities. Other people with transsexual histories choose to identify as women or men without any qualifying reference to this history.

transmisogyny A term coined by Julia Serano (2007) to denote the unique oppression experienced by people on the trans female/feminine spectrum (such as transsexual women) due to both transphobia and the societal devaluation of women and femininity (see misogyny).

transsexual (n.) A person who identifies and/or lives as a sex which is other than the sex they were assigned at birth. The difference between 'transgender' and 'transsexual'—being the most common terms in this area—is often based on the specifics of one's transition, i.e., 'transsexual' is a term most commonly used by people who have sought out surgical and/or hormonal changes.

transsexualism/transsexuality Nouns of the adjectival term 'transsexual' that refer to the phenomenon of people identifying or living as a sex other than the one they were assigned at birth.

transphobia The irrational fear or hatred of all individuals who transgress or blur the dominant gender categories in a given society. In addition to harming trans people, transphobic attitudes and behaviors can also lead to discrimination, violence, and oppression against gay, lesbian, bisexual, trans, queer, and intersex people as well as all gender-nonconforming individuals, regardless of their gender or sexual identity. See also genderism, which has a relationship to transphobia similar to that of heterosexism to homophobia.

transphobic harassment See harassment for gender-nonconformity.

two-spirit An identity term used by some Native American and First Nations (in Canada) people whose gender and/or sexuality does not conform to constructions of hetero- and/or cisgender norms prescribed by white settler colonial societies. For more on two-spirit, see Cruz (2011) as well as writings by Gregory Scofield and Qwo-Li Driskill.

ze/zie See pronouns.

Contributor Biographies

Lee Airton (Managing Editor) is a doctoral candidate in Language, Culture, and Teaching and an instructor in the concurrent teacher education program at York University in Toronto, Canada. Lee's dissertation uses affect, assemblage, and radical ethical theory to explore the micropolitics of social justice teacher education, with an eye to developing micropolitically focused pedagogy and curricula in this area. Lee's publications include articles in the journals *Sex Education* and *Curriculum Inquiry* (forthcoming), and a chapter on gender diversity for use in teacher education courses (in *Diversity and Multiculturalism: A Reader*, Peter Lang, 2009). Lee holds degrees in education and gender studies from McGill University, and blogs about gender-neutral pronoun usage in everyday life at http://theyismypronoun. tumblr.com/. Lee's doctoral research is funded by the Social Sciences and Humanities Research Council of Canada.

Arwyn Daemyir is a writer, activist, parent, and licensed massage therapist in Portland, Oregon, USA. Her work on parenting in kyriarchy has appeared in the anthologies *Trans Bodies, Trans Selves* and *The Good Mother Myth*. She was profiled on NPR.org and interviewed on the radio program *Think Out Loud* on Oregon Public Broadcasting for her expertise in Gender Diverse Parenting. Despite neither speaking nor reading Portuguese, she's been interviewed and published in national online and print publications in Brazil. Arwyn's work has also appeared in *Bitch* magazine, the online newspaper *Global Comment*, and in feminist and pro-choice zines. For three years she wrote about parenting, privilege, and rethinking social norms on her blog, *Raising My Boychick*, and helped broaden the global conversation around gender and parenting from neutrality to diversity. Arwyn currently focuses on the role of bodywork in improving resiliency and body-relationship for transgender and gender-creative adults, children and families in her private massage practice.

Diane Ehrensaft, Ph.D., is an Associate Professor at the University of California–San Francisco in the Department of Pediatrics, serving as the psychologist on the interdisciplinary team at the Child and Adolescent Gender Center Clinic. Dr. Ehrensaft is a developmental and clinical psychologist in the San Francisco Bay Area, specializing in research, psychotherapy, and consultation with gender-nonconforming children and their families. She is the author of *Gender Born, Gender Made: Raising Healthy Gender-Nonconforming Children* (The Experiment, May 2011), and lectures and publishes internationally on the subject of children's gender development and gender-nonconformity. Dr. Ehrensaft is the Director of Mental Health of the Child and Adolescent Gender Center, a University of California–San Francisco/community partnership and leads the Mind the Gap consortium of child gender mental health specialists under the umbrella of the Child and Adolescent Gender Center. Dr. Ehrensaft is also on the board of Gender Spectrum, a U.S. educational and advocacy organization. She received her Ph.D. from the University of Michigan in 1974 and has served on the faculty of Sir George Williams University, University of California–Berkeley, Lone Mountain College, the Wright Institute, Berkeley, Psychoanalytic Institute of Northern California, and the University of California–San Francisco.

Lorraine Gale, MSW, has developed unique expertise on providing safe, positive, and equitable services for LGBTIQ and gender-independent children, youth, and families through her work in the Out and Proud Program at the Children's Aid Society of Toronto (CAS-Toronto) since 1996. At CAS-Toronto, Lorraine designs and facilitates LGBTIQ-related training and education; provides consultation; develops policy, resources, and tools; and organizes pride celebrations. She authored CAS-Toronto's groundbreaking *Out and Proud Affirmation Guidelines: Practice Guidelines for Equity in Gender and Sexual Diversity*, using a strength-based, anti-oppressive approach. The *Guidelines* introduce a new framework, "Expanding the Circle," a comprehensive and essential tool for anyone serving children, youth, or families.

Lorraine has designed and delivered workshops for older LGBTQ adults to tell their personal stories in trainings for service providers, through the 519 Church St. Community Centre in Toronto. She has also designed and piloted leading-edge workshops for parents and families of LGBTQ youth through Delisle Youth Services in Toronto. Lorraine is passionate about social change and creative ways to re-frame the human experience with a new lens.

Lyndsey Hampton is a registered psychologist who is currently working with children and adolescents in an urban community mental health clinic. Previously she spent more than five years working in a rural setting where she created and facilitated a youth group for rural LGBTQ youth. She is also the mother to newborn twins.

Jennifer C. Ingrey is a doctoral candidate in Education in the field of Gender, Equity, and Social Justice at the University of Western Ontario. Her dissertation topic surrounds the issues of subjectivity in youth as it is practiced and understood in school spaces, namely the school washroom, which she investigates through the works of Michel Foucault and Judith Butler, as well as transgender studies. She is a teaching assistant in the Bachelor of Education program, teaching equity issues to/for teacher candidates, with a special interest in gender equity. She is also a certified Ontario teacher with teaching experience in the secondary school level in the areas of English and Visual Arts where gender issues were infused throughout her programming and curriculum, among other equity concerns. She is the grateful recipient of the Joseph-Armand Bombardier Canada Graduate Scholarship for doctoral studies.

Kimberley Ens Manning, Associate Professor in Political Science at Concordia University, studies social movements, gender politics, and social policy reform. Drawing on extensive fieldwork in rural Chinese villages and county archives, Dr. Manning has published articles on the origins of gender conflict in China's Great Leap Forward (1958–1960), co-edited a volume, *Eating Bitterness*, on the grassroots politics at work in China's Great Leap Famine (1959–1961), and is completing a monograph on gender politics before, during, and after the Chinese Communist revolution. Her current project looks at parental activism and advocacy on behalf of gender-creative children in Canada and the United States.

Elizabeth J. Meyer, Ph.D. (Co-Editor), is an Assistant Professor in the School of Education at California Polytechnic State University in San Luis Obispo and a Research Associate at the Simone de Beauvoir Institute at Concordia University in Montreal, Canada. She is the author of *Gender, Bullying, and*

Harassment: Strategies to End Sexism and Homophobia in Schools (Teachers College Press, 2009) and *Gender and Sexual Diversity in Schools* (Springer, 2010). She is a former high school teacher and Fulbright Teacher Exchange Program Grantee. She completed her M.A. at the University of Colorado–Boulder and Ph.D. at McGill University in Montreal, Quebec. Her research has been published in academic journals such as *Gender and Education; McGill Journal of Education; The Clearinghouse;* and *The Journal of LGBT Youth.* She blogs for *Psychology Today* and is also on Twitter: @lizjmeyer.

Audrey-Anne Dumais Michaud is a MSW student in the School of Social Work at the Université de Montréal. Her research interests include marginality, social problems, mental health, social action, and the sociology of health. She is a research assistant on several projects including the Gender Creative Kids research project, where she facilitated the parents' group modeled on social action methodology.

Karleen Pendleton Jiménez is a writer and Associate Professor in the School of Education and the Department of Gender and Women's Studies at Trent University. She is currently conducting a study on gender transgression as perceived by grade 4–12 students in Ontario rural schools. She has written on issues of sexual orientation and gender identity in schools, Latina community and identity, and lesbian experience. Selected publications include the co-edited (with Isabel Killoran) collection *"Unleashing the Unpopular": Talking about Sexual Orientation and Gender Diversity in Education,* and the book chapters "The Breastfeeding Curriculum: Stories of Queer, Female, Unruly Learning," and "'Start with the Land': Groundwork for Chicana Pedagogy." Her two books *Are You a Boy or a Girl?* (children's book) and *How to Get a Girl Pregnant* (memoir) were both Lambda Literary finalists. She wrote the screenplay for the award-winning short film *Tomboy,* the story of a young Latina-Canadian navigating school bullying, and finding comfort in her mother's love.

Jake Pyne is a community-based researcher, trans activist, and dad, who has worked on a number of research and community development projects in Toronto's trans community over the past 12 years. Most recently, his work focuses on supporting gender-independent children and transgender parents, through projects based at Concordia University, Rainbow Health Ontario, the LGBTQ Parenting Network at the Sherbourne Health Centre, the Re:-Searching for LGBTQ Health team at the Centre for Addiction and Mental Health and the Centre for the Study of Gender, Social Inequities and Mental Health at Simon Fraser University. In the fall of 2013, Jake will begin a Ph.D. program in Social Work and Gender Studies at McMaster University.

Marie-Joëlle Robichaud is a Ph.D. student in Social Work at the Université de Montréal. She has a B.A. from McGill University's School of Environment. Her humanitarian experiences persuaded her to restructure her studies in Social Work, where she experienced a fast-track from the Masters to the Ph.D. program. Marie-Joëlle's work revolves around interculturalism, child protection services, and ethics. She was a research assistant and group co-facilitator in the Gender Creative Kids research project.

Annie Pullen Sansfaçon, Ph.D. (Co-Editor), is Associate Professor in the School of Social Work at the Université de Montréal. Her research interests include social work ethics and professional identity as well as Social Action/Self-Directed Groupwork. In her writing she argues for a universal professional identity steeped in values and ethical thinking, and offers strategies for action anchored in social action and Self-Directed Groupwork methodologies. Lately, Annie has transferred findings on social workers' ethical practice while navigating the system in their clients' best interest to the experiences of parents with gender-nonconforming children; both groups navigate oppressive conditions and similar challenges in voicing the concerns of those they care for. She has applied Social Action methodologies to various strands of a funded research project aimed at better understanding the experience of gender-nonconforming children.

Françoise Susset is a clinical psychologist and couples and family therapist working in Montreal, Quebec. Her principal areas of interest are trauma and sexual minority issues. For several years, she participated in the general mental health training and clinical supervision of residents in Family Medicine from the Université de Montréal Medical School. During her many years in Minnesota, she was a member of the original clinical team of Pride Institute, the first drug and alcohol-dependency treatment center in the world serving the LGB community. She is the co-founder of the Institute for Sexual Minority Health, http://www.ismh-isms.com/, dedicated to training and education. Although her clinical work is mainly with trans adults and teens, she also focuses specifically on the question of gender-variant behavior in prepubescent children, helping families and schools challenge notions regarding sexuality, sexual orientation, gender identity, and gender expression. She works closely with several community organizations involved in improving access and quality care for individuals belonging to sexual minority groups in Quebec. She is a member of WPATH and serves on the Board of the Canadian Professional Association for Transgender Health (CPATH).

Haley Syrja-McNally enjoys the outdoors and has a great love of dance—both of which strongly inform who she is as a person. She completed her Bachelor of Social Work with Ryerson University and is entering York University's Master of Social Work program. Haley completed a thoroughly enjoyable placement with the Out and Proud program at the Children's Aid Society of Toronto, where she was able to expand her knowledge about working with LGBTQ+ and gender-independent children, youth, and families, and where she was also graciously given the opportunity to co-write this chapter!

Jemma Tosh is a Lecturer in Psychology at the University of Chester, UK. Her research incorporates critical psychology, feminist, queer, trans, and intersex perspectives with a particular focus on gender, sexual violence, and related psychiatric diagnoses. She is the General Representative for the Psychology of Women Section of the British Psychological Society and Assistant Editor for the Psychology of Women Section Review. She is currently writing her first book on the critical psychology of transgenderism and sexual violence, due to be published in 2014. Jemma is also active in feminist, trans, and intersex activism and has written extensively about her activism against psychiatric treatment that discourages gender-creativity in children.

Ann Travers is Associate Professor of Sociology in the Department of Sociology and Anthropology at Simon Fraser University in Vancouver, Canada. Dr. Travers' current research activities reflect an interest in the role of sport in constructing gender identity, the relationship between sport and gender injustice, transgender issues within and without queer communities, and social safety nets for gender-variant children and youth. In her groundbreaking (2008) article, "The Sport Nexus and Gender Injustice," published in the *Studies in Social Justice Journal*, Travers makes a compelling case for the elimination of male-only sex-segregated sporting spaces. Her most recent publications include (2013) "Thinking the Unthinkable: Imagining an 'un-American,' Girl-friendly, Women- and Trans-Inclusive Alternative for Baseball," *Journal of Sport & Social Issues*, and (2011) "Women's Ski Jumping, the 2010 Olympic Games and the Deafening Silences of Sex Segregation, Whiteness and Wealth," *Journal of Sport & Social Issues*. Dr. Travers, who now identifies as queer/trans, was also a gender-nonconforming child and now finds herself parenting one.

Michelle Walks recently earned her Ph.D. from the University of British Columbia (Okanagan campus). Her doctoral work focused on the reproductive desires, choices, and experiences of butch lesbians, transmen, and genderqueer individuals in British Columbia. This research illuminated and critiqued the assumed link between femininity and reproduction, and brought attention to masculine experiences of pregnancy, breastfeeding, mothering, and queer experiences of infertility. Michelle co-edited *An Anthropology of Mothering* (Demeter Press, 2011), and is a guest editor for a special issue of *Anthropologica* on "Queer Anthropology" (May 2014). Michelle currently works as a sessional instructor, and lives in Kelowna, BC, with her partner and son.

References

Achenbach, T. M. (1991). *Manual for behavioral behavior checklist/4–18 and 1991 profile*. Burlington, VT: University of Vermont Department for Psychiatry.

Airton, L. (2009). Untangling 'gender diversity': Genderism and its discontents (i.e., everyone). In S. Steinberg (Ed.), *Diversity and multiculturalism: A reader* (pp. 223–245). New York: Peter Lang.

Ajeto, D. (2009). *A soul has no gender: Love and acceptance through the eyes of a mother of sexual and gender minority children*. Rotterdam, The Netherlands: Sense.

Ali, A. (2004). The intersection of racism and sexism in psychiatric diagnosis. In P. Caplan & L. Cosgrove (Eds.), *Bias in psychiatric diagnosis* (pp. 71–76). Oxford, UK: Rowman & Littlefield.

Ali, R. (2010) *Dear Colleague Letter*. Washington, DC: Department of Education, Office for Civil Rights. Retrieved August 1, 2013 from http://www2.ed.gov/about/offices/list/ocr/letters/colleague-201010.html

Allison, D. (1994). Believing in literature. In *Skin: Talking about sex, class & literature* (pp. 165–181). Ithaca, NY: Firebrand Books.

American Civil Liberties Union. (2011). Sturgis v. Copiah County School District Retrieved January 3, 2013, from: http://www.aclu.org/lgbt-rights/sturgis-v-copiah-county-school-district

American Educational Research Association. (2013). *Prevention of bullying in schools, colleges, and universities: Research report and recommendations*. Washington, DC: Author.

American Psychiatric Association. (1952). *Diagnostic and statistical manual of mental disorders*. Washington, DC: Author.

American Psychiatric Association. (1968). *Diagnostic and statistical manual of mental disorders* (2nd ed.). Washington, DC: Author.

American Psychiatric Association. (1973). Homosexuality and sexual orientation disturbance: Proposed change in DSM-II, 6th Printing, page 44, Position Statement. Retrieved March 8, 2011 from: http://www.psychiatryonline.com/DSMPDF/DSM-II_Homosexuality_Revision.pdf

American Psychiatric Association. (1980). *Diagnostic and statistical manual of mental disorders* (3rd ed.). Washington, DC: Author.

American Psychiatric Association. (1987). *Diagnostic and statistical manual of mental disorders* (3rd ed., rev.). Washington, DC: Author.

American Psychiatric Association. (1994). *Diagnostic and statistical manual* (4th ed.). Washington, DC: Author.

American Psychiatric Association. (2000a). *Diagnostic and statistical manual of mental disorders* (4th ed., text rev.). Washington, DC: Author.

American Psychiatric Association. (2000b). Position statement on therapies focused on attempts to change sexual orientation (reparative or conversion therapies). Retrieved October 1, 2010, from: http://www.psych.org/Departments/EDU/Library/APAOfficial-DocumentsandRelated/PositionStatements/2000001.aspx

American Psychiatric Association. (2013). *Diagnostic and Statistical Manual of Mental Disorders, Fifth Edition*. Washington DC: Author.

American Psychiatric Association. (2013). Gender Dysphoria Fact Sheet. Retrieved August 7, 2013, from: http://www.dsm5.org/Documents/Gender%20Dysphoria%20Fact%20Sheet.pdf

American Psychiatric Association. (2013a). Changes from DSM-IV-TR to DSM-5. Retrieved June 26, 2013, from http://www.psychiatry.org/practice/dsm/dsm5

American Psychiatric Association. (2013b). Gender Dysphoria. Retrieved June 26, 2013, from http://www.psychiatry.org/practice/dsm/dsm5

Anguksuar, L. R. (1997). A postcolonial perspective on Western [mis]conceptions of the cosmos and the restoration of indigenous taxonomies. In S. E. Jacobs, W. Thomas & S. Lang (Eds.), *Two-spirit people: Native American gender identity, sexuality, and spirituality* (pp. 217–222). Chicago: University of Illinois Press.

Angus Reid Public Opinion. (2010). Same-sex relations: Canadians and Britons are more open on same-sex relations than Americans. Retrieved January 8, 2013, from: http://www.angus-reid.com/polls/43149/canadians-and-britons-are-more-open-on-same-sex-relations-than-americans/

Arnot, M. (2002). *Reproducing gender? Essays on educational theory and feminist politics*. London: RoutledgeFalmer.

Balsam, K. F., Huang, B., Fieland, K. C., Simoni, J. M., & Walters, K. L. (2004). Culture, trauma, and wellness: A comparison of heterosexual and lesbian, gay, bisexual, and two-spirit Native Americans. *Cultural Diversity and Ethnic Minority Psychology, 10*(3), 287–301.

Balsam, K. F., Rothblum, E. D., & Beauchaine, T. P. (2005). Victimization over the life span: A comparison of lesbian, gay, bisexual, and heterosexual siblings. *Journal of Consulting and Clinical Psychology, 73*(3), 477–487.

Banda, P. S. (2013, June 24). Colorado rights case ruling favors transgender student Retrieved June 26, 2013, from: http://www.pressherald.com/news/Colorado-ruling-lets-transgender-student-use-girls-bathroom.html

Bannerji, H. (2000). *The dark side of the nation: Essays on multiculturalism, nationalism and gender.* Toronto, ON: Canadian Scholar's Press.

Bartlett, N. H., & Vasey, P. L. (2006). A retrospective study of childhood-atypical behavior in Samoan Fa'afafine. *Archives of Sexual Behavior, 35*(6), 659–666.

Bartlett, N., Vasey, P., & Bukowski, W. (2000). Is Gender Identity Disorder in Children a mental disorder? *Sex Roles, 43,* 753–785.

Bauer, G., Hammond, R., Travers, R., Kaay, M., Hohenadel, K., & Boyce, M. (2009). "I don't think this is theoretical; this is our lives": How erasure impacts health care for transgender people. *Journal of the Association of Nurses in AIDS Care, 20*(4), 348–361.

Bauer, G., Pyne, J., Francino, M., & Hammond, R. (in press). La suicidabilité parmi les personnes trans en Ontario: Implications en travail social et en justice sociale. *Revue Service Social, 59*(1).

Beard, J., & Bakeman, R. (2000). Boyhood gender-nonconformity: Reported parental behavior and the development of narcissistic issues. *Journal of Gay and Lesbian Psychotherapy, 4*(2), 81–97.

Beemyn, G., & Rankin, S. (2011). *The lives of transgender people.* New York: Columbia University Press.

Benjamin, H. (1966). *The transsexual phenomenon.* New York: Jullian Press.

Berkowitz, D., & Ryan, M. (2011). Bathrooms, baseball, and bra shopping: Lesbian and gay parents talk about engendering their children. *Sociological Perspectives, 54*(3), 329–350.

Besnier, N. (1994). Polynesian gender liminality though time and space. In G. Herdt (Ed.), *Third sex, third gender: Beyond sexual dimorphism in culture and history.* New York: Zone Books.

Bill 13: Accepting Schools Act. (2012). Royal assent June 19, 2012. 40th Legislature, 1st Session. Retrieved February 12, 2013, from: http://ontla.on.ca/web/bills/bills_detail.do?locale=en&BillID=2549

Bill 33: Toby's Act (Right to Be Free from Discrimination and Harassment Because of Gender Identity or Gender Expression). (2012). Royal assent June 19, 2012. 40th Legislature, 1st Session. Retrieved February 12, 2013, from: http://www.ontla.on.ca/web/bills/bills_detail.do?locale=en&BillID=2574&isCurrent=&detailPage=bills_detail_status

Bill C-279: An Act to Amend the Canadian Human Rights Act and the Criminal Code (Gender Identity and Gender Expression). (2011). 1st Reading Sept. 21, 2011. 41st Parliament, 1st Session. Retrieved on February 12, 2013, from: http://www.parl.gc.ca/HousePublications/Publication.aspx?DocId=5127590

Bill C-389: An Act to Amend the Canadian Human Rights Act and the Criminal Code (Gender Identity and Gender Expression). (2011). 3rd Reading Feb. 9, 2011. 40th Parliament, 3rd Session. Retrieved February 12, 2013, from: http://openparliament.ca/bills/40-3/C-389/

Bird, J. D., Kuhns, L., & Garofalo, R. (2012). The impact of role models on health outcomes for lesbian, gay, bisexual, and transgender youth. *Journal of Adolescent Health, 50*(4), 353–357.

Blackwood, E. (2005). Gender transgression in colonial and postcolonial Indonesia. *Journal of Asian Studies, 64*(4), 849–879.

Blaise, M. (2005). *Playing it straight: Uncovering gender discourses in the early childhood classroom.* New York: Routledge.

Blanchard, R. (1985). Typology of male-to-female transsexualism. *Archives of Sexual Behaviour, 14,* 247–261.

Blanchard, R. (1989a). The classification and labeling of nonhomosexual gender dysphorias. *Archives of Sexual Behavious, 18,* 315–334.

Blanchard, R. (1989b). The concept of autogynephilia and the typology of male gender dysphoria. *Journal of Nervous and Mental Disease, 177,* 616–623.

Blanchard, R. (2005). Early history of the concept of autogynephilia. *Archives of Sexual Behavior, 34*(4), 439–446.

Boler, M. (1999). *Feeling power: Emotions and education.* New York: Routledge.

Bornstein, K. (1994). *Gender outlaw.* New York: Routledge.

Bradley, S., & Zucker, K. (2004). Gender identity and psychosexual disorders. In J. Wiener & M. Dulcan (Eds.), *The American Psychiatric Publishing textbook of child and adolescent psychiatry* (pp. 813–835). Washington, DC: American Psychiatric Publishing.

Brill, S., & Pepper, R. (2008). *The transgender child: A handbook for families and professionals.* San Francisco: Cleis Press.

British Columbia Teachers' Federation. (2006–13). Code of ethics. Retrieved May 10, 2013, from: http://www.bctf.ca/ProfessionalResponsibility.aspx?id=4292

British Psychological Society. (2010). *Proceedings of the 2010 Division of Clinical Psychology Annual Conference.* Retrieved September 24, 2010, from: http://www.dcpconference.co.uk

Browne, K. (2008). Selling my queer soul or queerying quantitative research? Sociological Research Online, 13(1). Retrieved March 14, 2012, from: http:www.socresonline.org.uk/13/1/11.html

Bruni, F. (2012, October 9). At long last, dignity. *The New York Times,* p. A23.

Bryan, J. (2012). *From the dress-up corner to the senior prom: Navigating gender and sexuality diversity in pre K–12 schools.* Lanham, MD: Rowman & Littlefield.

Bryant, K. (2006). Making gender identity disorder of childhood: Historical lessons for contemporary debates. *Sexuality Research & Social Policy, 3*(3), 23–39.

Bryant, K. (2008). In defense of gay children? "Progay" homophobia and the production of homonormativity. *Sexualities, 11*(4), 455–475.

Bucar, E., & Enke, A. (2011). Unlikely sex change capitals of the world: Trinidad, United States, and Tehran, Iran, as twin yardsticks of homonormative liberalism. *Feminist Studies, 37*(2), 301–328.

Buechner. S. D. (2012). 41st Parliament, 1st Session Standing Committee on Justice and Human Rights. House of Commons. Retrieved from: http://www.parl.gc.ca/HousePublications/Publication.aspx?DocId=5851475&Language=E&Mode=1

Burke, P. (1996). *Gender shock: Exploding the myths of male and female.* New York: Anchor Books.

Burleton, J. (2008). DSM-V and Kenneth Zucker. Retrieved October 1, 2010, from: http://transactive.blogspot.com/2008/05/dsm-v-kenneth-zucker.html

Butler, J. (1990). *Gender trouble: Feminism and the subversion of identity.* New York: Routledge Falmer.

Butler, J. (1993). *Bodies that matter: On the discursive limits of "sex."* New York: Routledge.

Butler, J. (2004). *Undoing gender.* New York: Routledge.

CA Bill SB-1772, § 835 (2012).

California Commission on Teacher Credentialing. (2008). *Cal TPA candidate handbook.* Sacramento, CA: Author. Retrieved from: http://www.ctc.ca.gov/educator-prep/tpa-files/candidatehandbook-appendixa-tpes.pdf

Callender, D. R. (2008). When Matt became Jade: Working with a youth who made a gender transition change in high school. In I. Killoran & K. P. Jimenez (Eds.), *Unleashing the unpopular: Talking about sexual orientation and gender diversity in education* (pp. 37–52). Olney, MD: Association for Childhood Education International.

Campaign Life Coalition is concerned that the "Bathroom Bill" C-389 could pass in Parliament. (2010, November 16). *Canada News Wire.*

Canadian Charter of Rights and Freedoms (s. 15) § Part I of the Constitution Act c. 11 (1982, 1985).

Caplan, P. (1995). *They say you're crazy: How the world's most powerful psychiatrists decide who's normal.* Reading, MA: Addison-Wesley.

Caplan, P. (2011). Psychiatric diagnosis arbiters decide how boys vs. girls should act and feel. *Psychology Today.* Retrieved October 3, 2011, from: http://www.psychologytoday.com/blog/science-isnt-golden/201106/psychiatric-diagnosis-arbiters-decide-how-boys-vs-girls-should-act-a

Carmichael, P., & Alderson, J. (2004). Psychological care in disorders of sexual differentiation and determination. In A. Balen, S. Creighton, M. Davies, J. MacDougall, & R. Stanhope (Eds.), *Paediatric and adolescent gynaecology: A multidisciplinary approach* (pp. 158–178). Cambridge: Cambridge University Press.

Carver, P. R., Yunger, J. L., & Perry, D. G. (2003). Gender identity and adjustment in middle childhood. *Sex Roles, 49,* 95–109.

Caudwell, D. (1949). Psychopathic transexualis. *Sexology, 16,* 274–280.

Centre for Social Action. (2012). *Social action research.* Retrieved December 11, 2012, from: http://www.dmu.ac.uk/research/research-faculties-and-institutes/health-and-life-sciences/centre-for-social-action/research.aspx

Chamberland, L., Émond, G., Julien, D., Otis, J., & Ryan, W. (2010). L'impact de l'homophobie et de la violence homophobe sur la persévérance et la réussite scolaires. *Fonds de recherche sur la société et la culture Québec; Rapport de recherche: Programmes actions concertées.* Retrieved from: http://www.fqrsc.gouv.qc.ca/upload/editeur/LineChamberland-resume-118474.pdf

Children's Aid Society of Metropolitan Toronto. (1995). We are your children too: Accessible child welfare services for lesbian, gay and bisexual youth. Toronto, ON: Author.

Children's Aid Society of Toronto. (2012). Out and proud affirmation guidelines: Practice guidelines for equity in gender and sexual diversity. Toronto, ON: Author.

Children's Hospital of Los Angeles. (2012). *Transforming Family program.* Retrieved July 20, 2012, from: http://transformingfamily.org/about-us/

Children's National Medical Centre. (2003). *If you are concerned about your child's gender Behaviour: A guide for parents.* Retrieved March 1, 2012, from: http://childrensnational.org/files/PDF/DepartmentsAndPrograms/Neuroscience/Psychiatry/GenderVariantOutreachProgram/GVParentBrochure.pdf

Choe, Y. (2008). The APA's DSM-V development: Kenneth Zucker's involvement. Retrieved October 1, 2010, from: http://www.exgaywatch.com/wp/2008/05/the-apas-dsm-development-kenneth-zuckers-involvement/

CLE Staff. (2005, April 8). BCCA: North Vancouver school board liable for homophobic harassment of student. *Stay Current: The Continuing Legal Education Society of British Columbia.* Retrieved from: http://www.cle.bc.ca/CLE

Clements-Nolle, K., Marx, R., & Katz, M. (2006). Attempted suicide among transgender persons: The influence of gender-based discrimination and victimization. *Journal of Homosexuality, 51*(3), 53–69.

Cloud, J. (2000, September 25). His name is Aurora. *Time.* Retrieved November 15, 2011, from: http://www.time.com/time/magazine/article/0,9171,998007,00.html

Cochrane, K. (2007, October 10). I'm considering a revolution. *The Guardian.* Retrieved November 18, 2012, from: http://www.guardian.co.uk/music/2007/oct/10/folk.gender

Cohen-Kettenis, P. T., & Gooren, L. J. (1999). Transsexualism: A review of etiology, diagnosis and treatment. *Journal of Psychosomatic Research, 46,* 315–333.

Cohen-Kettenis, P. T., & Kuiper, A. J. (1984). Transseksualiteit en psychotherapie. *Tijdschrift Voor Psychotherapie, 10,* 153–166.

Cohen-Kettenis, P. T., & Pfäfflin, F. (2003). *Transgenderism and intersexuality in childhood and adolescence.* Thousand Oaks, CA: Sage.

Cohen-Kettenis, P. T., & van Goozen, S. H. (1997). Sex reassignment of adolescent transsexuals: A follow-up study. *Journal of the American Academy of Child and Adolescent Psychiatry, 36,* 263–271.

Cohen-Kettenis, P. T., Owen, A., Kaijser, V. G., Bradley, S. J., & Zucker, K. J. (2003). Demographic characteristics, social competence, and behavior problems in children with gender identity disorder: A crossnational, cross-clinic comparative analysis. *Journal of Abnormal Child Psychology, 31*(1), 41–53.

Cohen-Kettenis, P. T., Schagen, S. E. E., Steensma, T. D., de Vries, A. L. C., & Delemarre-van de Waal, H. A. (2011). Puberty suppression in a gender-dysphoric adolescent: A 22-year follow-up. *Archives of Sexual Behavior, 40*(4), 843–847.

Cohen-Kettenis, P., & Pfafflin, F. (2009, October 17). The DSM diagnostic criteria for Gender Identity Disorder in adolescents and adults. *Archives of Sexual Behavior.* doi:10.1007/s10508-009-9562-y

Cohen-Kettenis, P., Delemarre-van de Waal, H., & Gooren, L. (2008). The treatment of adolescent transsexuals: Changing insights. *Journal of Sexual Medicine, 5,* 1892–1897.

Colapinto, J. (2000). *As nature made him: The boy who was raised as a girl.* Toronto, ON: Harper Perennial.

Cole, C. M., O'Boyle, M., Emory, L. E., & Meyer, W. J. (1997). Comorbidity of gender dysphoria and other major psychiatric diagnoses. *Behavioral Science, 26*(1), 13–26.

Collins, S. (2010). *The hunger games.* London: Scholastic Press.

Community Health Systems Resource Group, the Hospital for Sick Children. (2005, May). *Early school leavers: Understanding the lived reality of disengagement from secondary school.* Toronto, ON: Ontario Ministry of Education and Training.

Connell, R. W. (1987). *Gender and power: Society, the person and sexual politics.* Cambridge: Polity

Connell, R. W. (1995). *Masculinities.* Sydney: Allen and Unwin.

Connell, R. W. (2009). *Gender in world perspective.* Cambridge: Polity Press.

Conrad, P., & Angell, A. (2004). Homosexuality and remedicalization. *Society, 41*(5), 32–39.

Conway, L. (2008). An investigation into the publication of J. Michael Bailey's book on transsexualism by the National Academies. Retrieved June 10, 2012, from: http://ai.eecs.umich.edu/people/conway/TS/LynnsReviewOfBaileysBook.html

Corbett, R. (2012). Including transgendered athletes in sport. *Sport and Law Strategy Group.* http://www.sportlaw.ca/2012/06/including-transgendered-athletes-in-sport/, June 28.

Corliss, H. L., Cochran, S. D., & Mays, V. M. (2002). Reports of parental maltreatment during childhood in a United States population-based survey of homosexual, bisexual and heterosexual adults. *Child Abuse and Neglect, 26*, 1165–1178.

Craven, C. (2010). *Pushing for midwives: Homebirth mothers and the reproductive rights movement.* Philadelphia: Temple University Press.

Croft, S., & Beresford, P. (1989). User-involvement, citizenship and social policy. *Critical Social Policy, 9*(26), 5–18.

Cruz, L. E. (2011). Medicine bundle of contradictions: Female-man, Mi'kmaq/Acadian/Irish diasporas, invisible disabilities, masculine-feminist. In J. Yee (Ed.), *Feminism for real: Deconstructing the academic industrial complex of feminism* (pp. 49–60). Ottawa, ON: Canadian Centre for Policy Alternatives.

Currah, P., & Minter, S. (2000). Unprincipled exclusions: The struggle to achieve judicial and legislative equality for transgender people," *William and Mary Journal of Women and the Law, 7*(37), 37–59.

Curtis, A. (2009). State rules in favor of young transgender. *Bangor Daily News.* Retrieved from: http://www.bangordailynews.com/detail/109732.html

D'Augelli, A. R., Pilkington, N. W., & Hershberger, S. L. (2002). Incidence and mental health impact of sexual orientation victimization of lesbian, gay, and bisexual youths in high school. *School Psychology Quarterly, 17*(2), 148–167.

D'Augelli, A., Grossman, A., & Starks, M. (2006). Childhood gender atypicality, victimization, and PTSD among lesbian, gay, and bisexual youth. *Journal of Interpersonal Violence, 21*(11), 1462–1482.

D'Augelli, A. R., Grossman, A. H., Salter, N. P., Vasey, J. J., Starks, M. T., & Sinclair, K. O. (2005) Predicting the suicide attempts of lesbian, gay and bisexual youth. *Suicide and Life-Threatening Behavior, 35*(6), 646–660.

Daemyir, A. (2012, October 25). *Not just their problem: Why parenting the next generation of trans kids is every parent's responsibility, and how gender diverse parenting can help.* Paper presented at the National Workshop on Gender Creative Kids, Concordia University, Montreal, Quebec.

Davison, K., & Frank, B. (2006). Masculinities and femininities and secondary schooling: The case for a gender analysis in the postmodern condition. In C. Skelton, B. Francis, & L. Smulyan (Eds.), *The Sage handbook of gender and education* (pp. 152–165). Thousand Oaks, CA: Sage.

Delemarre-van de Waal, H. A., & Cohen-Kettenis, P. T. (2006). Clinical management of gender identity disorder in adolescents: A protocol on psychological and paediatric endocrinology aspects. *European Journal of Endocrinology, 155*(1), S131–S137.

Denney, D. (1998). *Social policy and social work.* Oxford, UK: Clarendon Press.

DePalma, R., & Atkinson, E. (Eds.). (2008). *Invisible boundaries: Addressing sexualities equality in children's worlds.* London: Trentham Books.

de Vries, A. L. (2010). *Gender dysphoria in adolescents: Mental health and treatment evaluation.* Unpublished doctoral dissertation. VU University, Amsterdam, The Netherlands.

de Vries, A. L. C., Steensma, T. D., Doreleijers, T. A. H., & Cohen-Kettenis, P. T. (2010). Puberty suppression in adolescents with gender identity disorder: A prospective follow-up study. *The Journal of Sexual Medicine, 8*(8), 2276–2283.

de Vries, A., & Cohen-Kettenis, P. (2012). Clinical management of gender dysphoria in children and adolescents: The Dutch approach. *Journal of Homosexuality. 59*, 301–320.

de Vries, A., Cohen-Kettenis, P., & Delemarre-van de Waal, H. (2006). Clinical management of Gender Dysphoria in adolescents. In *Caring for transgender adolescents in BC: Suggested guidelines.* Vancouver, BC: Vancouver Coastal Health, Transcend Transgender Support & Education Society & the Canadian Rainbow Health Coalition. Retrieved July 20, 2012, from: http://transhealth.vch.ca/resources/library/tcpdocs/guidelines-adolescent.pdf

Diamond, M., & Sigmundson, H. (1997). Sex reassignment at birth: Long-term review and clinical implications. *Archives of Pediatrics and Adolescent Medicine, 151*, 298–304.

DiNovo, C. (2012). Second reading of Bill 33. *Legislative Assembly of Ontario.* Retrieved February 13, 2013, from: http://www.ontla.on.ca.

Doe v. Brockton Sch. Comm. (No. 2000-J-638 Mass. App. 2000).

Dorais, M., & Lajeunesse, S. L. (2000). *Mort ou fif: La face cachée du suicide chez les garçons.* Montréal, QC: VLB Éditeur.

Douard, J. (2009). Sex offender as scapegoat: The monstrous other within. *New York Law School Law Review, 53*, 32–52.

Drescher, J. (2010). Queer diagnoses: Parallels and contrasts in the history of homosexuality, gender variance, and the *Diagnostic and Statistical Manual. Archives of Sexual Behavior, 39*, 427–460.

Drummond, K. D., Bradley, S. J., Peterson-Badali, M., & Zucker, K. J. (2008). A follow-up study of girls with gender identity disorder. *Developmental Psychology, 44*(1), 34–45.

Duggan, L. (2003). *The twilight of equality? Neoliberalism, cultural politics, and the attack on democracy.* Boston: Beacon Press.

Durso, L. E., & Gates, G. J. (2012). *Serving our youth: Findings from a national survey of service providers working with lesbian, gay, bisexual, and transgender youth who are homeless or at risk of becoming homeless.* Los Angeles: The Williams Institute with True Colors Fund and Palette Fund.

Eckholm, E. (2012, September 30). California is first state to ban gay "cure" for minors. *The New York Times*. Retrieved November 21, 2012, from: http://www.nytimes.com/2012/10/01/us/california-bans-therapies-to-cure-gay-minors.html? r=0

Edwards Leeper, L., & Spack N. P. (2012). Psychological evaluation and medical treatment of transgender youth in an interdisciplinary "Gender Management Service" (GeMS) in a Major Pediatric Center. *Journal of Homosexuality, 59*, 321–336.

Egan v. Canada (2 S.C.R. 513–1995).

Egge, C. (n.d.). God is not a Christian. Interview of Desmond Tutu. Herald of Europe, 3. Retrieved May 5, 2013, from: www.heraldofeurope.co.uk/Article.aspx?ArticleID=566857151

Ehrensaft, D. (2007). Raising girlyboys: A parent's perspective. *Studies in Gender and Sexuality, 8*(3), 269–302.

Ehrensaft, D. (2009). One pill makes you boy, one pill makes you girl. *International Journal of Applied Psychoanalytic Studies, 6*(1), 12–24.

Ehrensaft, D. (2011a). Boys will be girls, girls will be boys: Children affect parents as parents affect children in gender-nonconformity. *Psychoanalytic Psychology, 28*(4), 528–548.

Ehrensaft, D. (2011b). *Gender born, gender made: Raising healthy gender-nonconforming children.* New York: The Experiment.

Ehrensaft, D. (2012). From Gender Identity Disorder to gender identity creativity: True gender self child therapy. *Journal of Homosexuality, 59*, 337–356.

Ekins, R., & King, D. (2001). Pioneers of transgendering: The popular sexology of David O. Cauldwell. *The International Journal of Transgenderism, 5*(2). Retrieved January 2, 2012, from: http://www.iiav.nl/ezines/web/ijt/97–03/numbers/symposion/cauldwell_01.htm

Eliot, L. (2010). *Pink brain, blue brain: How small differences grow into troublesome gaps—and what we can do about it.* Boston: Mariner Books.

Elliot, P. (2010). *Debates in transgender, queer, and feminist theory: Contested sites.* Farnham, UK: Ashgate.

Epstein, R. (2009a). Introduction. In R. Epstein (Ed.). *Who's your daddy? And other writings on queer parenting* (pp. 13–32). Toronto, ON: Sumach Press.

Epstein, R. (Ed.). (2009b). *Who's your daddy? And other writings on queer parenting.* Toronto, ON: Sumach Press.

Ettelbrick, P. (2007). Since when is marriage a path to liberation? In G. Kirk & M. Ozakawa-Rey (Eds.), *Women's lives: Multicultural perspectives* (4th ed.). New York: McGraw-Hill.

Everyone wants Justin Bieber's hair. (2013). Kidz World. Retrieved April 21, 2013, from: http://www.kidzworld.com/article/22583-everyone-wants-justin-beibers-hair#

Fausto-Sterling, A. (2000). *Sexing the body: Gender politics and the construction of sexuality.* New York: Basic Books.

Fausto-Sterling, A. (2012). The dynamic of gender variability. *Journal of Homosexuality, 59*, 398–421.

Feder, E. K. (1997). Disciplining the family: The case of Gender Identity Disorder. *Philosophical Studies, 85*, 195–211.

Feder, E. K. (1999). Regulating sexuality: Gender Identity Disorder, children's rights, and the state. In U. Narayan & J. J. Bartowiak (Eds.), *Having and raising children: Unconventional families, hard choices, and the social good* (pp. 163–176). University Park: The Pennsylvania State University Press.

Feinberg, L. (1998). *Trans liberation: Beyond pink or blue*. Boston: Beacon Press.

Feinstein, R., Greenblatt, A., Hass, L., Kohn, S., & Rana, J. (2001). *Justice for all? A report on lesbian, gay, bisexual, and transgendered youth in the New York juvenile justice system*. New York: Lesbian and Gay Project of the Urban Justice Center.

findlay, b. (n.d.). Proud of pride days: Queers defeat homophobic mayors. Retrieved February 8, 2012, from: http://www.barbarafindlay.com/new.htm

Fisk, N. (1973). Gender Dysphoria Syndrome (the how, what, and why of a disease). In D. Laub & P. Gandy (Eds.), *Proceedings of the Second Interdisciplinary Symposium on Gender Dysphoria Syndrome* (pp. 7–14). Palo Alto, CA: Stanford University Press.

Fisk, N. (1974). Gender Dysphoria Syndrome: The conceptualization that liberalizes indications for total gender reorientation and implies a broadly based multi-dimensional rehabilitative regimen. *The Western Journal of Medicine, 120*(5), 386–391.

Fleming, J., & Ward, D. (1997). *Research as empowerment: The Social Action approach*. Leicester, UK: Centre for Social Action.

Fleming, J., & Ward, D. (2004). Methodology and practical applications of the Social Action Research model. In F. Rapport (Ed.), *New qualitative methodologies in health and social care: Putting ideas into practice* (pp. 162–178). London: Routledge.

Foibey. (2010). Protest writeup for Zucker's appearance before the BPS. Retrieved January 3, 2011, from: http://foibey.livejournal.com/583609.html

Foucault, M. (1975). *Discipline and punish: The birth of the prison* (2nd ed.) (A. Sheridan, Trans.). New York: Vintage Books.

Foucault, M. (1980). *Power-knowledge: Selected interviews and other writings, 1972–1977* (C. Gordon, Ed., C. Gordon, L. Marshall, J. Mepham, & K. Soper, Trans.). New York: Harvester Press.

Foucault, M. (1982). Afterword: The subject and power. In H. L. Dreyfus & P. Rabinow (Eds.), *Michel Foucault: Beyond structuralism and hermeneutics*. Chicago: University of Chicago Press.

Foucault, M. (1988). *Technologies of the self: A seminar with Michel Foucault* (L. Martin, H. Gutman, & P. Hutton, Eds.). Amherst: University of Massachusetts Press.

Fralic, S. (2012, August 6). Hey, Vancouver: Show some pride and keep your pants on. *The Vancouver Sun*.

Frankfuert, K., (2000) A place for everyone. *Principal Leadership, 1*(2), 64–67.

Fraser, N. (2007). Feminist politics in the age of recognition: A two-dimensional approach to gender justice. *Studies in Social Justice, 1*(1), 23–35.

Gale, L. (2012). *Out and proud affirmation guidelines: Practice guidelines for equity in gender and sexual diversity*. Toronto, ON: Children's Aid Society of Toronto.

Garafalo, R., Wolf, R. C., Kessel, S., Palfrey, J., & DuRant, R. J. (1998) The association between health risk behaviors and sexual orientation among a school-based sample of adolescents. *Pediatrics, 1010*(5), 895–902.

Garrow, H. B. (2012a, March 9). Suffolk schools OK new dress code, omit gender. *The Virginian-Pilot*.

Garrow, H. B. (2012b, February 9). Suffolk weighs ban on cross-gender clothing for students. *The Virginian Pilot*.

Gelder, M. G., & Marks, I. M. (1969). Aversion treatment in transvestism and transsexualism. In R. Green & J. Money (Eds.), *Transsexualism and sex reassignment* (pp. 383–413). Baltimore: Johns Hopkins University Press.

Gender Spectrum. (2012a). *Gender training for schools.* Retrieved July 20, 2012, from: http://www.genderspectrum.org/education/school-training-program

Gender Spectrum. (2012b). *Parent support groups.* Retrieved July 20, 2012, from: http://www.genderspectrum.org/outreach/support-groups.

GID Reform Advocates. (n.d.). Retrieved July 2, 2012, from: http://www.gidreform.org/

Gillis, L. (2012, October 25). *Building capacity for community support in Ontario: The Gender-Independent Children Project.* Paper presented at the National Workshop on Gender Creative Kids. Concordia University, Montreal. Quebec.

Giroux, H., & Purpel, D. (Eds.). (1983). *The hidden curriculum and moral education: Deception or discovery.* Berkeley, CA: McCutchan.

Glavinic, T. (2010). Research shows lack of support for transgender and gender-nonconforming youth in U.S. school systems. *Student Pulse, 2*(1), 1–2.

Global News. (2013, April 7). Michelle and Garfield. *AM/BC.* Retrieved from: http://global-news.ca/video/459161/ambc-michelle-and-garfield

GLSEN & Harris Interactive. (2012). *Playgrounds and prejudice: Elementary school climate in the United States; A survey of students and teachers.* New York: GLSEN.

GLSEN. (2012). The 2011 national school climate survey: Key findings on the experiences of lesbian, gay, bisexual and transgender youth in our nation's schools. New York: Author.

GLSEN. (2013). Nondiscrimination laws protecting students by state Retrieved June 24, 2013, from: http://www.glsen.org/sites/default/files/non-discrim-states.pdf

Goebel, B. L., & Brown, D. R. (1981). Age differences in motivation related to Maslow's need hierarchy. *Developmental Psychology, 17,* 809–815. doi:10.1037/0012–1649.17.6.809

Goodbaum, J., Huot, J., & Patterson, D. (2012). Let people be who they are: Best practices when working with gender-independent children and their families in Ottawa. Ottawa, ON: Family Services Ottawa. Retrieved from: http://familyservicesottawa.org/wp-content/uploads/2012/07/Let-People-Be-Who-They-Are.pdf

Grant, J. M., Mottet, L. A., Tanis, J., Harrison, J., Herman, J. L., & Keisling, M. (2011). *Injustice at every turn: A report of the National Transgender Discrimination Survey, executive summary.* Washington, DC: National Center for Transgender Equality, National Gay and Lesbian Task Force. Retrieved from: http://transequality.org/PDFs/Executive_Summary.pdf

Gray, M. (2007). From websites to Wal-Mart: Youth, identity work, and the queering of boundary publics in small town USA. *American Studies, 48*(2), 49–59.

Gray, S. A. O., Carter, A. S., & Levitt, H. (2012). A critical review of assumptions about gender-variant children in psychological research. *Journal of Gay & Lesbian Mental Health, 16,* 4–30.

Gray, W. (2012, May 30). Interview by Chris Walker. *CBC Daybreak.* Retrieved January 8, 2013, from: http://www.cbc.ca/daybreaksouth/2012/05/#igImgId_39780

Green, F. (2011). Practicing feminist mothering. Winnipeg, MB: Arbeiter Ring.

Green, R. (1987). *The "sissy boy syndrome" and the development of homosexuality.* New Haven, CT: Yale University Press.

Green, R., & Fuller, M. (1973). Group therapy with feminine boys and their parents. *International Journal of Group Psychotherapy, 23*(1), 54–68.

Greenson, R. R. (1964). On homosexuality and gender identity. *International Journal of Psycho-Analysis, 45,* 217–219.

Greenson, R. R. (1966). A transvestite boy and a hypothesis. *International Journal of Psycho-Analysis, 47,* 396–403.

Greytak, E. A., Kosciw, J. G., & Diaz, E. M. (2009). *Harsh realities: The experiences of transgender youth in our nation's schools.* New York: GLSEN.

Griffin, P., & Carroll, H. (2010 *On the team: Equal opportunity for transgender student athletes.* Women's Sports Foundation. available at: http://www.wiaa.com/ConDocs/Con550/TransgenderStudentAthleteReport.pdf

Griffin, P. (2007). Neoliberalism and the World Bank: Economic discourse and the (re)production of gendered identity(ies). *Policy Futures in Education,* 5(2), 226–238.

Grossman, A. H., & D'Augelli, A. R. (2006). Transgender youth: Invisible and vulnerable. *Journal of Homosexuality, 51*(1), 111–128.

Grossman, A. H., & D'Augelli, A. R. (2007). Transgender youth and life-threatening behaviors. *Suicide and Life-Threatening Behavior, 37,* 527–537.

Hacking, I. (1995). The looping effect of human kinds. In D. Sperber, D. Premack, & A. Premack (Eds.), *Causal cognition: A multidisciplinary debate* (pp. 351–383). Oxford, UK: Oxford University Press.

Halberstam, J. (1998). *Female masculinity.* Durham, NC: Duke University Press,

Halberstam, J. (2004). Oh bondage up yours! Female masculinity and the tomboy. In S. Bruhm & N. Hurley (Eds.), *Curiouser: On the queerness of children* (pp. 191–214). Minneapolis: University of Minnesota Press.

Halberstam, J. (2005). *In a queer time and place: Transgender bodies, subcultural lives.* New York: New York University Press.

Halberstam, J. (2011). *The queer art of failure.* Durham, NC: Duke University Press.

Halberstam, J. J. (2012). *Gaga feminism: Sex, gender, and the end of normal.* Boston: Beacon Press.

Haldeman, D. C. (2000). Gender atypical youth: Clinical and social issues. *School Psychology Review, 29*(2), 192–200.

Hampton, L. (2007). *Sexual identity development in transwomen.* Unpublished master's thesis. University of Calgary, Calgary, Alberta.

Haraway, D. (1991). *Simians, cyborgs, and women: The reinvention of nature.* New York: Routledge.

Hatzenbuehler, M. L. (2011) The social environment and suicide attempts in lesbian, gay, and bisexual youth. *Pediatrics, 127*(5), 896–903.

Hegarty, P. (2009). Toward an LGBT-informed paradigm for children who break gender norms: Comment on Drummond et al. (2008) and Rieger et al. (2008). *Developmental Psychology, 45*(4), 895–900.

Hellen, M. (2009). Transgender children in schools. *Liminalis: Journal for Sex/Gender Emancipation and Resistance,* 81–99.

Hembree, W. C., Cohen-Kettenis, P., Delemarre-van de Waal, H. A., Gooren, L. J., Meyer, W. J., III, Spack, N. P., et al. (2009). Endocrine treatment of transsexual persons: An Endocrine Society clinical practice guideline. *Journal of Clinical Endocrinology & Metabolism, 94*(9), 3132–3154.

Henkle v. Gregory (150 F. Supp. 2d 1067 (Nev. Dist. 2001).

Hill Collins, P. (1998). *Fighting words: Black women and the search for justice.* Minneapolis: University of Minnesota Press.

Hill Collins, P. (2005). *Black sexual politics: African Americans, gender, and the new racism.* New York: Routledge.

Hill, D. B., & Menvielle, E. (2009). "You have to give them a place where they feel protected and safe and loved": The views of parents who have gender-variant children and adolescents. *Journal of LGBT Youth, 6*(2–3), 243–271. doi:10.1080/19361650903013527

Hill, D. B., Menvielle, E. J., Sica, K. M., & Johnson, A. (2010). An affirmative intervention for families with gender-variant children: Parental ratings of child mental health and gender. *Journal of Sex & Marital Therapy, 36*(1), 6–23.

Hill, D. B., Rozanski, C. Z., Carfagnini, J., & Willoughby, B. (2005). Gender identity disorders in childhood and adolescence: A critical inquiry. In D. Karasic & J. Drescher (Eds.), *Sexual and gender diagnoses of the "Diagnostic and Statistical Manual" (DSM): A reevaluation* (pp 7–34). Binghamton, NY: Haworth Press.

Hird, M. (2003). A typical gender identity conference? Some disturbing reports from the therapeutic front lines. *Feminism & Psychology, 13*, 181–199.

Holmes, C. (2012). Violence denied, bodies erased: Towards an interlocking spatial framework for queer anti-violence organizing. Unpublished doctoral dissertation. Interdisciplinary Studies. University of British Columbia (Okanagan campus), Kelowna, BC.

hooks, b. (1994). *Teaching to transgress: Education as the practice of freedom.* New York: Routledge.

Ibbitson, J. (Feb 10, 2011). Transgendered-rights bill headed for defeat in Tory-held Senate.

Intersex in Australia. (2010). iPetition: Petition Ken Zucker's invitation as a keynote speaker to the DCP annual conference 2010. Retrieved November 16, 2010, from: http://oiiaustralia.com/12199/ipetition-petition-ken-zuckers-invitation-keynote-speaker-dcp-conference-2010/

Intersex in Australia. (2011a). About us. Retrieved July 8, 2011, from: http://oiiaustralia.com/

Intersex in Australia. (2011b). OII Australia and "ISGD" : A response to the debate. Retrieved June 2, 2011, from: http://oiiaustralia.com/13750/oii-australia-isgd-response-debate/

Intersex Initiative Portland. (2003). *Introduction to intersex activism: A guide for allies.* Portland, OR: Author. Retrieved from: http://www.intersexinitiative.org/publications/pdf/intersex-activism2.pdf

iPetitions. (2010). Petition Ken Zucker's invitation as a keynote speaker to the DCP conference 2010. Retrieved November 12, 2010, from: http://www.ipetitions.com/petition/zucker2010/signatures

Isay, R. A. (1997). Remove Gender Identity Disorder from DSM. *Psychiatric News, 32*(9), 13.

Istar-Lev, A. (2004). *Transgender emergence: Therapeutic guidelines for working with gender-variant people and their families.* Binghamton, NY: Haworth Press.

Jeffreys, S. (1997). Transgender activism: A lesbian feminist perspective. *Journal of Lesbian Studies, 1*, 55–74.

Jeffreys, S. (2005). *Beauty and misogyny: Harmful cultural practices in the West.* London: Routledge.

Jewkes, Y., & Wykes, M. (2012). Reconstructing the sexual abuse of children: "Cyber-Paeds," panic and power. *Sexualities, 15*(8), 934–952.

Johnson, M. (2012, April 10). Canada Miss Universe changes rules to allow transgender women. DNAinfo. Retrieved from: http://www.dnainfo.com/new-york/20120410/manhattan/miss-universe-changes-rules-allow-transgender-women?gclid=CNDGhvTxg7QCFW-GnPAodGUgAZg#ixzz2ECg7mX1F

Jordan, K. M. (2000). Substance abuse among gay, lesbian, bisexual, transgender, and questioning adolescents. *School Psychology Review, 29*(2), 201–206.

Kaitlin. (2011). "Anti-homophobia policy: Fighting homophobia in Burnaby schools," *Gender Focus*. Retrieved April 15, 2013, from: http://www.gender-focus.com/tag/anti-homophobia-policy

Kane, E. W. (2012). *The gender trap: Parents and the pitfalls of raising boys and girls*. New York: New York University Press.

Kazyak, E. (2012). Midwest or lesbian? Gender, rurality, and sexuality. *Gender & Society, 26*(6), 825–848.

Kelly, F. (2011). Transforming law's family: The legal recognition of planned lesbian motherhood. Vancouver, BC: University of British Columbia Press.

Kennedy, N., & Hellen, M. (2010). Transgender children: More than a theoretical challenge. *Graduate Journal of Social Science, 7*(2), 25–43.

Kennedy, S. (2008). Preventing sexual risk behaviors among gay, lesbian, and bisexual adolescents: The benefits of gay sensitive HIV instruction in schools. *Journal of Gay & Lesbian Issues in Education, 4*(2), 107–109.

Kilodavis, C. (2011). *My princess boy: A mom's story about a young boy who loves to dress up*. New York: Aladdin.

Kimmel, M., & Mahler, M. (2003). Adolescent Masculinity, Homophobia, and Violence: Random School Shootings, 1982-2001. *American Behavioral Scientist, 46*, 1439–1458.

Klomek, A. B., Marrocco, F., Kleinman, M., Schonfeld, I. S., & Gould, M. (2008). Peer victimization, depression, and suicidality in adolescents. *Suicide and Life-Threatening Behavior, 38*(2), 166–180.

Knafo, A., Iervolino, A., & Ploming R. (2005). Masculine girls and feminine boys: Genetic and environmental contributions to atypical gender development in early childhood. *Journal of Personality and Social Psychology, 88*(2), 400–412.

Knopp, L. (2004). Ontologies of place, placelessness, and movement: Queer quests for identity and their impacts on contemporary geographic thought. *Gender, Place and Culture, 11*(1), 121–134.

Kosciw, J., & Diaz, E. (2006). *The 2005 National School Climate Survey: The experiences of lesbian, gay, bisexual and transgender youth in our nation's schools*. New York: The Gay, Lesbian, and Straight Education Network.

Kosciw, J., Greytak, E., Diaz, E. M., & Bartkiewicz, M. J. (2010). *The 2009 School Climate Survey: The experiences of lesbian, gay, bisexual and transgender youth in our nation's schools*. New York: GLSEN.

Koyama, E. (2003). The transfeminist manifesto. In R. Dicker & A. Piepmeier (Eds.), *Catching a wave: Reclaiming feminism for the 21st century* (pp. 244–262). Boston: Northeastern University Press.

Krafft-Ebing, R. (1892). *Psychopathia sexualis with especial reference to contrary sexual instinct: A medico-legal study*. Philadelphia: F. A. Davis.

Kranz, K. C., & Daniluk, J. C. (2002). We've come a long way baby … or have we? Contextualizing lesbian motherhood in North America. *Journal of the Association for Research on Mothering, 4*(1), 58–69.

Kreukels, B., & Cohen-Kettenis, P. T. (2011). Puberty suppression in gender identity disorder: The Amsterdam experience. *Nature Reviews Endocrinology, 7*, 466–472.

Kuiper, B., & Cohen-Kettenis, P. (1988). Sex reassignment surgery: A study of 141 Dutch transsexuals. *Archives of Sexual Behavior, 17*(5), 439–457.

Kumashiro, K. (2000). Toward a theory of anti-oppressive education. *Review of Educational Research, 70*(1), 25–53.

Lambda Legal (2002, August 28) Groundbreaking legal settleent is first to recognize constitutional right of gay and lesbian students to be out at school and protected from harassment. New York: Lambda Legal. Retrieved August 1, 2013 from www.lambdalegal.org/news/ ca_20020828_groundbreaking-legal-settlement-first-to-recognize

Land, D. (2003). Teasing apart secondary students' conceptualizations of peer teasing, bullying and sexual harassment. *School Psychology International, 24*(2), 147–165.

Landolt, M. A., Bartholomew, K., Saffrey, C., Oram, D., & Perlman, D. (2004). Gender-nonconformity, childhood rejection, and adult attachment: A study of gay men. *Archives of Sexual Behavior, 33*(2), 117–128.

Langer, S., & Martin, J. (2004). How dresses can make you mentally ill: Examining gender identity disorder in children. *Child and Adolescent Social Work Journal, 21*(1), 5–23.

Langlois, J. H., & Downs, A. C. (1980). Mothers, fathers, and peers as socialization agents of sex-typed play behaviors in young children. *Child Development, 51*, 1237–1247.

Lather, P. (1991). *Feminist research in education: Within/against*. Victoria, Australia: Deakin University Press.

Lather, P. (2008, February 14). *Getting lost: Reading for difference in qualitative research*. A lecture presented at Ohio State University, Columbus, OH. Retrieved July 19, 2009, from: iTunes.

Lawrence, A. (2008). Gender identity disorders in adults: Diagnosis and treatment. In D. Rowland & L. Incrocci (Eds.), *Handbook of sexual and gender identity disorders* (pp. 423–456). Hoboken, NJ: John Wiley & Sons.

Lemert, C. (2002). *Dark thoughts: Race and the eclipse of society*. New York: Routledge.

Lesbian & Gay Foundation. (2010). Ken Zucker protest. Retrieved March 3, 2011, from: http:// www.lgf.org.uk/ken-zucker-protest/

Letts, W. J., & Sears, J. T. (Eds.). (1999). *Queering elementary education: Advancing the dialogue about sexualities and schooling*. Lanham, MD: Rowman & Littlefield.

Lev, A. (2004). *Transgender emergence: Therapeutic guidelines for working with gender-variant people and their families*. New York: Haworth Clinical Practice Press.

Lev, A. (2005). Disordering gender identity: Gender identity disorder in the DSM-IV-TR. *Journal of Psychology and Human Sexuality, 17*, 35–69.

Lewin, E. (1993). *Lesbian mothers: Accounts of gender in American culture*. Ithaca, NY: Cornell University Press.

Lewin, E. (2009a). *Gay fatherhood: Narratives of family and citizenship in America*. Chicago: University of Chicago Press.

Lewin, E. (2009b). Who's gay? What's gay? Dilemmas of identity among gay fathers. In E. Lewin & W. Leap (Eds.), *Out in public: Reinventing lesbian/gay anthropology in a globalizing world* (pp. 84–103). Malden, MA: Wiley-Blackwell.

Lindemalm, G., Korlin, D., & Uddenberg, N. (1987). Prognostic factors versus outcome in male-to-female transsexualism: A follow-up study of 13 cases. *Acta Psychiatrica Scandinavica, 75*, 268–274.

Lock, J. (2002) Violence and sexual minority youth. *Journal of School Violence, 1*(3), 77–89.

Lockhart, A. (2010). Protests planned as "gender repair clinic" psychiatrist is invited to Manchester. Retrieved November 30, 2010, from: http://manchestermule.com/article/protests-planned-as-'gender-repair-clinic'-psychiatrist-is-invited-to-manchester

Luce, J. (2004). Imaging bodies, imagining relations: Narratives of queer women and "assisted conception." *Journal of Medical Humanities, 25*(1), 47–56.

Luce, J. (2010). *Beyond expectation: Lesbian/bi/queer women and assisted conception*. Toronto, ON: University of Toronto Press.

Luecke, J. C. (2011). Working with transgender children and their classmates in pre-adolescence: Just be supportive. *Journal of LGBT Youth, 8*(2), 116–156.

Lytton, H., & Romney, D. M. (1991). Parents' differential socialization of boys and girls: A meta-analysis. *Psychological Bulletin, 109*, 267–296.

Maccoby, E. E. (1998). *The two sexes: Growing up apart, coming together*. Cambridge, MA: Belknap Press of Harvard University Press.

Macgillivray, I. K. (2007). *Gay-straight alliances: A handbook for students, educators, and parents*. Binghamton, NY: Harrington Park Press.

Macionis, J., & Gerber, L. (2011). *Sociology* (7th ed.). Toronto, ON: Pearson.

Mallon, G. (1999a). A call for organizational trans-formation. In G. P. Mallon (Ed.), *Social services with transgendered youth* (pp. 131–142). Binghamton, NY: Haworth Press.

Mallon, G. (1999b). Knowledge for practice with transgendered persons. In G. P. Mallon (Ed.), *Social services with transgendered youth* (pp. 1–18). Binghamton, NY: Haworth Press.

Mallon, G. (1999c). Practice with transgendered children. In G. P. Mallon (Ed.), *Social services with transgendered youth* (pp. 49–64). Binghamton, NY: Haworth Press.

Mallon, G. P. (1999). Practice with transgendered children. *Journal of Gay & Lesbian Social Services, 10*(3–4), 49–64.

Malpas, J. (2011). Between pink and blue: A multi-dimensional family approach to gender non-conforming children and their families. *Family Process, 50*(4), 453–470.

Marksamer, J. (2008). And by the way, do you know he thinks he's a girl? The failures of law, policy, and legal representation for transgender youth in juvenile delinquency courts. *Sexuality Research & Social Policy, 5*(1), 72–92.

Marksamer, J. (2011). A place of respect: A guide for group care facilities serving transgender and gender non-conforming youth. San Francisco: National Center for Lesbian Rights and Sylvia Rivera Law Project.

Martin, C. L. (1990). Attitudes and expectations about children with nontraditional and traditional gender roles. *Sex Roles, 22*, 151–165.

Maslow, A. H. (1943). A theory of human motivation. *Psychological Review, 50*, 370–396.

McConaghy, N., & Silove, D. (1992). Do sex-linked behaviors in children influence relationships with their parents? *Archives of Sexual Behavior, 2*(5), 469–479.

McDonald, M., & Zeichner, K. M. (2009). Social justice teacher education. In W. Ayers, T. Quinn, & D. Stovall (Eds.), *Handbook of social justice in education* (pp. 595–610). New York: Routledge.

McGill, J., & Kirkup, K. (2013). Locating the trans legal subject in Canadian law: XY v. Ontario. *Windsor Review of Legal and Social Issues, 33*(96), 46.

McGuire, J. K., Anderson, C. R., Toomey, R. B., & Russell, S. T. (2010). School climate for transgender youth: A mixed method investigation of student experiences and school responses. *Journal of Youth Adolescence, 39*(10), 1175–1188.

McIntosh, P. (1990). White privilege: Unpacking the invisible knapsack. *Independent School 49*, 31–35.

Meadow, T. (2011). "Deep down where the music plays": How parents account for childhood gender variance. *Sexualities, 14*(6), 725–747.

Menvielle, E. (2012). A comprehensive program for children with gender-variant behaviors and gender identity disorders. *Journal of Homosexuality, 59*(3), 357–368.

Menvielle, E., & Hill, D. (2011). An affirmative intervention for families with gender-variant children: A process evaluation. *Journal of Gay and Lesbian Mental Health, 15*, 94–123.

Menvielle, E., & Tuerk, C. (2002). A support group for parents of gender-nonconforming boys (clinical perspectives). *Journal of the American Academy of Child and Adolescent Psychiatry, 41*(8), 1010–1014.

Menvielle, E., Tuerk, C., & Perrin, E. (2005). To the beat of a different drummer: The gender-variant child. *Contemporary Pediatrics, 22*(2), 38–45.

Menz, K. (2011). CIS in no rush to mirror NCAA transgender policy. Canadian University Press, http://cupwire.ca/articles/47902, September 30.

Metcalfe, W., & Caplan, P. (2004). Seeking "normal" sexuality on a complex matrix. In P. Caplan & L. Cosgrove (Eds.), *Bias in psychiatric diagnosis* (pp. 121–126). Oxford, UK: Rowman & Littlefield.

Meyer, E. J. (2006). Gendered harassment in North America: School-based interventions for reducing homophobia and heterosexism. In C. Mitchell & F. Leach (Eds.), *Combating gender violence in and around schools* (pp. 43–50). Stoke-on-Trent, UK: Trentham Books.

Meyer, E. J. (2007). Lessons from Jubran: Reducing school board liability in cases of peer harassment. *Proceedings of the 17th Annual Conference of the Canadian Association for the Practical Study of Law in Education, 1*, 561–576. Retrieved from: https://www.academia.edu/2751018/Lessons_from_Jubran_Reducing_school_board_liability_in_cases_of_student_harassment

Meyer, E. J. (2008a). A feminist reframing of bullying and harassment: Transforming schools through critical pedagogy. *McGill Journal of Education, 43*(1), 33–48.

Meyer, E. J. (2008b). Gendered harassment in secondary schools: Understanding teachers' (non) interventions. *Gender & Education, 20*(6), 555–570.

Meyer, E. J. (2009). *Gender, bullying, and harassment: Strategies to end sexism and homophobia in schools.* New York: Teachers College Press.

Meyer, E. J. (2010). *Gender and sexual diversity in schools*. New York: Springer.

Meyer, E. J. (2013, October 25). *Supporting gender diversity in schools: Legal and ethical perspectives*. Paper presented at the National Workshop on Gender Creative Kids. Concordia University, Montreal, Quebec.

Meyer, I. H. (2003). Prejudice, social stress, and mental health in lesbian, gay, and bisexual populations: Conceptual issues and research evidence. *Psychological Bulletin, 129*, 674–697.

Meyer, W. (2012). Gender Identity Disorder: An emerging problem for pediatricians. *Pediatrics. 129*(3), 571–573.

Meyer-Bahlburg, H. (2002). Gender identity disorder in young boys: A parent- and peer-based treatment protocol. *Clinical Child Psychology and Psychiatry, 7*(3), 360–376.

Miedzian, M. (2005). How rape is encouraged in American boys and what we can do to stop it. In E. Buchwald, P. Fletcher, & M. Roth (Eds.), *Transforming a rape culture* (pp. 159–172). Minneapolis, MN: Milkweed.

Mohanty, C. (2012, February 20). *On walls, borders, and occupations: Securitized regimes, anatomies of violence, and feminist critique*. Paper presented at Simon Fraser University, Vancouver, BC.

Moller, B., Schreier, H., Li, A., & Romer, G. (2009). Gender identity disorder in children and adolescents. *Current Problems in Pediatric and Adolescent Health Care, 39*, 117–143.

Money, J. (1975). Ablatio penis: Normal male infant sex-reassigned as a girl. *Archives of Sexual Behavior, 4*(1), 65–71.

Money, J. (1986). *Venuses penuses: Sexology, sexosophy and exigency theory*. New York: Prometheus Books.

Montgomery v. Independent School District No. 709, (2000) 109 F. supp. 2d 1081, 1092 (D. Minn)

Montreuil v. Canadian Human Rights Commission and Canadian Forces, 2009 CHRT 28 (Canadian Human Rights Tribunal 2009).

Moon, M. W., Fornili, K. , & O'Briant, A. L. (2007) Risk comparison among youth who report sex with same-sex versus both-sex partners. *Youth & Society, 38*(3), 267–284.

Moore, M. (2011). *Invisible families: Gay identities, relationships, and motherhood among black women*. Berkeley: University of California Press.

Moore, S. M. (2002). Diagnosis for a straight planet: A critique of gender identity disorder for children and adolescents in the DSM-IV. *Dissertation Abstracts International, 63*(4) (UMI No. 3051898).

Morgan, Wilson, G., & O'Brien, M. (2012). Submission on the draft *Diagnostic and Statistical Manual of Mental Disorders* 5th edition and the World Professional Association for Transgender Health 7th *Standards of Care*. Organisation Intersex International Australia Limited.

Moy, L. C. (2008). *Disrupting "bully" talk: Progressive practices and transformative spaces for anti-violence work in schools*. Vancouver, BC: University of British Columbia Press.

Mullaly, R. (2010). *Challenging oppression and confronting privilege*. Toronto, ON: Oxford University Press.

Mullender, A., & Ward, D. (1991) *Self-directed group: Users take action for empowerment*. London: Whiting & Birch.

Mullender, A., Ward, D., & Fleming, J. (2013). *Empowerment in action: Self-directed groupwork.* Basingstoke, UK: Palgrave Macmillan.

My son's Christmas dress. (2012, December 18). *Raising My Rainbow* [Weblog]. Retrieved January 2, 2013, from: http://raisingmyrainbow.com/2012/12/18/my-sons-christmas-dress/#comment-9164

Namaste, V. (2005). *Sex change, social change: Reflections on identity, institutions, and imperialism.* Toronto, ON: Women's Press.

Namaste, V. (2009). Undoing theory: The "transgender question" and the epistemic violence of Anglo-American feminist theory. *Hypatia, 24*(3), 11–32.

Namaste, V. K. (2000). Chapter 1: Tragic misreadings: Queer theory's erasure of transgender subjectivity; Chapter 2: Theory trouble: Social scientific research and trangendered people. In *Invisible lives: The erasure of transsexual and transgendered people* (pp. 9–23, 24–38). Chicago: University of Chicago Press.

National Children's Hospital. (2012). *Children's Gender and Sexuality Advocacy and Education Program.* Retrieved July 20, 2012, from: http://www.childrensnational.org/DepartmentsandPrograms/default.aspx?Id=6178&Type=Program&Name=Gender%20and%20Sexuality%20Psychosocial%20Programs#advocacy

National Collegiate Athletic Association (NCAA). (2011). NCAA inclusion of transgender student-athletes. NCAA Office of Inclusion.

National Gay and Lesbian Task Force. (2007, September 17). *State nondiscrimination laws in the U.S.* Retrieved January 3, 2008, from: http://www.thetaskforce.org/downloads/reports/issue_maps/non_discrimination_09_07.pdf

Noble, J. B. (2006). *Sons of the movement: FtMs risking incoherence on a post-queer cultural landscape.* Toronto, ON: Women's Press.

Nuttbrock, L., Hwahng, S., Bockting, W., Rosenblum, A., Mason, M., Macri, M., et al. (2010). Psychiatric impact of gender-related abuse across the life course of male-to-female transgender persons. *Journal of Sex Research, 47*(1), 12–23.

O'Hartigan, M. D. (1994). A rose is a rose: The nomenclature of sex and oppression. *TransSisters: The Journal of Transsexual Feminism, 7,* 39–44.

O'Reilly, A. (Ed.). (2004). Mother outlaws: Theories and practices of empowered mothering. Toronto, ON: Women's Press.

Olyslager, F., & Conway, L. (2007, September 7). *On the calculation of the prevalence of transsexualism.* Paper presented at the WPATH 20th International Symposium, Chicago, IL. Retrieved from: http://ai.eecs.umich.edu/people/conway/TS/Prevalence/Reports/Prevalence%20of%20Transsexualism.pdf

Ontario College of Teachers. (n.d.). Ethical standards. Retrieved May 9, 2013, from: http://www.oct.ca/public/professional-standards/ethical-standards

Ontario Human Rights Commission (OHRC). (2012). The Ontario Human Rights Code. Retrieved from: http://www.ohrc.on.ca/en/ontario-human-rights-code

Ontario Ministry of Education. (2006, June). *Safe schools policy and practice: An agenda for action.* Toronto: Author.

Ontario Ministry of Education. (2009a). *Equity and inclusive education in Ontario schools: Guidelines for policy development and implementation.* Toronto: Author.

Ontario Ministry of Education. (2009b, June 24). *Policy/program memorandum no. 119: Developing and implementing equity and inclusive education policies in Ontario schools.* Toronto: Author.

Ontario Ministry of Education. (2009c). *Realizing the promise of diversity: Ontario's equity and inclusive education strategy.* Toronto: Author.

Owen, M. (2001). "Family" as a site of contestation: Queering the normal or normalizing the queer? In T. Goldie (Ed.), *In a queer country: Gay and lesbian studies in the Canadian context* (pp. 86–102). Vancouver, BC: Arsenal Pulp Press.

Paechter, C. (2001). Using poststructuralist ideas in gender theory and research. In C. Skelton & B. Francis (Eds.), *Investigating gender* (pp. 41–51). Buckingham, UK: Open University Press.

Paoletti, J. B. (2012). *Pink and blue: Telling the boys from the girls in America.* Bloomington: Indiana University Press.

Park, M. (2011, September 27). Transgender kids: Painful quest to be who they are. CNN.com. Retrieved July 3, 2013, from: http://www.cnn.com/2011/09/27/health/transgender-kids

Pascoe, C. J. (2007). *Dude you're a fag: Masculinity and sexuality in high school.* Berkeley: University of California Press.

Pauly, I. B. (1965). Male psychosexual inversion: Transsexualism; A review of 100 cases. *Archives of General Psychiatry, 13*(2), 172–181.

Peletz, M. (2006). Transgenderism and gender pluralism in Southeast Asia since early modern times. *Current Anthropology, 47*(2), 309–340.

picaVpica/pica pica's androgyne videos. (2008, May 1). *Labels.* Retrieved December, 12, 2012, from: http://www.youtube.com/watch?v=ouRUBvb7tVk

Pickstone-Taylor, S. (2003). Children with gender-nonconformity. *Journal of the American Academy of Child and Adolescent Psychiatry, 42*, 266.

Pleak, R. R. (2009). Formation of transgender identities in adolescence. *Journal of Gay & Lesbian Mental Health, 13*(4), 282–291.

Poisson, J. (2011, December 26). The "genderless baby" who caused a storm of controversy in 2011. *Toronto Star.* Retrieved April 15, 2013, from: http://www.thestar.com/news/gta/2011/12/26/the_genderless_baby_who_caused_a_storm_of_controversy_in_2011.html

Preston-Shoot, M. (1992). On empowerment, partnership and authority in groupwork practice: A training contribution. *Groupwork, 5*(2), 5–30.

Pubertal blockade safe for pediatric patients with gender identity disorder. (2012). *Endocrine Today.* Retrieved July 20, 2012, from: http://www.healio.com/endocrinology/pediatric-endocrinology/news/print/endocrine-today/%7B69C4C36A-37C3-4053-A856-22A27F8DF62C%7D/Pubertal-blockade-safe-for-pediatric-patients-with-gender-identitydisorder

Pullen Sansfaçon, A. (with the collaboration of Dumais Michaud, A. A., Robichaud, M. J., & Clegg, A.). (2012). Princess boy, trans girl, queer youth: Social Action Research Project—Parenting a "gender-creative" child in today's society. Unpublished research report prepared for the Social Sciences and Humanities Research Council of Canada (SSHRC). Retrieved from: http://academia.edu/2305931/Princess_Boys_Trans_Youth_Queer_Girl_-_Social_Action_Research_Project_Parenting_a_gender_creative_child_in_todays_society

Pullen Sansfaçon, A., Ward, D., Robichaud, M. J., Dumais-Michaud, A. A., & Clegg, A. (in press). Working with parents of gender-variant children: Using social action as an emancipatory research framework. *Journal of Progressive Human Services.*

Pullen-Sansfaçon, A. (2012). Socratic dialogue and self-directed group work: Strengthening ethical practice in social work. *Social Work with Groups, 35*(3), 253–266.

Pyne, J. (2012a). *"Parenting is not a job … it's a relationship": Recognition and relational knowledge among parents of gender non-conforming children. An epistemological grounded theory study.* Paper presented at the National Workshop on Gender Creative Kids, Concordia University, Montreal, Quebec.

Pyne, J. (2012b). RHO Fact sheet: Supporting gender-independent children and their families. Retrieved from: www.rainbowhealthontario.ca

Queerty. (2009). Dr. Kenneth Zucker's war on transgenders. Retrieved October 1, 2010, from: http://www.queerty.com/dr-kenneth-zuckers-war-on-transgenders-20090206/

Rainbow Health Ontario. (2012). *Reproductive options for trans people.* Retrieved January 2, 2013, from: http://www.rainbowhealthontario.ca/admin/contentEngine/contentDocuments/Reproductive_Options_for_Trans_People_.pdf

Raymond, J. (1979). *The transsexual empire.* Boston: Beacon Press.

Rayside, D. (2009). Two pathways to revolution: The difference that context makes in Canada and the United States. In R. Epstein, (Ed.), *Who's your Daddy? And other writings on queer parenting* (pp. 202–209). Toronto, ON: Sumach Press.

Rekers, G. A. (1972). *Pathological sex-role development in boys: Behavioral treatment and assessment.* Unpublished doctoral dissertation, University of California, Los Angeles, CA.

Rekers, G. A. (1975). Stimulus control over sex-typed play in cross-gender identified boys. *Journal of Experimental Child Psychology, 20,* 136–148.

Rekers, G. A. (1977). Atypical gender development and psychosocial adjustment. *Journal of Applied Behavior Analysis, 10*(3), 559–571.

Rekers, G. A. (1979). Sex-role behavior change: Intrasubject studies of boyhood gender disturbance. *Journal of Psychology, 103,* 255–269.

Rekers, G. A., & Lovaas, O. I. (1974). Behavioral treatment of deviant sex-role behaviors in a male child. *Journal of Applied Behavior Analysis, 7,* 173–190.

Rich, A. (1978/1993). Compulsory heterosexuality and lesbian existence. In H. Abelove, D. Halperin, & M. A. Barale (Eds.), *The lesbian and gay studies reader* (pp. 227–254). New York: Routledge.

Rich, A. (1980). Compulsory heterosexuality and lesbian existence. *Signs, 5*(4), 631–660.

Richardson, M., & Meyer, L. (2011, Summer). Preface. *Transgender Studies, 37*(2), 247–253.

Richmond, K., et al. (2010). Gender Identity Disorder: Concerns and controversies. In J. C. Chrisler & D. R. McCreary (Eds.), *Handbook of gender research in psychology* (pp. 111–131). New York: Springer.

Riley, E. A., Sitharthan, G., Clemson, L., & Diamond, M. (2011). The needs of gender-variant children and their parents: A parent survey. *International Journal of Sexual Health, 23,* 181–195.

Rimmer, A. (2005). What is professional social work? Social work and social justice. In S. Shardlow & P. Nelson (Eds.), *Introducing social work.* Lyme Regis, UK: Russell House.

Roberts, A. L., Rosario, M., Corliss, H. L., Koenen, K. C., & Austin, S. B. (2012). Childhood gender-nonconformity: A risk indicator for childhood abuse and posttraumatic stress in youth. *Pediatrics*. doi:10.1542/peds.2011–1804

Rochman, B. (2013, March 1). A 6-year-old boy becomes a girl: Do schools need new rules for transgender students? *Time*. Health and Family. Family Matters. Retrieved April 15, 2013, from http://healthland.time.com/2013/03/01/do-schools-need-new-rules-for-transgender-students/

Roen, K. (2006). Transgender theory and embodiment: The risk of racial marginalization. In S. Stryker & S. Whittle (Eds.), *The transgender studies reader*. New York: Routledge.

Roen, K. (2011). The discursive and clinical production of trans youth: Gender-variant youth who seek puberty suppression. *Psychology & Sexuality*, *2*(1), 58–68.

Rose, N. (2006). Disorders without borders? The expanding scope of psychiatric practice. *BioSocieties*, *1*, 465–484.

Ross, M. W., & Need, J. A. (1989). Effects of adequacy of gender reassignment surgery on psychological adjustment: A follow-up of fourteen male-to-female patients. *Archives of Sexual Behavior*, *18*, 145–153.

Roughgarden, J. (2004). *Evolution's rainbow: Diversity, gender, and sexuality in nature and people*. Berkeley: University of California Press.

Ryan, C. (2009a). Helping families support their lesbian, gay, bisexual, and transgender (LGBT) children. Washington, DC: National Center for Cultural Competence, Georgetown University Center for Child and Human Development.

Ryan, C. (2009b). Supportive families, healthy children: Helping families with lesbian, gay, bisexual & transgender children. San Francisco: Marion Wright Edelman Institute, San Francisco State University. Retrieved from: familyproject.sfsu.edu/files/English_Final_Print_Version_Last.pdf.

Ryan, C., Huebner, D., Diaz, R., & Sanchez, J. (2009). Family rejection as a predictor of negative health outcomes in White and Latino lesbian, gay, and bisexual young adults. *Pediatrics*, *123*(1), 346–352.

Ryan, C., Russell, S., Huebner, D., Diaz, R., & Sanchez, J. (2010). Family acceptance in adolescence in the health of LGBT young adults. *Journal of Child and Adolescent Psychiatric Nursing*, *23*(4) 205–213.

Saketopoulou, A. (2011). Minding the gap: Intersections between gender, race, and class in work with gender-variant children. *Psychoanalytic Dialogues*, *21*(2), 192–209.

Sandberg, D. E., Meyer-Bahlburg, H. F., Ehrhart, A. A., & Yager, T. J. (1993). The prevalance of gender atypical behavior in elementary school children. *Journal of the American Academy of Child and Adolescent Psychiatry*, *32*, 306–314.

Saulny, S., & Steinberg, J. (2011, June 12). On college forms, a question of race, or races, can perplex. *The New York Times*, p. A1.

Savin-Williams, R. (2001). Suicide attempts among sexual-minority youths: Population and measurement issues. *Journal of Counselling and Clinical Psychology*, *69*(6), 983–991.

Scanlon, K., Travers, R., Coleman, T., Bauer, G., & Boyce, M. (2010). Ontario's trans communities and suicide: Transphobia is bad for our health. *Trans PULSE*, *1*(2). Retrieved July 20, 2012, from: http://transpulseproject.ca/wp-content/uploads/2012/04/E2English.pdf

School District No. 44 (North Vancouver) v. Jubran, 2005 BCCA 201, Docket: L021700 (BCSC 6 2005).

Schreibman, L. (2005). *The science and fiction of autism.* Cambridge, MA: Harvard University Press.

Scott-Dixon, K. (2006). *Trans/forming feminisms: Trans-feminist voices speak out.* Toronto, ON: Sumach Press.

Seattle Children's Hospital. (2012). Gender Diversity Parent Support Group. Retrieved July 20, 2012, from: http://www.genderdiversity.org/family-support-groups/

Senate. In *The Globe and Mail.* Retrieved January 14, 2013, from http://www.theglobeandmail.com/news/politics/ottawa-notebook/transgendered rights bill.

Sensoy, O., & DiAngelo, R. (2012). *Is everyone really equal? An introduction to key concepts in social justice education.* New York: Teachers College Press.

Serano, J. (2007). *Whipping girl: A transsexual woman on sexism and the scapegoating of femininity* (1st ed.). Berkeley, CA: Seal Press.

Sharp, D. (2013, June 12). Transgender student suit goes to Maine high court. *ABC News.* Retrieved June 26, 2013, from: http://abcnews.go.com/US/wireStory/transgender-student-suit-maine-high-court-19382762-.UctFTD73JbU

Shildrick, M. (2002). *Embodying the monster: Encounters with the vulnerable self.* Belfast: Sage.

Skidmore, E. (2011). Constructing the "good transsexual": Christine Jorgensen, whiteness, and heteronormativity in the mid-twentieth-century press. *Feminist Studies, 37*(2), 270–300.

Smith, M. (1999). *Lesbian and gay rights in Canada: Social movements and equality-seeking, 1971–1995.* Toronto, ON: University of Toronto Press.

Smith, Y. L. S., Van Goozen, S. H. M., Kuiper, A. J., & Cohen-Kettenis, P. T. (2005). Sex re-assignment: Outcomes and predictors of treatment for adolescent and adult transsexuals. *Psychological Medicine, 35*(1), 89–99.

Smith, Y. L., van Goozen, S. H., & Cohen-Kettenis, P. T. (2001). Adolescents with gender identity disorder who were accepted or rejected for sex reassignment surgery: A prospective follow-up study. *Journal of the American Academy of Child and Adolescent Psychiatry, 40,* 472–481.

Snively, C. A. (2004). Building community-based alliances between GLBTQQA youth and adults in rural settings. *Journal of Gay & Lesbian Social Services, 16*(3–4), 99–112.

Solomon, A. (2012). *Far from the tree: Parents, children, and the search for identity.* New York: Scribner.

Solomon, B. B. (1976). *Black empowerment.* New York: Columbia University Press.

Spack, N. P., Edwards-Leeper, L., Feldman, H. A., Leibowitz, S., Mandel, F., Diamond, D. A., et al. (2012, February 20). Children and adolescents with gender identity disorder referred to a pediatric medical center. *Pediatrics.* doi:10.1542/peds.2011–0907 http://pediatrics.aappublications.org/content/early/2012/02/15/peds.2011–0907

Spade, D. (2003). Resisting medicine, re/modeling gender. *Berkeley Women's Law Journal, 7,* 15–37.

Spade, D. (2011). *Normal life: Administrative violence, critical trans politics, and the limits of law.* Brooklyn, NY: South End Press.

Speake, J. (Ed.). (2009). *The Oxford dictionary of proverbs.* Oxford, England: Oxford University Press.

Spiegel, A. (2008). Two families grapple with sons' gender preferences. Retrieved November 11, 2010, from: http://www.nrp.org/templates/story/story.php?storyId=90247842

Stacey, J., & Biblarz, T. J. (2001). (How) does the sexual orientation of parents matter? *American Sociological Review, 66*(2), 159–183.

Statistics Canada. (2010, January 11). Community belonging. Retrieved August 23, 2012, from: http://www.statcan.gc.ca/pub/82-229-x/2009001/envir/cob-eng.htm

Steensma, T., Biemond, R., de Boer, F., & Cohen-Kettenis, P. (2010). Desisting and persisting gender dysphoria after childhood: A qualitative follow-up study. *Clinical Child Psychology and Psychiatry, 16*(4), 499–516.

Stein, N. (2003). Bullying or sexual harassment? The missing discourse of rights in an era of zero tolerance. *Arizona Law Review, 45*, 783–799.

Steup, M. (2012). Epistemology. In E. N. Zalta (Ed.), *The Stanford encyclopedia of philosophy* Stanford, CA: Stanford University Press. Retrieved from: http://plato.stanford.edu/archives/win2012/entries/epistemology/

Stieglitz, K. A. (2010). Development, risk, and resilience of transgender youth. *Journal of the Association of Nurses in AIDS Care, 21*(3), 192–206.

Stockton, K. B. (2009). *The queer child; or, Growing sideways in the twentieth century.* Durham, NC: Duke University Press.

Strier, R. (2007). Anti-oppressive research in social work: A preliminary definition. *British Journal of Social Work, 37*(5), 857–871.

Stryker, S. (2006). (De)subjugated knowledges: An introduction to transgender studies. In S. Stryker & S. Whittle (Eds.), *The transgender studies reader* (pp. 1–17). New York: Routledge.

Stryker, S. (2008). Transgender history, homonormativity and disciplinarity. *Radical History Review, 100*, 145–157.

Sycamore, M. (2012). Why are faggots so afraid of faggots? An introduction. In M. Sycamore, (Ed.), *Why are faggots so afraid of faggots? Flaming challenges to masculinity, objectification, and the desire to conform* (pp. 1–4). Oakland, CA: AK Press.

Sykes, H. (2004). Genderqueer: Transphobia and homophobia in schools. *Orbit, 34*(1), 21–25.

Szasz, T. (1960). The myth of mental illness. *The American Psychologist, 15*, 113–118.

2-Spirited People of the First Nations. (2008). *Our relatives said: A wise practices guide: Voices of Aboriginal trans-people.* Toronto, ON: Author.

Tanner, L. (2012). Asperger's dropped from diagnosis manual. Retrieved January 2, 2013, from: http://news.msn.com/science-technology/aspergers-dropped-from-diagnosis-manual

Taylor, C., Peter, T., McMinn, T. L., Elliott, T., Beldom, S., Ferry, A., et al. (2011). *Every class in every school: The First National Climate Survey on Homophobia, Biphobia, and Transphobia in Canadian Schools. Final report.* Toronto, ON: Egale Canada Human Rights Trust.

Taylor, C., Peter, T., Schachter, K., Paquin, S., Beldom, S., Gross, Z., et al. (2008). *Youth speak up about homophobia and transphobia: The First National Climate Survey on Homophobia in Canadian Schools. Phase one report.* Toronto, ON: Egale Canada Human Rights Trust.

Theno v. Tonganoxie Unified School Dist. No. 464 (WL 3434016, (D. Kan. 2005).

Toomey, R. B., Ryan, C., Diaz, R. M., & Russell, S. T. (2011). High school gay-straight alliances (GSAs) and young adult well-being: An examination of GSA presence, participation, and perceived effectiveness. *Applied Developmental Science, 15*(4), 175–185.

Toomey, R. B., Ryan, C., Diaz, R. M., Card, N. A., & Russell, S. T. (2010). Gender-nonconforming lesbian, gay, bisexual, and transgender youth: School victimization and young adult psychosocial adjustment. *Developmental Psychology, 46*(6), 1580–1589.

Toronto District School Board. (2010, April 14). *Policy P071: Gender-based violence.* Retrieved February 12, 2013, from: http://www.tdsb.on.ca/ppf/uploads/files/live/98/1762.pdf

Toronto District School Board. (2012). *TDSB guidelines for the accommodation of transgender and gender non-conforming students and staff: An administrative guideline of the Toronto District School Board Human Rights Policy P031.* Retrieved February 12, 2013, from: http://www.tdsb.on.ca/_site/ViewItem.asp?siteid=10471&menuid=40696&pageid=34075

Tosh, J. (2011a). "Zuck off"! A commentary on the protest against Ken Zucker and his "treatment" of childhood gender identity disorder. *The Psychology of Women Section Review, 13(1),* 10–16.

Tosh, J. (2011b). Professor Zucker's invitation as a keynote speaker to the Division of Clinical Psychology annual conference: A response. *PsyPAG Quarterly, 79*(1), 14–19.

Tosh, J. (2013). *"Rape is …": A feminist analysis of the production and transformation of rape discourses.* Unpublished doctoral dissertation, Research Institute for Health and Social Change, Manchester Metropolitan University, UK.

Trans Youth Family Allies. (2013). Understanding through education: A guide to supporting trans youth and their families. Retrieved January 3, 2013, from: http://imatyfa.org/permanent_files/images/tyfa-brochure-out-june-08.jpg

Travers, A. (2008). The sport nexus and gender injustice. *Studies in Social Justice Journal, 2*(1), 79–101.

Travers, R., Bauer, G., Pyne, J., Bradley, K., Gale, L., & Papadimitriou, M. (2012). *Impacts of strong parental support for trans youth: A report prepared for Children's Aid Society of Toronto and Delisle Youth Services.* Retrieved February 7, 2013, from: http://transpulseproject.ca/wp-content/uploads/2012/10/Impacts-of-Strong-Parental-Support-for-Trans-Youth-FINAL.pdf

Trinity Western University v. British Columbia College of Teachers (S.C.R. 772, 2001 2001).

Trowbridge, C. (2005, December 29). Former student, district settle lawsuit. *The Tonganoxie Mirror.* Retrieved from: http://www.tonganoxiemirror.com

Tuerk, C. (Speaker). (2004). *Critical perspectives on gender identity disorders in children and adolescents, part 3* (CD No. 04APA/CD-S51A). Valencia, CA: Mobiltape.

UK Community Psychology Discussion List. (2010). Statement of concern sent. Retrieved December 1, 2010, from: https://www.jiscmail.ac.uk/cgi-bin/webadmin?A2=ind1012&L=COMMUNITYPSYCHUK&F=&S=&P=62

Ussher, J. (1991). *Women's madness: Misogyny or mental illness?* London: Harvester Wheatsheaf.

Valentine, D. (2007). *Imagining transgender: An ethnography of a category.* Durham, NC: Duke University Press.

Van Manen, M., McClelland, J., & Plihal, J. (2007). Naming student experiences and experiencing student naming. In D. Thiessen & A. Cook-Sather (Eds.), *International handbook of student experience in elementary and secondary school* (pp. 85–98). Dordrecht, The Netherlands: Springer.

Vincent, J. (2011, October 18). The lives of gender-variant children. Panel presentation for Sexual Diversity Studies Program, University of Toronto, Toronto ON.

Walker, R. (1992). *To be real: Telling the truth and changing the face of feminism*. New York: Anchor House.

Walks, M. (2012, October 25). *Gender-creativity via parent initiative*. Paper presented at the National Workshop on Gender Creative Kids, Montreal, Quebec.

Walks, M. (2013). Gender identity and in/fertility. Unpublished doctoral dissertation. Interdisciplinary Studies. University of British Columbia (Okanagan campus), Kelowna, BC.

Wallien, M. S., & Cohen-Kettenis, P. T. (2008). Psychosexual outcome of gender-dysphoric children. *Journal of the American Academy of Child and Adolescent Psychiatry, 47*(12), 1413–1423.

Warner, M. (1991). Introduction: Fear of a queer planet. *Social Text, 29*, 3–17.

Warner, T. (2002). *Never going back: A history of queer activism in Canada*. Toronto, ON: University of Toronto Press.

Watkinson, A. (1999). *Education, student rights and the Charter*. Saskatoon, SK: Purich.

Weathers, H. (2011, September 16). Why I let my son live as a girl: Mother of boy who returned to school in a skirt bravely tells her extraordinary story. *UK Daily Mail*. Retrieved October 3, 2011, from: http://www.dailymail.co.uk/femail/article-2038392/Why-I-let-son-live-girl-Mother-boy-returned-school-skirt.html

Wei, S. (2004). Whole. In *Hear me out: True stories of teens educating and confronting homophobia: A project of Planned Parenthood of Toronto* (pp. 103–107). Toronto, ON: Second Story Press.

Weiss, P. (2012, August 31). Dad protects son from bullies by wearing a skirt. Guess what? It works. *Shine Parenting*. http://ca.shine.yahoo.com/blogs/parenting/dad-protects-son-bullies-wearing-skirt-guess-works-153600107.html

Wells, K. (2009). *Supporting trans-identified students: Strategies for a successful in-school transition*. Paper presented at the Queer Issues in the Study of Education and Culture, Ottawa, ON.

Wells, K., Roberts, G., & Allan, C. (2012). *Supporting transgender and transsexual students in K–12 schools: A guide for educators*. Ottawa, ON: Canadian Teachers' Federation.

Weston, K. (1996). *Render me, gender me: Lesbians talk sex, class, color, nation, studmuffins*. New York: Columbia University Press.

White Holman, C., & Goldberg, J. (2006, January). *Ethical, legal, and psychosocial issues in care of transgender adolescents* (pp. B1–B17). Vancouver, BC: CRHC, Transcend and Vancouver Coastal Health. January.

Wherry, A. (Oct 4, 2012). The vast bathroom conspiracy. In *Maclean's*. Retrieved January 13, 2013, from http://www2.macleans.ca/2012/10/04/the-vast-bathroom-conspiracy

Whitelocks, S. (2013, February 27). "It was the best day of my life": Transgender teen on being voted Homecoming Queen after keeping her original sex a secret. *Mail Online*. Retrieved April 15, 2013, from: http://www.dailymail.co.uk/femail/article-2285357/It-best-day-life-Transgender-teen-voted-Homecoming-Queen-keeping-original-sex-secret.html

Whittle, S., Turner, L., & Al-Alami, M. (2007). Engendered penalties: Transgender and transsexual people's experiences of inequality and discrimination. *The Equalities Review*. Manchester Metropolitan University, Press for Change.

Wilber, S., Ryan, C., & Marksamer, J. (2006). *CWLA best practice guidelines: Serving LGBT youth in out-of-home care*. Washington, DC: Child Welfare League of America.

Wilson, I., Griffin, C., & Wren, B. (2002). The validity of the diagnosis of gender identity disorder (Child and Adolescent Criteria). *Clinical Child Psychology and Psychiatry,* 7(3), 335–351.

Wilson, K. (2000). Gender as illness: Issues of psychiatric classification. In E. Paul (Ed.), *Taking sides: Clashing views on controversial issues in sex and gender* (pp. 31–38). Guilford, UK: Dushkin McGraw-Hill.

Wingerson, L. (2009, May 19). Gender identity disorder: Has accepted practice caused harm? *Psychiatric Times.* Retrieved September 3, 2010, from: http://www.psychiatrictimes.com/display/article/10168/1415037

Winnicott, D. W. (1965a). Ego distortion in terms of true and false self. In D. W. Winnicott, *Maturational processes and the facilitating environment* (pp. 140–152). Madison, CT: International Universities Press.

Winnicott, D. W. (1965b). *Maturational processes and the facilitating environment.* Madison, CT: International Universities Press.

Winnicott, D. W. (1970). *Playing and reality.* London: Tavistock.

Winters, K. (2005). Gender dissonance: Diagnostic reform of gender identity disorder for adults. *Journal of Psychology & Human Sexuality, 17,* 71.

Winters, K. (2008). Maligning terminology in the DSM: The language of oppression. Retrieved June 1, 2012, from: http://gidreform.wordpress.com/2008/06/24/maligning-terminology-in-the-dsm-the-language-of-oppression/

Winters, K. (2009). Transvestic disorder and policy dysfunction in the DSM-V. Retrieved June 1, 2012, from: http://www.gidreform.org/blog2009Apr22.html

Winters, K. (2011a). The proposed gender dysphoria diagnosis in the DSM-5. *GID Reform.* Retrieved October 3, 2011, from: http://gidreform.wordpress.com/2011/06/07/the-proposed-gender-dysphoria-diagnosis-in-the-dsm-5/

Witterick, K. (2011). Genderless baby's mother responds to media frenzy. *Toronto Star.* Retrieved October 3, 2011, from: http://www.thestar.com/news/article/998960--genderless-baby-s-mother-responds-to-media-frenzy?bn=1

Witterick, K., & Stocker, D. (2012, October 25). *Gender engaged parenting: Nurturing identity self determination in children.* Paper presented at the National Workshop on Gender Creative Kids, Montreal, Quebec.

Women's Legal Education and Action Fund (LEAF). (2010). Gender identity in human rights statutes: Gender identity and gender expression in human rights legislation. *Equality Rights Central.* Retrieved December 12, 2012, from: http://www.equalityrightscentral.com/canada_equality_rights_law.php?page=statutory_human_rights&subtopic=Analysis&id=20101208145417&doc=Gender+Identity+Amendments+in+Canada+and+Ontario+%28final%29.htm

Wood, K. L. (2009). Chapter 11: Pre-service teachers' experiences in teacher education: What we taught and what they learned about equitable education. In R. Milner (Ed.), *Diversity and education* (pp. 163–174). Springfield, IL: Charles C. Thomas.

World Professional Association for Transgender Health (WPATH). (2011). *Standards of care for the health of transsexual, transgender and gender-nonconforming people* (7th ed.). Retrieved October 6, 2011, from: www.wpath.org

World Professional Association for Transgender Health. (2012). *Standards of care for the health of transsexual, transgender, and gender-nonconforming people* (7th Version). Retrieved from http://www.wpath.org/documents/SOC%20V7%2003-17-12.pdf

Woronoff, R., Estrada, R., & Sommer, S. (2006). *Out of the margins: A report on regional listening forums highlighting the experiences of lesbian, gay, bisexual, transgender, and questioning youth in care.* Washington, DC: Child Welfare League of America & Lambda Legal.

Wren, B. (2002). "I can accept my child is transsexual but if I ever see him in a dress I'll hit him": Dilemmas in parenting a transgendered adolescent. *Clinical Child Psychology and Psychiatry, 7*(3), 377–397.

Wyss, S. (2004). "This was my hell": The violence experienced by gender non-conforming youth in US high schools. *International Journal of Qualitative Studies in Education, 17*(5), 709–729.

Youdell, D. (2005). Sex-gender-sexuality: How sex, gender and sexuality constellations are constituted in secondary schools. *Gender and Education, 17*(3), 249–270.

Yunger, J. L., Carver, P. R., & Perry, D. G. (2004). Gender identity and adjustment in middle childhood. *Sex Roles, 49*(3–4), 95–109.

Zosuls, K. M., Miller, C. F., Ruble, D. N., Martin, C. L., & Fabes, R. A. (2011). Gender development research in *Sex Roles*: Historical trends and future directions. *Sex Roles, 64*, 826–842.

Zucker, K. J. (1999). Commentary on Richardson's (1996) "Setting Limits on Gender Health." *Harvard Review of Psychiatry, 7*(1), 43–50.

Zucker, K. J. (2004). Gender identity development and issues. *Child and Adolescent Clinics of North America, 13*, 551–568.

Zucker, K. J. (2005). Gender identity disorder in children and adolescents. *Annual Review of Clinical Psychology, 1*, 467–492.

Zucker, K. J. (2006a). Commentary on Langer and Martin's (2004) "How Dresses Can Make You Mentally Ill: Examining Gender Identity Disorder in Children." *Child and Adolescent Social Work Journal, 23*, 533–555.

Zucker, K. J. (2006b). Gender identity disorder in children and adolescents. Retrieved November 11, 2010, from: http://www.health.am/sex/more/gid_in_children_and_adolescents/

Zucker, K. J. (2008). Children with gender identity disorder: Is there a best practice? *Neuropsychiatrie de l'enfance et de l'adolescence, 56*, 358–364.

Zucker, K., Bradley, S. (2004). Gender Identity and Psychosexual Disorders. In J. Wiener & M. Dulcan (Eds.), *The American Psychiatric Publishing Textbook of Child and Adolescent Psychiatry*, pp. 813–835. Washington: American Psychiatric Publishing.

Zucker, K. J., & Bradley, S. J. (1995). *Gender identity disorder and psychosexual problems in children and adolescents.* New York: Guilford Press.

Zucker, K. J., & Bradley, S. J., & Sanikhani, M. (1997). Sex difference in the referral rates of children with gender identity disorder: Some hypotheses. *Journal of Abnormal Psychology, 25*, 217–227.

Zucker, K. J., Wood. H., Singh, D., & Bradley, S. (2012). A developmental, biopsychosocial model for the treatment of children with gender identity disorder. *Journal of Homosexuality, 59*, 369–397.

Gender AND Sexualities IN Education

GENERAL EDITORS: ELIZABETH J. MEYER & DENNIS CARLSON

Part of the Peter Lang Diversity series, the Gender and Sexuality in Education series seeks to publish high quality manuscripts that address the complex interrelationship between gender and sexuality in shaping young people's schooling experiences, their participation in popular youth cultures, and their sense of self in relation to others. Books published might include: a study of hip-hop youth culture, Latina/o students, white working class youth, or LGBTQQ community groups—in each case asking how they explore, challenge, and perform gender and sexualities as part of learning and "becoming somebody." Other books might address issues of masculinities, gender and embodiment, trans and genderqueer youth, sexuality education, or the construction of heteronormativity in schools. We invite contributions from authors of ethnographic and other qualitative studies, theoretical texts, as well as critical analyses of popular culture "texts" targeted at or produced by youth—including an analysis of popular music and fan culture, video and film, and gaming culture. While the focus of the series is on original research or theoretical monographs, exceptionally well-crafted proposals for thematically coherent edited volumes and textbooks will also be considered.

For additional information about this series or for the submission of manuscripts, please contact:

> Dennis Carlson, Miami University: carlsodl@muohio.edu
> Elizabeth J. Meyer, California Polytechnic State University:
> ejmeyer@calpoly.edu

To order other books in this series, please contact our Customer Service Department:

> (800) 770-LANG (within the U.S.)
> (212) 647-7706 (outside the U.S.)
> (212) 647-7707 FAX

Or browse by series:

> WWW.PETERLANG.COM